STUDIES IN IMPERIALISM

founding editor John M. MacKenzie and general editor Andrew S. Thompson

When the 'Studies in Imperialism' series was founded more than twenty-five years ago, emphasis was laid upon the conviction that 'imperialism as a cultural phenomenon had as significant an effect on the dominant as on the subordinate societies'. With well over a hundred titles now published, this remains the prime concern of the series. Cross-disciplinary work has indeed appeared covering the full spectrum of cultural phenomena, as well as examining aspects of gender and sex, frontiers and law, science and the environment, language and literature, migration and patriotic societies, and much else. Moreover, the series has always wished to present comparative work on European and American imperialism, and particularly welcomes the submission of books in these areas. The fascination with imperialism, in all its aspects, shows no sign of abating, and this series will continue to lead the way in encouraging the widest possible range of studies in the field. 'Studies in Imperialism' is fully organic in its development, always seeking to be at the cutting edge, responding to the latest interests of scholars and the needs of this ever-expanding area of scholarship.

Citizenship, nation, empire

Manchester University Press

SELECTED TITLES AVAILABLE IN THE SERIES

EMPIRE OF SCHOLARS
Universities, networks and the British academic world, 1850–1939
Tamson Pietsch

WRITING IMPERIAL HISTORIES
(ed.) Andrew S. Thompson

VISIONS OF EMPIRE
Patriotism, popular culture and the city, 1870–1939
Brad Beaven

EMPIRE CAREERS
Working for the Chinese Customs Service, 1854–1949
Catherine Ladds

HEROIC IMPERIALISTS IN AFRICA
The promotion of British and French colonial heroes, 1870–1939
Berny Sèbe

Citizenship, nation, empire

THE POLITICS OF HISTORY TEACHING IN ENGLAND, 1870–1930

Peter Yeandle

MANCHESTER UNIVERSITY PRESS

Copyright © Peter Yeandle 2015

The right of Peter Yeandle to be identified as the author of this work has been asserted by him in accordance with the Copyright, Designs and Patents Act 1988.

Published by MANCHESTER UNIVERSITY PRESS
ALTRINCHAM STREET, MANCHESTER M1 7JA
www.manchesteruniversitypress.co.uk

British Library Cataloguing-in-Publication Data
A catalogue record for this book is available from the British Library

Library of Congress Cataloging-in-Publication Data applied for

ISBN   978 0 7190 8012 8 hardback

First published 2015

The publisher has no responsibility for the persistence or accuracy of URLs for any external or third-party internet websites referred to in this book, and does not guarantee that any content on such websites is, or will remain, accurate or appropriate.

Typeset
by Toppan Best-set Premedia Limited

This book is dedicated to my son, Alex

CONTENTS

Founding editor's introduction — viii
Acknowledgements — x
Note on the text — xii

Introduction   1

Part I – Contested histories: the teaching of history in its 'golden age'   17

1 Enlightened patriotism: or, what was history for?   19
2 The renaissance of the child: educational theory and the teaching of history   50

Part II – Imperial values and enlightened patriotism in the teaching of history, c. 1880–1930   73

3 Imperial values in the teaching of history I: national origins, seafaring and the Christian impulse   77
4 Imperial values in the teaching of history II: the English 'race'   97
5 Enlightened patriots: heroes, heroines and 'pioneers of progress' in the teaching of history   118
6 History in war and peace   147

Conclusion   171

Select bibliography — 184
Index — 207

FOUNDING EDITOR'S INTRODUCTION

Education is the major means by which nations seek to socialise the young into the norms and values of adults, as well as provide them with the necessary economic and personal skills. In some centrist societies, the state is closely involved in these processes. In others, the state remains at arm's length. But in many, including Britain, the balance between state and locality, between central control and devolved powers, between politicians and schools, teachers and parents is a subject for constant debate. This is despite the fact that the educational system is very much a pluralist one, with state and private schools, Christian denominational – and more recently other religious affiliations – and secular governance. Yet the development of educational provision, in terms of the expansion of the availability of schooling, compulsion, and the age range of pupils and leaving times, has of course been established through the succession of education acts commencing in 1870 (1872 in Scotland), with repeated further major pieces of legislation in the twentieth century. In perhaps a typically British way, educational provision has often seemed both controlled and casual, both regulated and regionalised. These apparently haphazard arrangements were in some respects transferred to the British empire, where colonial governments (particularly in so-called dependent territories) often remained aloof from educational provision until they established greater authority in the twentieth century.

If all this is true of education in general, it has been equally true of the curriculum. And in curricular matters, no subject has tended to produce more controversy than history. The reason for this is readily apparent. The variety of ways in which societies view their history is perceived to be central to the formation of identities, to the creation of the 'nation', to concepts of citizenship, to notions of both personal and collective morality, and to the manner in which apparently dominant ideologies are transmitted to the young. Each generation, at least from the late nineteenth century (and in more general ways at earlier periods too), has debated how the young should be introduced to the past, how histories should be taught, and what lessons in good citizenship should be imparted. Each society invariably has a central idea of what has contributed to its current qualities or concepts of greatness. For the British this became the formation of the idea and the geographical and ethnic reality of Britain itself, as well as the dispersal of the British people – and of their language – across the globe from the sixteenth century onwards, a process that became more and more bound up with the development of empire. The great paradox of the notion of the 'island story', a phrase that achieved fresh currency in the recent past, is that the story was actually about an entire archipelago as well as connections with a congeries of countries spread across continents.

It has long been clear that, despite the attention of a number of scholars, the controversies surrounding the provision of a history curriculum required

FOUNDING EDITOR'S INTRODUCTION

to be revisited. Moreover, it has also been apparent that the subject of history should not be viewed in isolation, that ideas about history are transmitted in many diverse ways as well as in association with other disciplines. Peter Yeandle has done this in a remarkably diverse, nuanced and accessible way. When in the early 1980s I turned to a consideration of the transmission of ideas about the British empire in schools, I quickly recognised that history texts were an inadequate source for a full understanding of the ways in which wider notions of citizenship, nation and empire were transmitted to the young. 'Readers' associated with the development of literacy, geographical study, perhaps even aspects of religious instruction, were also important, in the case of the readers centrally so. Moreover, teacher manuals and training methods in the developing colleges were additionally significant. It was also essential to consider the age groups at which these materials were aimed. But my efforts were preliminary and tentative given the relatively pioneering nature of the work.

Yeandle's study is much more profound and he has revealed just how inadequate it is to consider only history texts when examining these issues. He recognises the ways in which the teaching of history has indeed been a constant source of controversy, but also reveals the manner in which the terms of the debate have often been both contradictory and paradoxical. Moreover, his major contribution is to chart the significance of educational theory and ideas about child psychology derived from continental models, originally and notably German. Through the spread of such influential models, he is able to unveil aspects of what he describes as 'the crisis of national confidence' in a variety of forms. He also examines the spread of arguments about the moral aspects of history teaching, the ways of imparting these to children of various ages, and the manner in which such notions contributed to communal values and the interests of the society. These debates seem, interestingly, to have intensified during the interwar years of the twentieth century. Above all he analyses the extent to which the British 'dominant ideology' of empire permeated these debates, methodologies and teaching practices. His conclusions are judicious and carefully balanced.

Interestingly, many of these issues have a habit of reappearing, as they have been doing in recent times under the influence of the former Secretary for Education Michael Gove and his historical advisers. This is even more complex with the devolution of educational provision – and concepts of citizenship, nation and community – to Scotland, Wales and Northern Ireland. Separating English/British history (as well as geographical and literary study) from global contexts remains problematic, not least because of the need to understand human migrations (outgoing and incoming, including the formation of today's multi-ethnic, if not multi-cultural, society – phenomena which seem to contribute to all sides of these arguments), the peopling of the world and the development of linguistic maps. It is quite clear that both the controversies and the studies of them will continue, but Yeandle's is a notable contribution to these highly significant and contentious issues.

John M. MacKenzie

ACKNOWLEDGEMENTS

Sincere thanks are owed to John MacKenzie and the anonymous readers who offered invaluable advice on the original book proposal and draft manuscripts. Emma Brennan and her team at MUP have been patient and supportive throughout. My research has taken me to several repositories, and my thanks go to staff at the British Library, the Institute of Education, Manchester John Rylands, the Brotherton, and the textbooks collection at Durham.

This manuscript has been several years in the making and I owe my sincere gratitude to many people for their encouragement and guidance along the way. Eric Evans and Yvette Solomon were excellent PhD supervisors. Steve Constantine, my internal examiner, continues to be a wonderful mentor. Robert Colls first persuaded me to propose the thesis as a book; Stephen Heathorn (for reasons which will become clear in the introduction) assured me that I was not reinventing the wheel. Kate Newey and Jeffrey Richards, who directed an AHRC project on the Cultural History of Pantomime on which I was a researcher, gave me time to undertake both further archival work and writing. I thank them both for their warmth and generosity. I am especially grateful to Jeffrey who frequently made his personal library available at short notice. Although he is no longer with us, I would also like to make clear my gratitude to Rob Phillips. I gained much from time spent working with him – both as researcher and then on the British Island Stories project. He was a great friend, an impeccable scholar and is sorely missed. Max Jones and Bertrand Taithe have given welcome support since I began teaching at Manchester. I have also benefitted greatly from the wisdom and comradeship of friends and colleagues over the last decade. Special thanks to (the following list is by no means exhaustive): Alan Booth, Thomas Dixon, Sarah Isherwood, Sarah Longair, John Marsh, Paul Miller, Mark Nixon, Sally Perkins, Sadiah Qureshi, Marcus Risdell, Sue Seddon, Gareth Stockey, James Taylor, Tereza Valny, Emma Vickers, Anne Witchard and Owain Wright.

Finally, my thanks to my family in general, and to my son, Alex, in particular. When Alex was at primary school, he wondered why Samuel Pepys hadn't dialled the emergency services. That led me to revisit sources, rethink some of my material and seek information on how educational psychologists from the late-Victorian period

ACKNOWLEDGEMENTS

contemplated children's conceptions of time. I found references in training manuals to the Herbartian method which started the process of research into the wider pedagogical culture of the late Victorian and Edwardian period, some of which is central to this book. Cheers matey!

NOTE ON THE TEXT

Michael Gove was Secretary of State for Education at the time this manuscript went into production. He was replaced by Nicola Morgan in a cabinet reshuffle on 15 July 2014.

Introduction

When we look at a map of the world, and we see how wide is the red that marks the British Empire, we may feel proud [. . .] Our race possesses the colonial spirit which French, Spaniards and Germans do not possess: the daring that takes men into distant lands, the doggedness that keeps them steadfast in want and difficulties, the masterful spirit that gives them power of Eastern races, the sense of justice that abuses them from abusing this power.[1]

This is a book about the politics of history teaching. The chronological period for this study ranges from the onset of mass schooling in the 1870s up to the end of the 1920s. Broadly put, research investigates the extent to which imperialism influenced those responsible for the creation of historical education. If previous studies of the history of history teaching are characterised by the tendency to focus on the content of textbooks alone, this book offers original insights drawn from investigations into the pedagogical culture of turn of the twentieth century England. Analysis of contemporary debates about the intended function of historical education demonstrate that the teaching of history in England has a far more complicated past than has often been assumed.

This book is timely for two predominant reasons. First (and writing in early 2013), the current British government perceives the teaching of history in England to be in need of a radical overhaul since it does not fulfil the objective of instilling national pride: a national curriculum, it is argued, should serve the ends of state. The suggested solution, now as in the 1980s, is a return to a 'golden age' of history teaching: a golden age characterised by a content-led curriculum, devoid of educational theory, and intended primarily to promote national identity.[2] One prompt for this study, then, is the desire to enquire what precisely constitutes this golden age. My findings suggest that the teaching of history was far from straightforwardly aimed at the delivery of state-prescribed patriotism. The cultivation of patriotism was a key ingredient underpinning rationales for the teaching of history; however, the 'patriotism' conceptualised by educationists was one which merged civic and imperial objectives. Significant weight was attached to the creation of a history curriculum which would promote 'enlightened patriotism': that is, an education which prioritised the needs of citizenship and morality above the inculcation of what contemporaries dubbed 'crude' or 'blind nationalism'.[3] Indeed, this book explains how educationists exercised far greater influence than has previously been recognised. This is the first study to trace the impact of pedagogical innovation, led by a little-known but prominent group of theorists called the Herbartians, on the teaching of history.

Second, recent debates about how far imperial propaganda pervaded popular culture at the turn of the twentieth century demand renewed attention to the teaching of history. These debates are twofold: on the nature of sources historians have used to reconstruct past practice; and on questions of intention and reception. It has long been held that history lessons served as a vehicle for the promotion of imperial patriotism. John MacKenzie's seminal *Propaganda and Empire* (1984) cited a series of examples demonstrating that school textbooks were one of the many sites of imperial propaganda. A number of scholars followed suit.[4] A shift in content towards the explicit teaching of imperial history is certainly evident in analysis of textbooks and syllabi for older children:[5] witness, for instance, the praise of Britain's imperial character evident in the extract from G.T. Warner's *A Brief Survey of British History* cited above. In 1892, the considerable efforts of the Royal Colonial Institute were rewarded when the Board of Education included the teaching of imperial studies as a subject for scholars in the higher standards in its Code of Regulations.[6] In *The Handbook of Suggestions* of 1905, the history of the empire was included in provision for older scholars, since it 'formed a stirring theme, full of interest to every young citizen'.[7] In the absence of a state-prescribed curriculum, the *Handbook* was as close as the state came to indicating best practice. Using such evidence, R.D. Bramwell maintains that 'the profound imperialistic fervour of the times penetrated history syllabuses'.[8] These interpretations, however, have been subjected to scrutiny in the last decade.

Overconcentration on subject-specific history textbooks can be misleading. Textbooks were, more often than not, used in subject-specific history lessons for older scholars who had stayed in school beyond the compulsory leaving age. Prior to the turn of the twentieth century, there was no such thing as the subject-specific history lesson in the vast majority of schools. Instead, children learnt their history from reading books designed for the teaching of literacy (one of the notorious, compulsory, 3 'R's of reading, writing and arithmetic). Stephen Heathorn's meticulous study into these primers, *For Home, Country and Race* (2000), demonstrates that it was these texts that were far likelier read by all children.[9] In 1882, lessons in literacy were rigorously reorganised on the premise that if children were to learn to read, then they were to learn to read from other less frequently taught subject material. One-third of all reading books used in literacy sessions needed to be historical.[10] These advances were endorsed by the 'Revised Instructions of 1896', issued to school inspectors, and which stipulated they ensure children read from at least two readers in their first and second standard, and at least three for Standard III and above. This doubled 1882 levels.[11] Historical topics featured heavily. In particular, reading from a 'history of England' was used in place of the study of the plays of Shakespeare, or texts by Milton, for scholars up to Standard IV and above.[12] This was to remain the case until well after the First World War.[13] Harry Withers, in his state-sponsored appraisal of historical education in his London elementary schools, confirms:

> It has no doubt been the case in many schools, in which History has not been presented as a class subject, that nevertheless, lessons in history have been given. And in every school without exception the rule had held good that out of the three reading books in every class above the Second Standard one has been a 'History reader'.[14]

The Education Committee of London County Council reported in 1911 that reading books were best used up to the end of Standard III (approximately aged ten), and for the want of better textbooks, used thereafter too.[15] One can be confident, therefore, that all elementary schoolchildren at some stage of their schooling were exposed to the historical reading book and few, prior to 1902 (after which history was introduced as a compulsory discrete subject for the first time), had formal subject-specific instruction in addition to their literacy lessons. Historical reading books incorporated cutting-edge developments in educational psychology and were subject to far more contemporary discussion than textbooks. The study of these, Heathorn correctly argues, should thus form the basis of research into common experiences of historical education.[16]

Heathorn finds that imperial ideology figured just as prominently in reading books as textbooks. This book confirms his findings through extending analysis into educational culture; indeed, this study would not be possible had he not laid the groundwork by providing such a detailed and methodical study of literacy primers.[17] Focus on how pedagogical intent shaped the content and tone of teaching resources reveals significant contemporary debate about what the teaching of history should aim to achieve. Across both genres of text used to teach history, children were presented with a series of lessons – explicit as well as inferred – in which they were intended to absorb prescribed values: values which, specifically, sought to inspire an emotional identification with England as the founder and home of a great empire. In his controversial *The Absent-Minded Imperialists* (2004), however, Bernard Porter contends that imperialism exercised much less of an impact on both the development and the practice of history teaching than previously argued.[18] In his preface he claims the empire 'was usually neglected in English schools':[19] in the remainder of his text he argues that where it did feature in history lessons (and according to him, it featured very little), it had little impact. My findings, to the contrary, indicate an abundance of evidence not merely demonstrating the intent to inculcate national-imperial values, but significant thought about how to translate this intent into practice. 'Intent', if one follows Porter's rationale, equates to a statement that it was desired children internalise knowledge of empire: what empire was, where it was, how it was and why it was; for imperialism to have affected popular culture, in Porter's rationale, it needed to be expressed unambiguously. Yet, as Stuart Ward identifies in his astute review, Porter's definition of 'imperialism' is at times so limited that he necessarily weakens his own argument that researchers need to pay more attention to the wider context.[20] If imperial content were missing, and Porter emphasises that it was, it need not indicate that imperial values were not being taught. On the contrary, the subtlety of imperialism – as an ideology expressed through the concept of 'enlightened patriotism' – is more than evident when one probes a little deeper into contemporary debates.

As will be demonstrated in the first chapter, educationists certainly emphasised that history teaching, especially in reading books, justified its place in the curriculum since it was uniquely positioned to teach citizenship above and beyond the inculcation of crude patriotism. What becomes apparent, when analysing debates in their educational context, was that history lessons were intended to teach a correlation of civic, national and imperial values. Chapters Three, Four and Five are organised thematically to demonstrate how imperial values were interwoven into the content of reading books: on stories of national origins and the medieval period, on stories about England's relationship with other British nations and colonial subjects, and in the use of history texts as lessons in moral biography. My argument is that material not specifically about the physical presence of the empire was still intended to teach imperial values: stories which concentrated on the period of Anglo-Saxon settlement, for instance, might not have instilled in children knowledge of the glories of nineteenth-century wars of territorial conquest, but they deliberately drew attention to a predisposition to seafaring and colonisation as innate ingredients in the English story. The study of the pedagogical culture in which texts were produced is vital both to assist understanding of the intended purpose of historical education as well as to contextualise thinking behind the selection of content. This study is particularly timely since David Cannadine, in *The Right Kind of History* (2011), both takes Bernard Porter's view regarding the paucity of teaching about empire at face value as well as incorrectly dismissing 'pedagogy [as] a largely undeveloped field'.[21]

It remains entirely possible to argue that history teaching was conceived of, and intended as, a vehicle of patriotism. 'Patriotism' – like 'imperialism' – was never a clear-cut concept. In the period of the making of a mass historical education between 1870 and 1930 debates raged between educationists, politicians and pressure groups about what history to teach, and how it should best be taught. Far from being divorced from educational psychology, I argue history gained credibility as a compulsory classroom subject only because it incorporated cutting-edge pedagogical developments. Educationists coined the concept of 'enlightened patriotism': for them, teaching history to young children should encourage an emotional relationship with the past; history should be presented as a narrative march from distant medieval origins towards the triumphant imperial present. Imperial values of mastery of the seas, love of liberty, courage, duty and hero worship were duly stitched into the narrative fabric of the complete duration of English history. In short, it is my argument that the imperial culture of late Victorian Britain did become manifest in the teaching of history, but in ways far more discreet than assumed and by use of methods which require further explication and analysis. The teaching of history was considered too politically sensitive in the formation of civic and national identities to leave to politicians alone.

The 'traditional' teaching of history?

It would be remiss, therefore, to carry out a study such as that presented in this book without reflecting on current developments in the National Curriculum in England. Since the election of the Coalition government in May 2010, the Conservative Secretary of State for Education, Michael Gove, has set about installing a narrative-based National Curriculum for History in which tales from 'our island story' take centre stage. As Terry Haydn explains, Gove's explicit aim is 'to use the school curriculum to shape the values, attitudes, and dispositions of future citizens and restore the Victorian Values of patriotism, service, duty and obedience'.[22] The phrase 'our island story' has appeared in every speech and interview given by Gove on the subject of history education. Writing on 10 November 2011, I have counted sixty-three instances these past eighteen months alone. For instance, on 5 October 2010, Gove announced:

> One of the under-appreciated tragedies of our time has been the sundering of our society from its past. Children are growing up ignorant of one of the most inspiring stories I know – the history of our United Kingdom. Our history has moments of pride, and shame, but unless we fully understand the struggles of the past we will not properly value the liberties of the present. The current approach we have to history denies children the opportunity to hear our island story. Children are given a mix of topics at primary, a cursory run through Henry the Eighth and Hitler at secondary and many give up the subject at 14, without knowing how the vivid episodes of our past become a connected narrative. This trashing of our past has to stop.[23]

According to Gove, the English do not teach enough of their own history and, when they do, it is rendered pointless by an overconcentration on skills above narrative content. Ultimately, the complaint is that the history curriculum in its current guise fails to promote national pride.[24] The former criticism – that not enough national history is taught – is blatantly false.[25] The latter criticism, that school history should serve the explicit ends of patriotism and national identity, arguably explains the yearning for a return to a presupposed golden age of history teaching in which lessons are presumed to reinforce patriotic sensibilities. It goes without saying that questions of how to teach Britain's imperial past remain hotly contested.[26]

Prior to the 1902 Education Act, discrete lessons in history were not compulsory in any school. Indeed, although the Board of Education published a series of *Suggestions* at regular intervals,[27] it was not until the introduction of a National Curriculum in 1990 that the government effected any statutory requirement for the *content* of history lessons. Yet, critics of contemporary historical education demand a return to past practice in which the narrative of continuous English national history was taught so that lessons (allegedly) served the ends of the state, all children were (supposedly) fed a bountiful feast of patriotic stories and grew up (it is assumed) to be proud members of the nation state. The 'traditional teaching of history' is identified as a product of the later nineteenth century, which found consensus in the interwar period but was believed wrongly abandoned in the 1970s as a result of educational psychologists exercising a pernicious influence on the schools by their prioritisation of child-centred learning.[28] 'New' style history modules, introduced by the Schools Council History Project in the 1970s, were variously labelled by (old) New Right critics as the 'Friendly Red Army' and the 'Shop Steward Syllabus' and were accused of 'peddling crackpot ideologies' and 'leaving our young people distrustful and confused'.[29] In 1987, New Right pamphleteer Stewart Deuchar yearned for a time when 'a school was a school and a teacher was a teacher and history was – more or less – history'.[30] In the words of the Education Secretary from 1980–86, Keith Joseph, 'an unholy alliance' of socialists, teachers and educationists had contributed to the dismantling of traditional teaching to the overall detriment of children's national self-understanding.[31] Jonathan Clark, lecturer in history at Oxford at the time, lent his support. In 1990, in a debate on 'History, the Nation and the Schools' held at Ruskin College,[32] he argued that this desire to return to a halcyon age of history teaching was owed to a modern crisis of British national identity demonstrating nostalgia for a time 'when "we" were more like "ourselves"'.[33] The restoration of a golden age of history teaching would, in Clark's summation, rescue children from the condescension of 'post-liberal', 'post-imperial' and 'postmodern' approaches to history: in doing so, the aim was that this would return to them a simple and politically expedient historical knowledge-base out of which to understand their nation and their place within it.[34] It is in this context that Gove revealed to *The Times*: 'I am an unashamed traditionalist'.[35]

It is the intention of this book to demonstrate the fragilities of such assumptions about past practice, especially since it is difficult not only to pin down *when* the golden age was, but also to decipher which 'tradition' critics are invoking. Peter Mandler has suggested the mobilisation of a 'golden age' itself is likelier a reference to critics' memories of their own education: that is, the history taught in grammar (or, one assumes, fee-paying) schools in the 1950s and 1960s.[36] Yet, in the 1950s, educationists bemoaned that they had inherited a system forged in the late nineteenth century. C.F. Strong (textbook author, school inspector and teacher educator), for instance, wrote that:

> current conceptions of history teaching have evolved in a period of less than a century. It is perhaps not surprising, therefore, that in no short time, the material and method of that teaching should have remained substantially what they were in the early days of their development in the last quarter of the nineteenth century.[37]

Maureen Bryant, similarly, in her Report of the History Syllabus Conference of 1967, stated: 'No-one in this country would advocate a prescribed course and yet there is a great deal of uniformity. Pressures from tradition – our own school days, courses at older universities, the whole apparatus of textbooks and examination syllabuses which we have inherited, all tend to produce uniformity'.[38] Both Strong and Bryant were aware that history teaching operated on two levels: the formalised system for older children in school beyond the compulsory leaving age, of whom there were relatively few, and a separate, simpler, system for the mass education of the many. Calls for the restoration of a golden age of history education conveniently both forget mass experience and neglect the crucial role of educational psychology in the development of compulsory history teaching.

In his analysis of the national education debates, Stephen Ball identified a restorationist impulse in the language of New Right critics which valorised 'traditional' teaching methods and denigrated progressive pedagogies.[39] Robert Phillips took this analysis one step further with particular regards to the teaching of history: 'it should come as no surprise to see attempts to define and cultivate certaintist notions of culture, identity and nationhood. A crucial arena in this process of cultural restorationism or cultural acclamation is the educational arena, particularly what is taught in the history classroom'.[40] Gove's insistence on a return to an island story narrative of national history constitutes precisely such an act of attempted restorationism. Theorists agree that shared history plays a vital function in the construction of both the 'nation' in general and national 'identity' in particular. Craig Calhoun, for instance, argues that central to identity formation is the notion of 'temporal depth' – that the peoples that make up a nation are linked through shared history.[41] Geoff Cubitt emphasises that nations are 'imagined as things enduring – endowed with origin, tradition, memory, heritage, history, destiny'.[42] Such arguments are not controversial. Rather, controversy emerges when one considers how those in the present *select* historical narratives from which to prescribe national identity. It has been over two decades since Eric Hobsbawm coined the phrase 'invention of tradition', a concept used to describe how – for political purpose – the past is shaped by the cultural, commercial or political demands of the present generation.[43] Anthony D. Smith, in contesting Hobsbawm's modernist approach to the making of nations and nationalisms, developed concepts of ethnosymbolism and myth-history, emphasising that selective stories of national ethnic origins generate nationalist sentiment since they tap into psychological symbols of belonging. Whether one subscribes to the modernist or ethnosymbolist point of view, it is hardly surprising that the teaching of history should excite so much debate: after all, the *national* curriculum for history denotes, hypothetically, control over a shared history out of which it is intended collective identification to the nation can be generated. It is no overstatement to argue that the battle to control the content of school history constitutes 'nothing less than a public and vibrant debate about the national soul'.⁴⁴

It is worth dwelling on Smith's identification of the three-part process invoked in how telling stories of national origins can dovetail political agendas.

1. Myth of a golden age – every nation requires a myth of origin, from which the 'people' emerge; the golden age is made up of stories of heroism, and a clear articulation of the accumulation of desirable national attributes. These stories should be connected together in a clear narrative demonstrating national progress over time.
2. Myth of decline – a need to show how the present was divorced from the past by enemies of the nation, or those who would seek to undermine national sentiment.
3. Myth of regeneration – requires the identification of why and how the nation lost its way; the restoration of the golden age to be achieved by a shift from 'explanatory myth to prescriptive ideology'.⁴⁵

Smith's taxonomy is reproduced here for three reasons. First, nostalgic accounts of history teaching in its 'golden age' produce and popularise false accounts which require investigation. Second, the identification of educationists as the folk devils responsible for decline is deliberately misleading; and, third, Gove's prescription of more Anglocentric history is troublesome in a context of multiculturalism and growing independence movements in Scotland, Wales and Northern Ireland. Calls to restore a 'traditional' teaching of history privilege English history. There is no explicit space in the New Right version of our island story for those other nations that make up the British and Hibernian Isles; nor – besides the tokenistic inclusion of post-1945 immigration – does Gove's narrative include space for the relationship between the English and those millions of people colonised as part of the imperial project. Even when taking into consideration timetable constraints and the day-to-day pressures of teaching, a history curriculum designed to promote a form of national identity which excludes as well as includes is worrying.

The role of the past in identity formation – of how 'we' represent 'us' to 'ourselves' – remains divisive. It is far from surprising that scholarship on four-nations historiography, prompted in the mid-1970s, has been reinvigorated in recent years.⁴⁶ 'National' histories were frantically rethought as a means to underpin constituent nationalisms in a manner that meant historians not only interrogated historical relationships between England, the metropole and 'her' peripheral nations,[47] but also wrote national histories which augmented independence movements.[48] In this context, the academic search for a distinctively *English* identity was revived. Paul Langford's *Englishness Identified* (2000), Robert Colls' *The Identity of England* (2002), Krishan Kumar's *The Making of English National Identity* (2003) and Peter Mandler's *The English National Character* (2006) are but a few. The English, in a context of political devolution, find it especially difficult to understand their particular 'identity' in a culture of post-imperial decline.[49] Following Colls and Mandler, that confusion is confounded by academic recognition that Englishness has never been constant and can only reliably be defined by its inconsistencies.[50] As Ernest Barker so presciently observed in 1927, 'not only is English national character made; it continues to be made and remade'.[51]

National identity is not a monolithic entity. It is an elusive, slippery and contested concept: it is shaped by a variety of factors; it is moulded to meet political concerns; it is often defined by the nature of questions asked by the researcher.[52] In the case of the relationship between history teaching and national identity formation, one must be aware that the reintroduction of perceived past practice is seen not only as a source of comfort but the means of reinvigoration. History teaching has been identified as a means for creating identity in 'new' nations.[53] In the case of an 'old' nation like England, the teaching of a single uncomplicated narrative is fraught with difficulties, especially if it incorporates, or seeks to revive, an outmoded version of *English* imperial history. To reintroduce the presupposed 'best' of past practice is but one of many ways to tell the story of English and British history. To teach only the one version, which is to the admitted ideological benefit of a particular political position, is not education but – to put it mischievously – the stuff of propaganda itself.

The past teaching of history was not as straightforward as made out by critics and it is the task of this book, therefore, to investigate what the teaching of history was like in its so-called 'golden age'. A series of important questions need to be asked. When taught, what was the content of and teaching methodology employed in historical education? If current critics bemoan the influence of educationists, what was the relationship between educationists and those fundamental to the creation of history syllabi and teaching resources a century or so ago? What types of resources were used in the classroom, both for the child to read, and to augment teachers' knowledge? And, on the question of teachers, how were they instructed to teach history and how were the key educational and political objectives of a historical education explained to them? The answers to these questions provide an alternative narrative to the presupposed 'history' of history teaching. Analysis of texts actually used in classrooms, and intended to be seen by all children, demonstrates that history was guaranteed a prized place on the curriculum precisely because of its unique contribution to citizenship education. It is a rich irony that critics of current historical education bemoan the influence of educationists as meddling and destructive; yet history gained a compulsory place on the curriculum in the early 1900s only because it embraced the most advanced, cutting-edge, pedagogical thinking of the period – a topic on which this book is the first to offer detailed analysis (see Chapter Two in particular).

The first half of this book investigates debates about the purpose and content of history teaching from the introduction of mass education in the 1870s to the onset of the First World War; in particular, I identify a dominant trend towards the incorporation of new educational theories in the 1890s. The second half examines how the content of reading books, with some contrast to textbooks, integrated pedagogical recommendations. More might be said on the social history of history teaching: for instance, if we had a better understanding of class sizes, classroom decoration, the relationship between history teaching and other subjects as well as extracurricular activities, and if we could read work produced by children, then we might learn more about the uptake of popular imperialism. That, again, is beyond the scope of a study which focuses on debates about purpose, but it is pleasing to note a number of historians of education are taking their research into the classroom.[54] The recent work of David Cannadine and his research team, though sketchy in its analysis of the first half of the twentieth century and mistakenly dismissive of the influence of pedagogical development, demonstrates that the story of history teaching can briefly be told by the capture of oral histories, administrative history and using children's classroom work.[55] The study of the comparable teaching of history in Irish, Scottish and Welsh schools, additionally beyond the scope of this book, would make for a fascinating insight into intra-British imperial understanding. Obviously, a study with a longer chronology would be welcome, but the pressure of word limit prevents me from taking the story – besides a few comments on legacies – beyond the 1920s. Although the majority of my focus is on the years leading up to the First World War, a chapter is provided on the effect of war and movements towards peace education in the early 1920s as a means to demonstrate that embedded practices remained largely unaltered. If there was any significant change in the 1920s, it was that the teaching of the history of the British Empire became more explicit.

In an impressive intervention into debates about English national identity, Robert Colls writes that '"England" is always up for debate, of course, but in recent years the debate has become critical. Because of this the revival of interest in national history is to be welcomed [...] It is my contention that we are living through a period of incomprehension [...] The English stand now in need of reassessment of who they are'.[56] Colls' objective is to provide an account of who the English *were*, so that some of the 'best and most useful parts of that history', much of which constitutes untold stories from English social history, can 'be carried forward into the future'. Taking a cue from Colls, it is my intention to provide a more nuanced analysis of the history of history teaching: how did the teaching of history tell the story of the development of English identity; and, what was the role of imperialism within that account? There are a number of untold stories and a number of lessons which might help us better understand the politics of both history teaching and post-imperial Britishness. With especial attention to the notion of 'enlightened patriotism', this book will hopefully contribute in its own way to early twenty-first century debate about the appropriate political purpose of history teaching.

Notes

1 G.T. Warner, *A Brief Survey of British History* (London: Blackie and Son, 1899), 248–9.
2 The most detailed discussion of what became dubbed 'The Great Debate' remains Rob Phillips' *History Teaching, Nationhood and the State: An Exploration of Policy Sociology* (London: Cassel, 1998). For a survey of twentieth-century developments, see R. Aldrich, 'New History: An Historical Perspective', in A.K. Dickinson, P.J. Lee and P.J. Rogers (eds), *Learning History* (London: Heinemann Educational, 1984), 210–24.
3 C.H.K. Marten, 'Some General Reflections on the Teaching of History', *History*, 2 (1913), 98. See Chapter One for elaboration.
4 J. MacKenzie, *Propaganda and Empire: The Manipulation of British Public Opinion* (Manchester: Manchester University Press, 1984), 174–97. Whereas MacKenzie recommended further research into training manuals and literacy primers (an invitation for further research which this book answers), subsequent scholars have tended to limit their surveys to textbooks alone. For example, Pamela Horn, 'English Elementary Education and the Growth of the Imperial Ideal', in J.A. Mangan (ed.), *Benefits Bestowed: Education and British Imperialism* (Manchester: Manchester University Press, 1988), 39–55; Michael Lieven, 'Bias in School History Textbooks', *Paradigm*, 2 (2000), 11–23; Steve Attridge, *Nationalism, Imperialism and Identity in Late Victorian Culture: Civil and Military Worlds* (Basingstoke: Palgrave, 2003), 44–8.
5 Valerie Chancellor's study of history teaching revealed much about the range of political opinion present in history textbooks *and* reading books, yet her study paid little attention to the actual number of scholars who studied history: as a study in textbook authorship it remains, however, a valuable resource in that it charts the whole of the nineteenth century and maps shifting attitudes. Chancellor, *History for their Masters: Opinion in the English History Textbook, 1800–1914* (London: Adams and Dart, 1970).

INTRODUCTION

6 MacKenzie, *Propaganda and Empire*, 175.
7 Board of Education, *Handbook of Suggestions for the Consideration of Teachers and Others Concerned with the Work of Public Elementary Schools* (HMSO, 1905), 61.
8 R.D. Bramwell, 'Curricular Determinants: An Historical Perspective', *History of Education Society Bulletin*, 12 (Autumn, 1973), 42. See also Kathryn Castle, *Britannia's Children: Reading Colonialism through Children's Books and Magazines* (Manchester: Manchester University Press, 1996), 4–6; Bill Marsden, '"Poisoned History": A Comparative Study of Nationalism, Propaganda and the Treatment of War and Peace in the Late Nineteenth and Early Twentieth-Century School Curriculum', *History of Education*, 29:1 (2000), 29–47.
9 S.J. Heathorn, *For Home, Country and Race: Constructing Gender, Class and Englishness in the Elementary School, 1880–1914* (Toronto: Toronto University Press, 2000); Heathorn, '"Let Us Remember that We, Too, Are English": Constructions of Citizenship and National Identity in English Elementary School Reading Books, 1880–1914', *Victorian Studies*, 38:4 (1995), 395–427.
10 Alec Ellis, *Educating Our Masters: Influences on the Growth of Literacy in Victorian Working Class Children* (Aldershot: Gower, 1985), 115; Heathorn, *For Home, Country and Race*, 11.
11 Alec Ellis, *History of Children's Reading and Literature* (London: Pergamon Press, 1968), 96.
12 Cited in Ellis, *History of Children's Reading*, 90.
13 Heathorn, *For Home, Country and Race*, 11.
14 H.L, Withers, 'Memorandum on the Teaching of History in the Schools of the London School Board' (1901), in Withers, *The Teaching of History and Other Papers* (Manchester: Sherrat and Hughes, 1904), 169.
15 London County Council, Education Committee, 'Report of a Conference on the Teaching of History in London Elementary Schools' (London: P.S. King and Son, [1911] 1923), 39.
16 For an earlier study that differentiated between textbooks and primers, though that differentiation was limited to analysis of age, see: Frank Glendenning, 'Attitudes to Colonialism and Race in British and French History Schoolbooks', *History of Education*, 3:2 (1974), 57–72.
17 Heathorn's work informs this study, as a scan of the endnotes will testify. It needs noting here, that my book expands analysis by extending chronological coverage into the 1920s, compares different types of texts used to teach history to children of different ages and class (textbooks for some older children and reading books intended for *all* children in compulsory schooling) and, most significantly, draws information from teacher-training manuals and texts on best practice. I elaborate upon the differences between these genres of text in Chapter One.
18 B. Porter, *The Absent-Minded Imperialists: What the British Really Thought About Empire* (Oxford: Oxford University Press, 2004).
19 Porter, *Absent-Minded Imperialists*, vii.
20 S. Ward, 'Echoes of Empire', *History Workshop Journal*, 62:1 (2006), 264–78.
21 David Cannadine, Jenny Keating and Nicola Sheldon, *The Right Kind of History: Teaching the Past in Twentieth-Century England* (Basingstoke: Palgrave, 2011), 37, 54–5.
22 Terry Haydn, '"Longing for the Past": Politicians and the History Curriculum in English Schools, 1988–2010', *Journal of Educational Media, Memory and Society*, 4:1 (2012), 14.
23 http://conservativehome.blogs.com/thetorydiary/2010/10/michael-gove-pupils-will-learn-our-island-story.html (accessed 12 August 2012).
24 See, for example, Niall Ferguson, 'History Has Never Been So Unpopular', *Guardian*, 29 March 2011.
25 An Ofsted (British State Office for Standards in Education) investigation into the teaching of history found that 'the view that too little British history is taught in secondary schools in England is a myth. Pupils in the schools visited studied a

considerable amount of British history and knew a great deal about the particular topics covered'. Cited in Richard Evans, '"The Wonderfulness of Us'" (the Tory Interpretation of History)', *London Review of Books*, 33:6 (March, 2011), 9–12.

26 Britain is not unique. Passionate debate about the content of school history textbooks is evident in 'culture wars' across the globe. See, for example, G. Nash, C. Crabtree and R.E. Dunn, *History on Trial: Culture Wars and the Teaching of the Past* (New York: Alfred A. Knopf, 1997); Terri Seddon, 'Politics and Curriculum: A Case Study of the Japanese History Textbook Dispute, 1982', *British Journal of Sociology of Education*, 8:2 (1987), 213–26; Marc Ferro, *The Use and Abuse of History, or, How the Past is Taught* (London: Routledge, 1984); Frank Furedi, *Mythical Past, Elusive Future: History and Society in an Anxious Age* (London: Pluto Press, 1992); David Tréfás, 'The Squaring of the Circle: The Reinvention of Hungarian History by the Communist Party in 1952', and Peter Rodgers, '(Re)Inventing the Past: The Politics of "National" History in the Ukrainian Classroom', both in *Studies in Ethnicity and Nationalism*, 6:2 (2006); Majid Al-Haj, 'National Ethos, Multicultural Education, and the New History Textbooks in Israel', *Curriculum Enquiry*, 35:1 (2005), 47–71; Elizabeth A. Cole (ed.), *Teaching the Violent Past: History Education and Reconciliation* (Plymouth: Powman and Littlefield, 2007).

27 D. Sylvester, 'A Historical Overview: Change and Continuity in History Teaching, 1900–1993', in H. Bourdillon (ed.), *Teaching History* (London and New York: Routledge, 1994), 9–23.

28 Aldrich, 'New History: An Historical Perspective', 210–24.

29 K. Crawford, 'A History of the Right: The Battle for Control of National Curriculum History, 1989–1994', *British Journal of Educational Research*, 43: 4 (1995), 442.

30 S. Deuchar, *History and GCSE History* (London: Centre for Policy Studies, 1987), 1.

31 Cited in D. Lawton, *The Tory Mind on Education, 1979–94* (London: Falmer, 1994), 144.

32 Some of the papers of which are reproduced as a special feature in *History Workshop Journal*, 29 (1990), 92–133, including short articles by Clark, Raphael Samuel, Janet Nelson, Alice Prochaska and Sylvia Collicott.

33 J.C.D. Clark, 'National Identity, State Formation and Patriotism: The Role of History in the Public Mind', *History Workshop Journal*, 29 (1990), 101.

34 Clark, 'National Identity, State Formation and Patriotism', 96.

35 Cited in Haydn, 'Longing for the Past', 14.

36 Peter Mandler, 'Is History in Danger'. Discussion piece for 'History, the Nation and the Schools', *History Workshop Online*, 19 March 2011. Available at: www.historyworkshop.org.uk/history-the-nation-and-the-schools/ (accessed 20 March 2014).

37 C.F. Strong, *History in the Secondary School* (London: University of London Press, 1958), 49.

38 Cited in A. Syriatou, 'Educational Policy and Educational Content: The Teaching of European History in Secondary Schools in England and Wales, 1945–1975' (unpublished PhD thesis, University of London, 1996), 47.

39 S.J. Ball, 'Education, Majorism and the Curriculum of the Dead', *Curriculum Studies*, 1:2 (1993), 195–214. See also Gary McCulloch, 'Privatising the Past: History and Education Policy in the 1990s', *British Journal of Education Studies*, 45:1 (1997), 69–82.

40 R. Phillips, 'History Teaching, Cultural Restorationism and National Identity in England and Wales', *Curriculum Studies*, 4:3 (1996), 387. See also G. Elwyn Jones, 'The Debate over the National Curriculum for History in England and Wales, 1989–90: The Role of the Press', *The Curriculum Journal*, 11:3 (2000), 299–322.

41 C. Calhoun, *Nationalism* (Buckingham: Open University Press, 1997), 5.

42 G. Cubitt (ed.), 'Introduction', *Imagining Nations* (Manchester: Manchester University Press, 1998), 8.

43 E. Hobsbawm, 'Introduction', in E. Hobsbawm and T. Ranger (eds), *The Invention of Tradition* (Cambridge: Cambridge University Press, 1992), 1–14.

INTRODUCTION

44 R. Phillips, P. Goalen, A. McCully and S. Wood, 'Four Histories, One Nation: History Teaching, Nationhood and a British Identity', *Compare*, 29:2 (1999), 153.
45 Anthony D. Smith, *Myths and Memories of the Nation* (Oxford: Oxford University Press, 1999), summarised from pages 64–8.
46 J.G.A. Pocock, 'British History: A Plea for a New Subject', *Journal of Modern History*, 47:1 (1975), 601–21. His ideas have been further advanced in two essays: 'The Limits and Divisions of British History: In Search of the Unknown Subject', *American Historical Review*, 87:2 (1982), 311–36; and, 'Conclusion: Contingency, Identity, Sovereignty', in Alexander Grant and Keith Stringer (eds), *Uniting the Kingdom? The Making of British History* (London and New York: Routledge, 1995), 292–302.
47 Debate on the 'new British historiography', or 'four-nations historiography' has received considerable attention: some of these edited collections contain excellent contributions (this list is by no means exhaustive): Grant and Stringer (eds), *Uniting the Kingdom?*; L. Brockliss and D. Eastwood (eds), *A Union of Multiple Identities: The British Isles, c.1750–1850* (Manchester: Manchester University Press, 1997); S. Caunce, E. Mazierska, S. Sydney-Smith and J.K. Walton (eds), *Relocating Britishness* (Manchester: Manchester University Press, 2004); H. Brocklehurst and R. Phillips (eds), *History, Nationhood and the Question of Britain* (Basingstoke: Palgrave, 2004); Raphael Samuel (ed.), *Patriotism: The Making and Unmaking of British National Identity*, 3 volumes (London: Routledge, 1989). For analysis of these debates, see John MacKenzie, 'Irish, Scottish, Welsh and English Worlds? The Historiography of a Four-nations Approach to the History of the British Empire' in Catherine Hall and Keith McClelland (eds), *Race, Nation and Empire: Making Histories,1750 to the Present* (Manchester: Manchester University Press, 2010), 133–53.
48 See, for example, the mobilisation of Rees Davies' and Gwyn Williams' work on Wales, and David McCrone's and Tom Devine's work on Scotland by Plaid Cymru and the Scottish National Party. Rees Davies, *The First English Empire: Power and Identities in the British Isles 1093–1343* (Oxford: Oxford University Press, 2000); Gwyn A. Williams, *When Was Wales? A History of the Welsh* (Harmondsworth: Penguin Books, 1991); Tom Devine, *The Scottish Nation* (London: Allen Lane, 1999); D. McCrone, *Understanding Scotland: The Sociology of a Stateless Nation* (London: Routledge, 1992).
49 Tom Nairn, *The Break-Up of Britain: Crisis and Neo-Nationalism*, second edition (London: New Left Books, 1977); Michael Hechter, *Internal Colonialism: The Celtic Fringe in British National Development* (Berkeley: University of California Press, 1975). See also Hugh Kearney, *The British Isles: A History of Four Nations* (Cambridge: Cambridge University Press, 1989).
50 Peter Mandler, *The English National Character: The History of an Idea from Edmund Burke to Tony Blair* (New Haven: Yale University Press, 2006); Robert Colls, *The Identity of England* (Oxford: Oxford University Press, 2002); Paul Langford, *Englishness Identified: Manners and Character, 1650–1850* (Oxford: Oxford University Press, 2000); Krishan Kumar, *The Making of English National Identity* (Cambridge: Cambridge University Press, 2003).
51 Ernest Barker, *National Character and the Factors in its Formation* (London: Methuen, 1927), 8.
52 Peter Mandler, 'What Is "National Identity"? Definitions and Applications in Modern British Historiography', *Modern Intellectual History*, 3:2 (2006), 271–97.
53 R. Guyver and T. Taylor (eds), *History Wars and the Classroom: Global Perspectives* (London and Charlotte, NC: Information Age Publishing, 2011).
54 I. Grosvenor, M. Lawn, and K. Rousmaniere (eds), *Silences and Images: The Social History of the Classroom* (New York: Peter Lang, 1999).
55 Cannadine, Keating and Sheldon, *The Right Kind of History*. Focus on pre-1939 largely reflects administrative history.
56 Colls, *Identity of England*, 6.

PART I

Contested histories: the teaching of history in its 'golden age'

CHAPTER ONE

Enlightened patriotism: or, what was history for?

In 1902, Liberal politician Richard Burdon Haldane prefaced the publication of a series of his lectures on *Education and Empire*:

> Today, at the beginning of the twentieth century, we as a nation have to face the problem of preserving our great commercial position, and with it the great Empire which the great men of past generations have won and handed down to us. That empire it is our duty to hold as a sacred trust, and to pass on in such a fashion that those who come after may be proud of us, as we are proud of the forefathers who did their work before our time. The duty which we have to discharge requires an effort. That effort must assume the form neither of swaggering along the High Street of the world, nor of sitting down with folded hands on a dust heap. It is rather to be sought in clear views and activity of the kind that is at once unhasting and unresting. Around us is surging up a flood of new competition. If we are to hold the ground which our predecessors won before the days of that competition, we shall require above all enlightened views.[1]

It is valuable to reproduce this since it encapsulates much contemporary thinking about the empire. There is an evident sense of paranoia: competitor nations threaten Britain's economic supremacy. Thus, Britain must take urgent action to maintain her position and, critically, if the correct actions are not taken the achievements of 'the great men of the past' will be undermined. The teaching of history was, explicitly, to inculcate 'enlightened views'. The significance of the word 'enlightened' within contemporaneous educational discourse will become clear below. In Haldane's lecture 'Great Britain and Germany: A Study in Education', he outlined how schooling in Germany was attuned to the needs of the state.[2] That, he argued, was a model the British should mimic. He urged those who had the power of influence in society to take action by manipulating what was taught in schools. For Haldane, Britain had for too long taken its international position for granted. Reverence for the past and responsibility to the future were key to Haldane's formulation of how to avert this worrying situation. If the nation were diagnosed as sick, the appropriate teaching of history was prescribed as a sure-fire antidote.

In this light, it becomes clear why the government sent a number of researchers to Germany to find out how such a newly created nation could economically advance so rapidly and thus threaten Britain's empire.[3] Michael Sadler, school inspector and made Director of the Office of Special Enquiries and Reports in 1895, was dispatched to Germany in 1906 with the task of researching how they taught Civics in particular. It was he who, upon his return, introduced to British educational jargon the phrase 'Education *for* Citizenship',[4] not the more recent think tanks who succeeded in 2002 in their aim of having citizenship introduced to the curriculum as a discrete secondary school subject.[5] From Sadler's advice, it was clear that much work was needed to continue inspiring children to *want* to do their best for their nation. The Germans, he argued (rather contentiously) in 1916, have 'made profitable use of second-rate intelligence [because they have] not neglected the mind' and had thus 'made systematic cooperation a habit'.[6] The conclusions which were returned cited education as an especially significant factor: to continue to compete in the global market the English, like the Germans, needed to fuse the ends of education and economic policy.[7] In 1913, W.H. Webb had fretted in *History*, the in-house journal of the Historical Association, that Germany, Japan, Italy and the 'regressive Balkan states' had put history to effective use whereas Britain had done too little to gear teaching towards the promotion of imperial pride. In 'our school code', he lamented, 'History is barely recognised and Patriotism, the twin sister of History, is ignored [...] the children of those countries imbibe the love of country with their mother's milk, and when they grew older, History and Patriotism took their hands and guided them into paths every true lover of his own land ought to go'.[8] On the evidence of such statements, it comes as no surprise that a number of studies have focused on the development of the history curriculum in Britain predominantly in the context of asking questions regarding the reach of imperial propaganda. The content of some texts used in classrooms may well have reflected that turn of the twentieth century Britain was an imperial nation concerned to instil patriotism in its young. Yet, closer attention to the history of history teaching, as well as debates about its intended purpose, demonstrates that these assumptions are fraught with methodological problems. Educationists, wary of the overt politicisation of the curriculum, pressed not for the teaching of patriotism *per se*, but 'enlightened patriotism'.

To do so, educationists concentrated their efforts on elementary school education – where the vast majority of the nation's children were taught their lessons in history through literacy primers. At the outset of our period, subject-specific lessons in history in state schools were significantly few in number. John Smith's analysis of Her Majesty's Inspectors' (HMI) reports finds that, prior to Education Acts of the earlier twentieth century, 'the take-up of history, despite various government initiatives, was derisory'.[9] History was considered poorly taught (strict emphases on rote-learning was lambasted) and poorly resourced (textbooks and teacher training was deemed woeful). One head teacher informed the Cross Commission in 1887 that history, in elementary schools, 'was almost extinct'.[10] By the 1900s, however, history's status as a low-ranking subject had quite reversed, to the extent that discrete lessons were made compulsory. In secondary schools, history was made a statutory part of the curriculum in 1900. For elementary schools, the regulation was implemented in 1901 and endorsed by the Balfour Act of 1902.[11] In the words of Olive Shropshire, a near-contemporary doctoral student researching history teaching in English schools for a Colombia thesis: '[t]he effect of the Act of 1902 was fairly electric. In 1901 history had been taught in 5,838 departments of the elementary schools. Almost overnight these figures leapt to 25,053'.[12] Prior to the 1902 Act, less than 5 per cent of children in London's Board Schools sat in subject-specific history lessons (only 26,781 out of 581,976) which became a compulsory minimum of two hours per week in 1901 for those children in Standard IV or above (above the age of seven).[13] C.H.K. Marten, one-time President of the Historical Association, recalled when writing in the 1930s that 'History may be said to be a creation of the twentieth century'.[14]

If discrete lessons in history were slight in number, and those that were taught were criticised, attitudes to historical stories in literacy primers, especially from the 1880s onwards, were markedly different. Educationists, and those who campaigned to influence the curriculum, recognised that reading books (designed for all children) could do much to serve ends beyond teaching the skill of reading. Reading books, as will be seen, not only sold in far higher number, but incorporated the latest developments in pedagogical theory. Unlike textbooks, they were designed with the aim to inculcate values rather than transmit knowledge. So embedded were reading books in the elementary system that, when history was made a compulsory part of the curriculum, it was this genre of text which was cited as the model for emulation. This chapter explores changing attitudes to the role of history: how could a subject, so infrequently taught in subject-specific lessons, become considered a vital constituent of the compulsory curriculum?

What precipitated this change? Why did teachers find making the transition to compulsory history education an easy, cost-free and convenient shift to make? Simply put, history had gained status because it had become identified as the subject best positioned to teach children their civic, national and – crucially – moral values. Debate may have raged about ideal content, but there was little disagreement with the view that all children should learn their historical lessons.

The first section of this chapter elaborates on the nature of history teaching before and after 1900–1 and justifies the sources used in this study. I demonstrate in more detail that the reading book, rather than textbook, is the more profitable source for studying the majority experience of historical education. This is especially so when taking into account texts produced for teachers: these method manuals provide unique insights into how educationists understood the usefulness of history. The second and third sections explore political and cultural attitudes to the teaching of history. Was this dramatic change in favour of history due to a perceived need to teach imperial values? Past studies assume history served to promote pro-imperial propaganda, yet closer attention to contemporary debates reveals history was rated highly for its contribution to citizenship – what educationists labelled 'enlightened patriotism'.

The development of historical education in English schools

The Revised Code of 1862 not only introduced the compulsory teaching of the 3 'R's – reading, writing and arithmetic – but introduced a system of payments by result. Schools received payment for children passing exams in these and other subjects. The teaching of subject-specific history had been castigated before the Code, and continued to be criticised after its introduction. When history was taught, inspection reports demonstrate profound disappointment. One noted in 1852 that 'I ought to except English History from those subjects in which I have witnessed any signal progress in our schools'.[15] When history *was* taught, the need for schools to attain the results required led to a rote-learning system of education which emphasised a factual curriculum. Such lessons, often based on teachers' use of densely packed textbooks, were lambasted. A witness reported to the Newcastle Commission (1861), that history lessons, when taken, suffered because 'there is much forced upon the memory that cannot be long remembered, and that would be useless if it were'.[16] The Bishop of Oxford lamented to the House of Lords in 1862 that this was 'the very worst criterion of the progress of education'.[17]

ENLIGHTENED PATRIOTISM?

Inspectors found little reason to praise the subject-specific history lesson following the Code's introduction. In his *General Report for the Year 1864*, Mr Birley noted with dismay that 'Geography, Grammar and History still occupy their places upon the "timetables", and that I fear is all'.[18] G.C. Williamson expressed his concern in 1891, complaining in his text on the teaching of history that 'to call history a collection of dates, to learn parrot-fashion by rote a series of dates, and to be able to repeat William I, 1066–1087, William II, 1087–100, and so on, is to degrade the very name of history'.[19] According to the academic Joshua Fitch, this was 'a joyless and useless mnemonic'.[20] 'The result [of rote learning] on pupils is generally disastrous', wrote James Welton in his popular teacher-training manual, continuing: 'nothing fatigues the brain so much as an attempt to acquire a large number of unsystemised facts'.[21] Another inspector, writing in 1872, observed:

> [O]ne aim was to 'cram' a certain amount of information into the brains of their scholars, which the latter should reproduce at the inspection. Reading lessons were given without a word of explanation, without a question to test how far the children had understood what they had been reading; spelling was taught mechanically, with as little reference as possible to the meaning of the words as affected by their form; arithmetic was not made interesting by the application of its principles to practical cases, but was dinned into the ears of the scholars in the same unvarying abstract form. Of geography, or grammar, or history I am persuaded that in the majority of schools not one word was spoken from year's end to year's end.[22]

Schools, obliged to focus on examination subjects, chose subjects deemed easier for the child to pass.[23] For older children, it was financially disingenuous to choose to teach subject-specific history as an examination subject in the context of payment by results. Little wonder that schools preferred instead to enter children for geography exams.[24] In 1874, history was made an optional 'class' subject, but its uptake was low. The combined number of scholars taught history in Warwick, Brighton, Blackburn and Kendal, between 1882 and 1884, for instance, was a paltry 4,215 out of a total 151,144 (geography and grammar both polled over 60,000). In 1898, only 5,133 schools across England – out of a sum number of nearly 50,000 – chose to teach history.[25]

The woeful standard of teaching resources compounded history's poor reputation. Subject-specific textbooks adopted the catechical frame, serving to underpin the rote method. Teacher educator Terence Raymont complained that the persistent use of outmoded textbooks 'furnish for sad reflection on our school system'.[26] Welton acknowledged in his manual that 'it is because many teachers know history only in the guise of an inferior school text-book that the subject has no attraction for them, and consequently is abhorred by their pupils'.[27] Moreover, up until reforms of the late century, it is hardly surprising that history was rejected in primary schools since teachers had little experience in it as a discrete timetabled subject. Specific training in history barely featured in teacher education, as J.M. Goldstrom's study of official state papers relating to the education of teachers reveals.[28] Stephen Colledge's short essay on history in the training college not only confirms that history was considered unimportant by tutors, but that even young teachers-in-training struggled to remember the 'basics'.[29]

When schools opted to teach history before the legislative amendments of 1900–2, it was usually for older children since the teaching grant was only available for upper standards.[30] As seen, however, teachers were compelled from 1882 to teach young children the art of reading through use of literacy primers.[31] In these lessons, children were examined on their ability to read, not recall content. This was significant: briefly put, history taught as story, rather than a compendium of dry facts, was imbued with a greater potential to inculcate values precisely because it was likelier to generate an emotional reaction in the child. Before analysing pedagogical developments in depth (in the next chapter), two contextual factors require further discussion. First, the economics of educational publishing are considered in order to demonstrate that reading books were used in far superior number than subject-specific textbooks. Second, more attention needs to be paid to late Victorian and Edwardian debates about the social utility of historical education.

By the beginning of the twentieth century, about 96 per cent of the 32.5 million inhabitants of England and Wales could read. This, Alexis Weedon argues, owed not only to the fact that learning how to read had been made compulsory in a mass education system, but also because the cost of books had declined so steeply that schools had ready access to mass-produced reading resources.[32] Paper value had decreased to two-thirds of its 1866 value, improvements to typesetting and publishing technologies increased the speed at which texts could be manufactured, so that for the general book market, the period between '1846 and 1916 saw a fourfold increase in production and a halving of book prices'.[33] Within the education market specifically, the Mundella revisions to the Educational Code of 1883 established a fixed grant per pupil which provided schools with enhanced powers for book purchase. 'Cheapness was a dominant criterion', Weedon maintains, and it is therefore significant that, in comparison to the lavishly illustrated and expensive to purchase textbooks, 'for the most part elementary school books were small and inexpensive'.[34] *Circular 233: Reading Books* (1884) outlined to inspectors that they should encourage schools to purchase reading books in bulk so that every child had the opportunity to use one.[35]

Sales figures for reading books far surpassed those for subject-specific textbooks, outnumbering them by a ratio of 10 to 1. Charles Oman's renowned textbook, *The History of England* (1895), sold only 6,000 copies between 1897 and 1902.[36] C.R.L. Fletcher's and Rudyard Kipling's *School History of England* (1911), referenced by Pamela Horn as an *elementary* school text, failed also to sell in high numbers.[37] Not only was it simply too expensive but it was never intended for an elementary school audience. In fact, this text was to unleash furious debate at the time about whether history should be used to promote national pride at all (I discuss the reception of Fletcher's text in more detail below). Bernard Porter's correspondence with the archivist at Oxford University Press reveals that the text sold 135,000 copies between the release of its first edition in 1911 and its last in 1954, including a release via a New York publisher in 1911 and a Parisian publisher in 1932.[38] These are respectable numbers, but they pale into insignificance when compared to reading book sales. Longman, for instance, published 480,000 *New Reading Books* between 1885 and 1902 alone, including 115,000 of its *Ship Historical Readers* between 1891 and 1902 and 120,000 *Ship Literary Readers* between 1894 and 1904. Reading books published by Macmillan numbered 263,000 sales between 1892 and 1895, while those published by Edward Arnold between 1898 and 1900 numbered just short of 123,000.[39] The London School Board alone purchased 95,520 sets of historical readers between 1897 and 1900.[40]

The statistical differences are thus significant. By weight of sales figures, state recommendation and teaching practice, it is imperative that historians – seeking to gauge the historical content read by the majority of the nation's schoolchildren – look to reading books rather than textbooks. Attention to reading books is especially important since educationists held these in higher regard than textbooks. Whereas textbooks were widely lambasted, educationists were keen to praise improvements to literacy primers. David Salmon reminded those teachers in training who read his manual that it was crucial they chose texts to teach history which would appeal to young children since these books might be the first – and possibly the only – reading they would undertake:

> Reading books should be chosen with great care. Poor children read few other books, and no children read any other books so slowly, so minutely, or so repeatedly. We cannot expect children to love books which are not worth loving; hence, whether the lessons in the reading book be continuous or detached, whether they be selected because they contain certain words, convey certain information, inculcate certain moral truths, or stimulate certain emotions, they should invariably be interesting.[41]

Some inspectors worried that reading books would not test the child's historical knowledge: T.W. Danby, reporting in 1894, was frustrated that he would listen to children read historical content yet was unable to decipher if they were learning 'a picture drawn out of perspective'.[42] Yet most, given the scant teaching of history as a timetabled subject in its own right, found satisfaction that some history was read. Withers was pleased that reading lessons 'excite[d] curiosity and stimulate[d] an appetite for increased knowledge'.[43] The Board of Education insisted that the historical reading book was cited as an example of best practice because it inspired both love for reading and interest in the subject matter.[44] J.J. Findlay, Professor of Education at Manchester, insisted historical reading books were the most effective resources for engaging the imagination of children, thus influencing their sense of duty as citizens and patriots.[45] The historical reading book had proved to be popular with children and teachers not only because it was written in a 'spirited and rigorous human style', but – according to another educationist – could be 'read for its own intrinsic interest', and would stimulate the 'emotions' and 'mental excitement'.[46] It is not surprising, furthermore, to find that when history was made compulsory, it was recommended that teachers use reading books, not textbooks.

A further reason for the increased status of the historical reading book owed to the closer alignment of schools and universities.[47] The Historical Association was established in 1906 in England (with a belated Scottish branch in 1912). Indeed, in 1928, C.H.K. Marten, in his then guise as Chairman of the Historical Association's Examinations Committee, commented that 'the great advance that has been made in history teaching in English schools in the last thirty years or so is due in no small part to the influence of university historians'.[48] The professionalisation of history in universities had three direct, and positive, consequences for history in schools. Academics involved themselves in the *practice* of school history teaching: first, by writing texts and delivering lectures for teachers; second, by writing reading books and textbooks for use in the classroom; and, third, by presiding over a new generation of graduates of degree schemes in modern history who would themselves form a new cadre of specialist author.[49]

Often, the leading academics of the day watered down their own publications to a suitable language pitch, including Mandell Creighton, Frederick York-Powell, T.F. Tout, S.R. Gardiner and Oscar Browning.[50] Whereas, in the mid-nineteenth century, textbook authors tended to be clergymen, or the wives of clergymen, by the First World War the majority of texts were written by either academics, those with degrees in history, or those, such as G.A. Henty and John Finnemore, who had made their names as popular authors of juvenile adventure fiction. G.D. Howat commented in his survey of authors that those who 'were now writing for schools were also producing the major works of historical research and criticism'.[51] Further comment on the relationship between university historians and the teaching of history in schools is found in Chapter Three. Most frequently, however, authors of reading books were drawn from the burgeoning ranks of history graduates. Large publishing houses employed subject-specialist graduates: the houses of Adam and Charles Black, Cassell, Collins, Longmans and Macmillan, to name but a few, made a great deal of money from the business of educational publishing.[52] Publishing houses required 'specialist' authors because their name (along with their well-publicised degree) added an air of expertise and professionalism to the texts, which made them more marketable, and thus more saleable.[53]

Perhaps the greatest effect on the teaching of history in elementary schools was wrought by those who taught in teacher-training colleges and education departments in universities: John Adams, Catherine Dodd and J.J. Findlay are but three names of those little known in previous studies of the history of history teaching, but whose influence, we will see in the next chapter, was of paramount significance. The Act of 1902 boosted the importance of those deemed to be 'experts' in pedagogical matters. In the absence of strict centralised demands, method manuals served ostensibly as textbooks of best teaching practice.[54] As a result, a large number of manual authors, and others renowned for their work in progressive educational methods, were invited to give special talks and lectures to introduce teachers to educational theory.[55] Their influence on a new generation of teachers must not be underestimated. The numbers of children attending school rose exponentially following the introduction of mass compulsory and then free education, rising from 4 million registered scholars in 1881 to 5,750,000 by 1900.[56] These children required teachers. Between 1870 and 1895 the number of certified teachers increased from approximately 12,000 to 53,000 and to 114,000 by 1900 if one includes those who had not studied for their certificate. In addition, in the same period, the number of pupil-teachers rose from 14,000 to 34,000, and the number of adult assistant teachers was raised from a thousand to

28,000.[57] New teachers needed to be trained how to teach. Dedicated training colleges increased in frequency so that there were 1,355 of these by 1900, to which were added sixteen specialist residential pupil-teacher training centres in the 'great cities' between 1890 and 1900 which were connected to university colleges.[58] It is no surprise that a new genre of text emerged towards the end of the nineteenth century aimed specifically at instructing teachers in best practice.

Teachers constitute an essential, yet under-researched, piece of our puzzle. Heathorn studies them, but only in passing. In Porter's story of the history of how the working classes were taught, teachers appear only briefly.[59] Yet, to understand the history taught in the classroom, we need to know how teachers were advised to teach. Educationists in this period devoted much more attention to children as individuals (the present generation might call them 'autonomous learners') than is generally realised. This is the core sentiment in the following lengthy extract from Oscar Browning. Browning, of course, was not just an academic historian of some repute; he also had his finger firmly on the pulse of the condition of history in schools. He wrote textbooks and some reading books (*The Newbery History Readers*) and kept his fellow historians and history teachers abreast of developments in educational theory. This is how, in 1881, he began his *Introduction to the History of Educational Theories*:

> [E]ducation has always been a favourite problem with philosophers. Those who have wished to reform or reorganise the world, meeting with many difficulties in dealing with the mass of grown-up people, have turned their eyes to the more hopeful body of ingenious youth, whose minds are like white paper or pliant wax. If only the rising generation can be directed in the proper path, the regeneration of the human race will be a reality instead of a dream. Experience ought by this time to have taught us that these hopes are misleading. From one point of view education can do much, from another it can do little. A child is born into the world with its faculties given to it once and for all. No power can be put into it which is not there already. Its parents and a long line of ancestors have determined of what nature it shall be. As it grows up, and we fancy that we can fathom its capabilities and gauge its strength, we forget the countless capacities which lie hidden in the simple germ.[60]

Educationists thought about children as individuals: they were not blind to the prejudices, talents and problems which accompanied children to the classroom.[61] Payment by results was dismantled in the 1890s, which reduced pressure on schools to deliver a knowledge-dominated curriculum. Instead, in 1896 the Inspectorate urged school managers and teachers to augment their teaching by incorporating pedagogical developments into their programmes.[62] History was often understood to be the subject in which the teacher's individuality was most obvious. Joseph Landon's view that 'there is probably no subject commonly taught in schools on the treatment of which the teacher's views of life, political bias, intellectual habits, and the extent of his reading exercise so powerful an influence as on the teaching of history' was common.[63] Despite the uncertainties of knowing the thoughts of individual teachers, and indeed the actualities of their individual teaching practice,[64] research into teaching manuals provides plenty of evidence for how it was intended they teach history.

Teaching manuals can tell us more about what teachers were told was effective practice, how teachers were recommended to teach certain subjects, and, crucially for this study, how teachers were informed on how to use reading books in their teaching. These manuals constitute the significant textual output of the 'New Education' movement of the 1890s, some of which was concerned with teaching manual skills, but most of which was geared towards the promotion of moral values. Written by Masters of Method at training colleges,[65] these texts came together to constitute a consensus view on why history teaching, especially through the medium of the literacy primer, was important. In discussions within manuals of the merits of history teaching, the most significant 'group' were the 'Herbartians'. Johann Friedrich Herbart (1776–1841), labelled by Browning as the 'father of scientific pedagogy',[66] had formulated a scientific approach to education. His aim, above all, was to use education to produce 'moral citizens'. His pedagogical principles were identified by English educationists to provide an especially useful rationale for an education geared toward civic values, rather than rote-learning.[67] Herbart's ideas had been popular in the newly unified Germany in the 1870s, and it did not take long both for the translation of his works into English, and for the emergence in England of texts governed by adaptations of his method. The significance of Herbartian views on the purpose of history education is discussed further in Chapter Two.

What needs to be noted here is that teaching manuals, and their authors who taught in day training colleges and pupil-teaching centres and universities, were heavily influenced by the Herbartian method. Edmond Holmes, one time Her Majesty's Chief Inspector of Schools and reactionary critic against the Herbartians, opened his text, *In Defence of What Might Be* (1914), with the grudging comment that the Herbartians had become too 'influential ... in virtue of their control of Training Colleges'.[68] J.J. Findlay observed in his *Principles of Class Teaching* (1911 edition) that 'most of the books on Method written in recent years reveal their obligations to the Herbartian pedagogy, even where they make no direct reference to it'.[69] We can be reasonably certain that Herbartian ideas were introduced to a majority of teachers. That Herbartians emphasised the centrality of historical stories to a curriculum which prioritised an education in moral and civic values, as we will see, explains why the teaching of history was *not* explicitly geared towards the promotion of imperialism alone. The introduction of mass education incurred a cost and involved such a level of state involvement in people's everyday lives that a study of educational change in this period, divorced from considerations of the social and political context, would be to ignore the competing forces which sought to influence the aims and methods of elementary schooling. In particular, we need to know more about the nature and influence of imperial forces on the teaching and learning of history. It is to these more general contextual issues out of which mass historical education emerged at the turn of the twentieth century that we now turn.

Imperial intentions and civic objectives in the teaching of history

A wide range of voices clamoured to influence the content, teaching methodology and objectives of mass education. In doing so, these voices generated significant debate about both the purpose of schooling generally and a historical education in particular. What, according to educationists at the time and others who would attempt to influence the curriculum, was history *for*? There was a general consensus that history should influence the child's perception of its national and civic duties, yet there was also disagreement about how best to achieve this. The term 'citizenship' was cited with a frequency which suggests the demands of immediate returns in the social domestic setting outweighed educational obligations to the national and imperial project. As is clear in the following extract from the educationist Terence Raymont, sensationalist celebrations of empire stood 'for a very small part of what we mean by trying to make good citizens'.

> By the making of citizens we must not be understood to mean the inculcation of a narrow and selfish patriotism. This warning is necessary, because it seems only too possible to take a parochial view even of a great empire. The waving of national flags and the singing of national anthems, though quite proper in their way, stand for a very small part of what we mean by trying to make good citizens.[70]

Withers berated those who insisted history should be used to inculcate jingoism: the teaching of history, he argued, should not be a vehicle for 'partisan feelings in home affairs, or for international grudges in the discussion of foreign politics'.[71]

History teaching, especially the history taught to young children in reading books, was identified as a particularly valuable method to instil values. In a lecture delivered to the Historical Association in 1913, F.J.C. Hearnshaw, textbook author and renowned Oxford Professor, commented:

> It may be admitted that all three ends [of education] – the training of hand, of head and of heart – are, in their due proportions, good. But it may be contended – indeed it is my contention here and now – that in practical education under present conditions their due proportions will not be observed unless they are all co-ordinated.

'Together', Hearnshaw continued, these three ends were 'subordinated to the one paramount purpose of the production of good citizens'.[72] Note how Hearnshaw argues the 'production of good citizens' to be the 'paramount purpose' of education. This was a reflection on how, in order to ensure value for money, educationists and teachers were charged to improve the physical health and manual skills of the nation's schoolchildren,[73] as well as to teach them constructive knowledge. When combined with contemporary studies into the physical health of children, emphasis was placed on using education to fix bodies as well as influence minds: it was central to the movement for national 'efficiency', itself a rhetorical device in which leaders could be taught to lead, and the led to learn how to obey.[74] Military drill became popular with teachers and imperialists alike since it emphasised discipline and obedience as well as creating fitter bodies.[75] Indeed, Stephen Humphries is quite correct to argue that the inclusion of games and sports in the school curriculum was intended not only to make healthy the body and indoctrinate the minds of male working-class youth, but also to create a body of children accustomed to the rules of duty and obedience established in the public schools.[76] Considerable effort was therefore placed on improving physical health. Lessons learnt from historical stories, however, were especially geared towards the 'heart': it was intended that children were to both learn how to *know* what it meant to be a good citizen, but also to *feel* it their personal obligation. That, as will become clear, was an objective shared by imperialists and educationists. It was the method by which this emotive identification with nation and empire could be arrived at which provoked disagreement.

Contemporary debates about history teaching reveal attitudes to England's position in the world as an imperial nation. Historical education had received 'an honoured place in the timetables of our Primary

Schools', according to Withers in his report on the teaching of history in London's elementary schools, 'because of its bearing on the future of our civic and national life'.[77] Imperialists wrestled to influence what went on in schools; this was especially so following a change of tack from pro-imperialists in the 1870s and 1880s. This was part and parcel of the 'new imperialism'. Public debates on foreign policy and domestic politics had combined in discussion of a number of events, all of which drew increasing attention to Britain's role overseas and the need for a reform of attitudes at home. Disraeli's and Gladstone's debates over foreign policy in Afghanistan made the ethics of imperialism public, especially significant since the widening reach of the news media indicated more would read of overseas events.[78] The Scramble for Africa similarly made foreign policy a matter for domestic politics.[79] Alarm at the poor health of recruits and poor execution of warfare in South Africa similarly led to public debate about the role education should play in training the next generation.[80] These are but a few of the many factors which convinced imperialists that the general public must be made to know of the empire, encouraged to feel collective pride in it and hence become keen to defend it to the hilt. The empire was repackaged as a national project: it could promote national pride through stories of heroism, bravado and derring-do, set either in the exotic overseas or in defence of the homeland. It is little wonder, therefore, that the demands of imperial propagandists who fought hard to influence the curriculum proved difficult to ignore.

Evidence of the demand that history teaching be better utilised to promote imperial patriotism is wide reaching. Imperial ideals had become manifest in adventure fiction of the time, aimed at boys and girls of all social classes.[81] So, too, was the inculcation of imperial patriotism central to the burgeoning popularity of extra-curricular youth movements.[82] The Imperial Federation League (1884), the British Empire League (1896), the Victoria League (1899), the League of Empire (1901), the Daughters of Empire (1901) and the Empire Day Movement (1903) are but a few examples of societies and organisations which existed, in name, to advance understanding and appreciation of the empire.[83] For some, however, the fervent imperialism on parade in the Boy Scouts movement (1907) was insufficient since it appealed mainly to boys of a certain class.[84] For others, the fervent imperialism on display in literature and extracurricular groups required replication in schools. It is no surprise, then, that pro-imperial mandarins bemoaned the lack of imperial content in school resources: C.P. Lucas, ex-Colonial Office and later a textbook author, fretted that 'nine out of ten workingmen' were indifferent to the empire since they 'have never been taught to know or care' (one assumes that by 'workingmen', Lucas meant those not educated beyond the minimum leaving age or in fee-charging schools).[85] He had earlier urged for 'strongly and soberly' teaching pride in empire since such appreciation was 'vital to our national existence'.[86]

In a letter to *The Times* of 1903, an anonymous contributor deplored the paucity of 'elementary Imperial knowledge' taught in conjunction with history and geography. Such lack of volunteers for the Boer War was owed, the writer argued, to a restricted curriculum which was concerned predominantly with the 'Right Here' to the extent that 'the British Empire is even less than a geographical expression – it is a phrase without meaning'. Having 'never [been] taught in the plastic years of youth anything about the duty and privilege – the two are inseparable – of British citizenship', educationists should be coerced to take swift action lest there be 'irreparable injury to himself [the scholar] and the Empire'.[87] For this letter-writer, all schools – but especially the nation's elementary schools – had a duty to teach content which would enhance pride in empire. This complaint was neither unique, nor new; nor was it the opinion of a maverick individual. There was much consternation that there was no specialist historian working in training colleges until 1905, and that history did not feature in examinations for trainee teachers until 1907.[88]

Campaigns met with some triumph. Inspectors were urged to oversee that schools addressed imperial history in lessons for older children.[89] Withers confirmed that, up to Standard V, children in London learned their history from reading books structured around moral biographies but that in Standards VI and VII (if the child stayed in school until then), scholars were likely to read about nineteenth-century imperial history.[90] Questions on imperial topics featured in examinations for privately educated and secondary schoolchildren sitting both grade exams and university entrance exams.[91] The following questions from a variety of exam boards in 1888 indicate that candidates needed to know a good deal of imperial history to pass their tests: 'Whom do you consider to be the three greatest generals England has produced?'; 'On what occasions has England owed her safety to her fleet?'; 'How and Why were Bombay, Malta and Quebec acquired by the English?'; 'Relate the chief events of Warren Hastings's government of India?'; 'Describe the beginning and earliest direction of colonial enterprise in England'.[92] The content and tone of textbooks changed in order to reflect this imperial zeal.[93] And for the older children in elementary schools, this excerpt from Pitman's *King Edward History Readers* (1901) reveals a similar message:

> The British Empire at the beginning of the twentieth century includes lands in every part of the globe, some gained by the valour of our soldiers, or by the patient toil and steady enterprise of colonists from the mother country. It embraces people of almost every race, colour and religion, all living peacefully and prospering under the British flag, and content with the knowledge that the strong arm and brave spirit that gained that freedom for them will always be ready to defend that precious gift.[94]

Concentration on texts which confirm the presence of propagandist material, however, is but to cherry pick evidence to fit an argument. Reading books for younger children – the majority of the nation's children – were decidedly *less* concerned with presenting explicit imperial content than textbooks. C.H.K. Marten reflected in 1913 that such attempts to promote national pride were symptomatic of 'blind patriotism'.[95] Five years later, by which time the First World War had led many to consider the pitfalls of stoking up nationalism in schools, Paul Mantoux commented that such approaches were 'unworthy' and 'really anti-patriotic'.[96] Concern that demands made of history teaching would lead to a crude nationalism, rather than a thoughtful and genuine patriotism, accounts for much of the reluctance shown by educationists to incorporate explicit imperial propaganda as part of the reading lesson. Joseph Cowham, for example, condemned crude imperialism in his training manual of 1894:

> The scholar who reads history as it is frequently written [in textbooks] must come to the conclusion that England, as she appears to-day, is the result of a series of unavoidable wars; that the most important personages in the past are either the statesmen who brought the wars about, or the generals who led the forces to victory; and that the most certain path to renown is to take a prominent part in the butchery of thousands who have quite as much right to live as those that slay them.[97]

Here is an educationist openly questioning the ethics of how imperial affairs were to be taught. However, like many of his peers, Cowham was palpably proud of the empire. Thomas Cox and R.F. Macdonald, in their manual, insisted teachers instil patriotism in the young since it 'causes the heart to beat high at our country's glorious past and the pricelessness of our inheritance' (that included the empire). But this carried the caveat that children should be made aware that the 'pages of our history are blotted with error and full of terrible warnings [...] and miseries untold'.[98] John Adamson, Professor of Education, was of similar mind. He wrote in his manual of 1912 that the German system of teaching Prussian history 'serves as a reminder of a possible danger following in the wake of a state control'. The English, he warned, must resist 'the inculcation of a spurious patriotism' caused by the teaching of a 'distorted history'.[99]

ENLIGHTENED PATRIOTISM?

If some textbooks did reflect the will of imperialists, they were often berated for being too jingoistic. For instance, one of the most fervently imperialist texts of the time, Rudyard Kipling and C.R.L. Fletcher's *A School History of England* (1911), can be analysed as a barometer of just how much crude patriotism educationists were prepared to tolerate.[100] Some praised the book, so much so that Pamela Horn has described it as an everyday example of a text used in elementary schools.[101] Yet, costing 2s. 6d., it was too expensive for elementary schools: it would, as Bernard Porter confirms, 'have used up most schools' per capita book budget for an entire year'.[102] As seen, Fletcher's *History* did remarkably poorly in the sales stakes, selling significantly less in its publishing longevity than most 'readers' did in a very short period. It is probable that the frequency of its citation owes to the fact it was hardbound, contained poems composed by Kipling (his only contribution) and was replete with lavish illustrations. Perhaps it has so frequently been cited as an example of an early twentieth-century school book since Kipling's name made it more attractive for retention in archives than the cheaply produced, often unattractive and always flimsy reading books, thus making it a more readily available to subsequent researchers. However, it had many more contemporary detractors than admirers. Although a letter writer to *The Times* could wax that 'Fletcher and Kipling's history may have faults; but there is one fault that can never be attributed to it – lack of a manly patriotism',[103] others were quick to criticise it for its overt nationalism and seeming call to prejudice. The *Educational Times* of 1911, not a radical publication by any means, was dominated by letters condemning the coarse imperialism of the text. Its editorial claimed 'it was not worthwhile to gibbet his [Fletcher's] Imperialistic judgements', since the text was 'crude [...] uncontrollable and irresponsible'.[104] Another paper declared 'we should be loath to place the book in the hands of a child'.[105]

Clearly, those pushing for more teaching of empire had reason to be dissatisfied. Even on the outbreak of war in 1914, the Board of Education refused to allow history to be used to fuel of patriotism: 'the events now proceeding in Europe and the crisis the nation has to face, call for knowledge as well as courage and devotion [...] Everything should be avoided which would encourage national animosities'.[106] Explicit imperial education, despite attempts of imperialists, had neither saturated the curriculum, nor dominated history teaching – especially in the nation's primary schools. When jingoism did rear its head in schools, such as 'Boers' versus 'English' in school playgrounds, many were quick to caution against formalising such 'militant orgies': so argued Reginald Bray of the London County Council in 1904. What was needed, Bray argued, was the deliberate 'development of that something in the child which is tuned to beat in sympathy with the throb of his country's life'; not through the 'bombast and swagger of a bastard patriotism' but through the teaching of love for community as a prerequisite for a meaningful emotional attachment to country.[107] Educationists were not against the empire *per se*, but identified in historical education the potential to address other, and far more pressing, social concerns. They were likelier to invoke the language of citizenship.

For a staunch imperialist, such as the Earl of Meath, the characteristics of 'good citizenship', included 'manly values', 'indomitable pluck', 'hard work', 'thrift', 'self-denial' and 'endurance'. These, he emphasised, were the 'hall-marks of an imperial race'.[108] Meath, renowned in the 1890s for his criticisms that schools did too little to promote imperial values, not only carried out a lecture tour in 1893 on the theme of the 'ideal citizen' and how to breed these in schools, but also financed a venture to have as many of London's schools who would accept them display maps of the world on their classroom walls (showing the size, scope and 'pink' of the empire). It was also Meath who proposed, and pushed for, the inauguration of Empire Day, in order that the nation's citizens could celebrate together their communal pride in the empire.[109] Citizenship, according to Meath's vision, was inextricably tied not only to patriotism, but also to *imperial* patriotism. Accepting that citizenship is the relationship between the people and the state, Meath pointed out that 'it is not the British Isles but the British Empire that has to be reckoned as the state'. Good citizenship was the 'bond of Empire' and the 'source of untold strength' which would keep people bound together in their national duty.[110] In some parts of the country, Empire Day was a huge success (one estimate suggests 6,000 schools took part in 1905),[111] but as Bernard Porter correctly reminds us, despite gaining limited support, Meath's campaigns were largely unsuccessful prior to the war.[112] As in the case of Fletcher and Kipling's text, many considered Meath's proposals too jingoistic for use in schools or resented his patronising attempt to impose his blatantly aristocratic ideals across the social spectrum.[113]

However, Meath had tapped into a definition of citizenship which already resonated within educational discourse. In the period under discussion, citizenship – as prescribed for children of the working class – represented a commitment to locality, state, nation and also, empire.[114] Eugenia Low has emphasised that, in contrast to constructions of post-Second World War citizenship (the duties of the state to the individual fostered through the development of welfare institutions), prior to the First World War citizenship instead meant the *active* and outwards performance by individuals – especially of individuals newly enfranchised – of their 'deservingness'. In Low's formulation, citizenship in the late Victorian context was defined as an organic 'body politic' in which the 'relationship between the individual and the state [existed only] within a specific moral framework'.[115] Brad Beaven and John Griffiths have extended this analysis, arguing that the performance of citizenship by individuals in this period was directed through the promotion of character traits such as manliness, service and duty. Such traits showed signs of becoming increasingly more 'imperial' in the two decades leading up to the First World War, to the extent that formal education served to bind civic responsibility (in one's locality and to one's family) to national duty. That is, in order to be a *good* citizen, one had to be both a committed member of the community and also a patriot performing the best of imperial values.[116]

Emphasis on the immediate demands of citizenship education justified the teaching of history: for educationists, the teaching of civic values was *the* vital precondition for the teaching of patriotism. In David Salmon's words, 'the study of History should be a necessary preliminary to the performance of civic obligations'.[117] Joseph Cowham informed teachers they should strive to bring out 'the practical lessons of history, that is, the lessons affording guidance in citizenship'.[118] For influential educationist John Adamson, history 'displays ideals of good citizenship and illustrations of its principles'.[119] Withers wrote in his report on London's elementary schools that he would have trainee teachers repeat, in unison, 'Without History, Citizenship has no Root; Without Citizenship, History has no Fruit'.[120] This, he explained, was to remind teachers that history should first and foremost serve the ends of citizenship. History and citizenship were thus intertwined, but how was this relationship between the two formulated?

Oscar Browning, in a textbook of 1893 for older scholars, explained that 'citizenship' could be held by all people of the nation/state irrespective of whether or not they had the right to vote. For him:

> Every Englishman is a citizen in several different ways. He is a citizen of the town or the county district to which he belongs; he is a citizen of England, as a Scotsman he is a citizen of Scotland and an Irishman of Ireland; he is a citizen of the United Kingdom, and he is also a citizen of the great British Empire. He has different duties in each of these capacities – they begin with him at home, and they gradually widen until they embrace the circuit of the world.

Browning was clear that the 'state', by his definition synonymous with the empire, should be the framework of belonging which bound all people together within a unifying civic identity.[121] This, then, was a definition of citizenship similar to Meath's, yet one which did not prioritise the imperial need above the civic: targeting a reform of the child's attitudes in its *own* immediate context was deemed both achievable but also socially necessary. That compelled every individual to do their best at home, since in Browning's formulation individual goodness was a core component of the health of the nation and empire writ large. In another school text for seniors, A.J. Waldegrave shed light on the links between the individual and the collective. For him, the aim of all education 'must be to teach children to think of the "we" rather than the "I"'.[122] Like Browning and Meath, he pushed the notion of 'duty' to the fore. Waldegrave drew comparison between the nation and the body: 'a small wound gets poisoned and very soon the whole system is diseased. Thus we are reminded that various parts of the body are united so that injury to one may mean injury to the whole'.[123] Browning continued:

> The duties of the citizen are of two kinds, private and public. The first mainly concerns ourselves and our family, the second the nation and the state. But the proper performance of private duties may also be matters of public interest, because a well-ordered life is a benefit to the whole community. The condition of the state depends very much upon that of the family. The character of a whole country will sooner or later be determined by the character of the family life within it.[124]

By promoting the value of character traits such as duty and obedience, the teaching of history was deemed especially well placed to inform children that, no matter their status, he or she, in his or her locality, could contribute to the national – and by extension, imperial – wellbeing. Moreover, the teaching of history could promote enlightened patriotism by encouraging an appreciation of abstract notions of home and empire through stories of the unstinting efforts of past actors who had earned these rights to citizenship. It would present children with stories of the gradual accumulation of these civic rights over time; it could teach children that the sum of the British nation (empire) was owing to the collective effort of *all* its parts. History could show children not only how to be good citizens, but also give them reasons to *want* to become so. And perhaps, most importantly, given concerns about class addressed below, history for the children of the workers could encourage allegiance, obedience and commitment to the national cause. As Richard Aldrich neatly summarises in his brief survey of twentieth-century history education, 'History was not only important in inculcating qualities of leadership' for those in public schools, but it was most valued by the state since 'it was also useful in promoting followership'.[125]

Enlightened patriotism

Julia Stapleton has shown how a number of intellectuals were concerned that patriotism had become corrupted by imperial chauvinism.[126] Debates in pedagogical circles were subject to similar contestation. The phrase 'enlightened patriotism' occurs too frequently in the training manuals to be a mere quirk of prose style: it occurs in every manual consulted and is almost unanimously cited as *the* overriding objective for the teaching of history. What was this enlightened patriotism? 'The true patriot', James Welton wrote, 'is he who does his duty manfully in both the public and private relations of his life, not he who most persistently blows the trumpet of self-gratification or beats the drum of ostentatious advertisement'.[127] For Welton, teaching tub-thumping jingoism and 'civic' values did not equate: pedagogical emphasis, in his opinion, had to be on influencing the child's conduct of its everyday life. We have heard how Haldane wished for schools to create adults with 'enlightened views'. John Gunn noted that 'History should not only be a preparation for the duties of citizenship; it should also be the *foundation of enlightened patriotism*', by which he meant the performance of those civic duties.[128] He sheds further light on the term's definition: 'The belief that our own country is the very best will do so much to transform that idea into an actual fact; while the *desire* to make it the very best, which is a more enlightened form of patriotism, is a still more powerful means to the same end'. For him, patriotism was to the nation what 'self-respect is in the life of the individual'.[129] Terence Raymont also used the phraseology, urging teachers not to 'evade opportunities of passing healthy moral judgements and of cultivating an enlightened patriotism'.[130] These civic responsibilities were local (that is, to work hard and know their place), but this also had benefits for nation and empire. Children were to be taught that, by doing their best in their daily lives, their actions and attitudes – no matter how insignificant these might seem –formed an important contribution to ongoing national and imperial greatness.

The concept of enlightened patriotism was not just used in counterpoint to propagandists' appeals for more explicit imperial education but, in the context of significant franchise reform, to raise political awareness. 'As the assimilation of the county and borough franchise is speedily approaching accomplishment', E. Pascoe-Williams emphasised in his letter of 1884 to *The Times*, and if the 'rising generations are to become intelligent and capable citizens [. . .] it is essential they should receive efficient instruction in historical subjects, for politicians of all parties are constantly appealing to the facts of history in proof of their respective arguments'.[131] He was not alone in feeling such anxiety. Commenting on the educational value of history, A.F. Pollard, historian and one time President of the Historical Association, claimed that 'in the first place, political power has been placed in the hands of the masses who are just beginning to feel that they possess it, but have little or no historical enlightenment on the ways in which it may be used'.[132] The establishment, concerned about the rise of working-class organisations (reflected in growing support for leftist political parties), sought to use history to promote identification with nation rather than social class. For older children, that meant lessons in constitutional history. For younger scholars, however, emphasis was placed on teaching children that the vote incurred great responsibilities. Manual authors, in explaining the social value of historical stories, argued that early years education should serve to instil reverence for English democratic traditions. For Landon, historical stories would 'assist in the understanding of the grounds upon which political opinion and practice should be based; and to afford guidance for the future'.[133] History should teach not only how to use the vote, wrote Cowham, but to understand the 'freedom by which our forefathers gained the privileges we now enjoy'.[134] 'It is generally contended', Collar and Crook informed their readers, 'that a knowledge of history will also enable him later on to exercise his political privileges and municipal duties in a more intelligent manner'.[135] This was a consensus view, evident not only in manuals but in the text of classroom resources. In *The English Homeland*, for example, children would read that they were the 'men and women of the future', and as such, had responsibilities since, 'if this country is to keep its greatness the children must be trained to think well and act well. That is what education is for, and that is why you go to school'.[136] John Finnemore, prolific author of texts for young children, was more explicit:

> The working classes of England have more votes than any other class, because there are more of them. So it is plain that no law is likely to be made now which would offend them. If such a law were passed, they would at the next election turn out the man who made it, and put in others who would promise to please them [...] But of what use is a vote? It is of very great use indeed. By means of your vote you can have your share in governing your country [...] many of the children that read this book will someday be voters. They should learn to respect their vote; it is strong weapon in their hands for good or ill. They should learn to use their vote. A vote should never be given without thought. Do your best to find out which is the best man to receive it. Remember that it lies with the voters to choose the rulers of their country. This is a great trust. You cannot be too careful in carrying out this duty.[137]

The teaching of history, then, should be studied not merely as an indicator of the influence of imperial propaganda. Historical education was held by contemporaries as especially valuable because of its capacity – unique according to some – to promote civic values. Despite the yoking of citizenship to patriotism as 'enlightened patriotism', empire lobbyists continued to bemoan the influence of educationists on curricula. For them, the empire needed to be presented more vibrantly and wrapped up in a rhetoric of celebration and pride. Their demands for more imperial *content* in textbooks blinded them to the extent to which enlightened patriotic – imperial – *values* had come to underpin the teaching of history in reading books which all children used.

Summary

Throughout this period, debates about the functions of the teaching of history were volatile and ongoing. The next chapter engages more closely with the dominant educational ideas of the time, especially Herbartianism which exercised increasing influence over the teaching of history. It was not insignificant that Herbartians identified elementary schools as potential sites for the transmission of moral education: for them, to wield any effect on how children conducted their lives, the teaching they received had to appeal to their emotions and inspire in them the will to do what was morally correct. Herbartianism appealed to government, educationists and teachers alike, according to one of its leading advocates, since its ambition to inculcate moral virtues was related closely to the Christian doctrine of goodwill, the loss of which many saw as an unfortunate flaw in the movement towards sectarian education.[138] As defined in the late nineteenth century, more pressingly, moral education could be made synonymous with civic values. One reviewer of Herbartian-influenced method manuals summarised general Herbartian intent thus:

> The ultimate purpose of the Herbartians may be said to be the development of 'character', not in a narrow subjective sense, but in a broad social one. They seek to fit the child for every important phase of family, social, civil, religious and economic life – to develop, in short, the whole boy or girl. In this broad aim they are, perhaps, not peculiar; but they have certainly made some contributions as to the means for accomplishing this end, so devoutly to be desired for public education [. . .] They believe that, properly selected, articulated and taught, the common branches of an elementary education are potent influences in training the child's moral insight and disposition.[139]

Little wonder, then, that many, concerned as we have witnessed in this chapter about the nation's moral values, were quick to advertise, adopt and implement this system. Indeed, as Richard Selleck argues, one reason which explains the widespread popularity of the Herbartian approach was that Herbartians 'spoke to those who were ready to hear'.[140] Or, as the school inspector Frank Hayward explained later, he was drawn towards Herbartianism because it was an 'aggressive' approach to education which invoked action rather than mere gesticulative discussion, and sought to produce moral 'conviction' in the face of the 'threat of chaos for society'.[141] In particular, he believed that 'the incapacity of churches to meet the human and spiritual needs of children needed to be challenged'.[142] In the context of turn of the twentieth century England, a pedagogy which promised to produce moral, loyal and obedient citizens was considered too good an opportunity to miss.

A series of objectives had therefore been attached to historical education: stories told in historical reading books, written in order to appeal to the emotions of their child readers, were intended to train the heart and inspire active participation in civic life, thereby promoting the child's physical allegiance to its community. Such a community, following models prevalent in educational discourses on citizenship, was the necessary precondition to the child feeling an emotional attachment to more abstract concepts of nation and empire. A sense of *emotional* attachment to the nation was to be the foundation upon which new identities, attitudes and aspirations were to be built. It could, educationists believe, transform all children into enlightened patriots. This was the core objective of historical education as experienced by the majority of English schoolchildren, and, as will be seen in the next chapter, such an approach was firmly grounded in educational theory. If enlightened patriotism was the aim, then how was this best achieved? It is to a closer investigation of the nature of pedagogy in late Victorian and Edwardian England that we now turn.

Notes

1 R.B. Haldane, *Education and Empire: Addresses on Certain Topics of the Day* (London: John Murray, 1902), vii–ix.
2 'Great Britain and Germany: A Study in Education', an address delivered in October 1901 at Liverpool, reproduced in Haldane, *Education and Empire*, 1–38.
3 Paul Kennedy, *The Rise of the Anglo-German Antagonism, 1860–1914* (London: G. Allen and Unwin, 1980); E.P. Hennock, *British Social Reform and German Precedents, 1880–1914* (Oxford: Clarendon, 1987).
4 For a narrative, see Jessie Wong's PhD, 'Continuity and Change in Citizenship Education in Twentieth Century England' (unpublished PhD thesis, University of Liverpool, 1991), 60–1; Roy Lowe, 'Personalities and Policy: Sadler, Morant and the Structure of Education in England', in Richard Aldrich (ed.), *In History and Education* (London: Woburn Press, 1996), 98–115.

5 J. Arthur, I. Davies, A. Wrenn, T. Haydn and D. Kerr, *Citizenship through Secondary History* (London: Routledge, 2001).
6 Quoted from David Phillips, 'Michael Sadler and Comparative Education', *Oxford Review of Education*, 32:1 (2006), 49.
7 R.J.W. Selleck, *The New Education: The English Background, 1870–1914* (London: Isaac Pitman, 1968), 104–6.
8 W.H. Webb, 'History, Patriotism and the Child', *History*, 2:1 (1913), 53–4.
9 John Smith, '"No Subject ... More Neglected": Victorian Elementary School History, 1862–1900', *Journal of Educational Administration and History*, 41:2 (2009), 136.
10 Smith, 'No Subject ... More Neglected', 145
11 Wendy Robinson, 'Historiographical Reflections on the 1902 Education Act', *Oxford Review of Education*, 28:2–3 (2002), 159–72.
12 Olive Shropshire, *The Teaching of History in English Schools* (New York: Teachers' College, 1936), 21.
13 H.L. Withers, 'Memorandum on the Teaching of History in the Schools of the London School Board' (1901), in Withers, *The Teaching of History and Other Papers* (Manchester: Sherrat and Hughes, 1904), 168, 185–6.
14 C.H.K. Marten, 'The Teaching of History in England', in Marten, *On the Teaching of History and Other Addresses* (Oxford: Basil Blackwell, 1938), 45.
15 Cited in T.D. Cook, 'Changing Attitudes to the Teaching of History in Schools, c.1900–1970' (unpublished MPhil thesis, University of Lancaster, 1970), 46.
16 Smith, 'No Subject ... More Neglected', 137.
17 Cited from B.A. Rapple, 'Payments by Results: An Example of Assessment in Elementary Education from Nineteenth Century Britain', *Education Policy Analysis Archives*, 2:1 (1994), 12. Available at: http://larrycuban.files.wordpress.com/2012/01/664-974-1-pb.pdf (accessed 21 March 2014), 4.
18 Cited in F. Sutton, 'An Investigation into the Impact of Imperialism on the Teaching of History in the Elementary Day Schools of England and Wales' (unpublished MA Dissertation, University of Lancaster, 1995), 36.
19 G.C. Williamson, *On Learning and Teaching History in Schools and on the Results Obtained by Such Teaching* (London: Longmans, Green & Co., 1891), 244.
20 J. Fitch, *Lectures on Teaching* (Cambridge: Cambridge University Press, 1881), 389.
21 J. Welton, *Principles and Methods of Teaching*, second edition (London: University Tutorial Press, 1909), 29.
22 Cited in Rapple, 'Payments by Results', 12.
23 On examinations in history, see J. Roach, 'History Teaching and Examining in the Secondary Schools, 1850–1900', *History of Education*, 5:2 (1976), 127–40.
24 In 1872, geography was by far the most popular specific subject, taken by 59,774 pupils, followed by English grammar with 18,426 and then history with 16,645. Although this statistic had risen to 17,710 by 1875, English literature had pushed history into the position of the fourth most popular specific subject. Statistics drawn from G.R. Batho, 'Sources for the History of History Teaching in Elementary Schools, 1833–1914', in T.G. Cook (ed.), *Local Studies and the History of Education* (London: Methuen, 1972), 139–43. See also I. Steele, 'A Study of the Formative Years of the Development of the History Curriculum in English Schools, 1833–1901' (unpublished PhD, University of Sheffield, 1974), 178–90.
25 Smith, 'No Subject ... More Neglected', 144–6.
26 T. Raymont, *The Principles of Education* (London: Longmans, Green and Co., 1904), 271.
27 Welton, *Principles and Methods of Teaching*, 221.
28 J.M. Goldstrom (ed.), *Education – Elementary Education, 1780–1900* (Newton Abbott: David and Charles, 1972).
29 Stephen Colledge, 'The Study of History in the Teacher Training College', *History of Education Society Bulletin*, 36 (1985), 45–51.

30 Prior to the 1900–1 Acts, most children left school having not studied history as a discrete subject. A study of London's Board Schools in 1893, for instance, found that only 8,026 children above the age of twelve attended school, whereas there were 237,484 registered scholars aged five–eleven (school attendance between the ages of five and fourteen, and beyond the age of twelve was only made compulsory in 1921). F. Smith, *History of English Elementary Education, 1760–1902* (London: University of London Press, 1931), 335.
31 J.J. Findlay, *History and its Place in Education* (London: University of London Press, 1923), 9–10.
32 Alexis Weedon, *Victorian Publishing: The Economics of Book Production for a Mass Market, 1836–1916* (Aldershot: Ashgate, 2003), 33.
33 Weedon, *Victorian Publishing*, 67, 57.
34 Weedon, *Victorian Publishing*, 115.
35 Weedon, *Victorian Publishing*, 127. Inspectors, however, were not allowed to recommend any particular publishers. Cases of bribery, or the attempted bribery of school boards and inspectors, were commonplace, thus demonstrating just how competitive the market for reading books had become. Weedon, *Victorian Publishing*, 125–7.
36 S.J. Heathorn, *For Home, Country and Race: Constructing Gender, Class and Englishness in the Elementary School, 1880–1914* (Toronto: Toronto University Press, 2000), 13.
37 P. Horn, 'English Elementary Education and the Growth of the Imperial Ideal', in J.A. Mangan (ed.), *Benefits Bestowed: Education and British Imperialism* (Manchester: Manchester University Press, 1988), 39–55. Kipling, of course, is perhaps the reason why this resource has taken such a significant role in the historiography of history teaching. Fletcher was a reactionary Oxford Don often criticised for his ultra-Conservative views.
38 Private correspondence with Bernard Porter.
39 Heathorn, *For Home, Country and Race*, 224–9. Longman, Edward Arnold and Macmillan constituted three of the most powerful publishing houses producing reading books and other paper resources for the education market. Cassell and Collins were also popular publishers, as were Blackie's and A. & C. Black.
40 Heathorn, *For Home, Country and Race*, 14.
41 David Salmon, *The Art of Teaching* (London: Longmans, Green and Co., 1898), 115.
42 Cited in Smith, 'No Subject ... More Neglected', 139.
43 Withers, 'The Teaching of History and Other Papers', 112.
44 For further discussion on the value of reading, see Gillian Galbraith, *Reading Lives: Reconstructing Childhood, Books and School in Britain, 1870–1920* (Basingstoke: Macmillan, 1997), 131.
45 J.J. Findlay, *Principles of Class Teaching*, second edition (London: Macmillan, 1904), 211.
46 A. Garlick, *A New Manual of Method*, sixth edition (London: Longmans, Green and Co., 1904), 267.
47 The Royal Historical Society was formed in 1868 with the intention to bring together professional historians, many of whom increasingly came to declare an interest in the school education of pupils. In the 1870s, separate Honours degrees were established at Oxford and Cambridge. The *English Historical Review* was founded in 1886. At Manchester from 1890 and London from 1903, T.F. Tout and A.F. Pollard respectively assisted in the development of important schools of history at the new universities. See V. Chancellor, *History for their Masters: Opinion in the English History Textbook, 1800–1914* (London: Adams and Dart, 1970), 22–5; R. Aldrich, 'Interesting and Useful', *Teaching History*, 47 (1987), 11–14; A. Taylor-Milne, 'History at the Universities: Then and now', *History*, 59:195 (1974), 33–46; Historical Association, *The Historical Association, 1906–56* (London: Historical Association, pamphlet, 1955), 5–6.

48 C.H.K. Marten, 'The First School Examinations and the Teaching of History', *History*, 13 (1928), 24.
49 W.E. Marsden, *The School Textbook: Geography, History and Social Studies* (London: Woburn Press, 2001), 33–43; Chancellor, *History for their Masters*, 11–13; Heathorn, *For Home, Country and Race*, 24–55.
50 Chancellor, *History for their Masters*, 22.
51 G.D. Howat, 'The Nineteenth-Century History Textbook', *British Journal of Educational Studies*, 13:2 (1965), 151.
52 For discussion, see Weedon, *Victorian Publishing*, 111–41.
53 Heathorn, *For Home, Country and Race*, 44–6.
54 Natalie Hole, 'Nineteenth-Century Method Manuals with Special Reference to English Literature', *Paradigm*, 7:2 (2003), available at: http://w4.ed.uiuc.edu/faculty/westbury/Paradigm/ (accessed 13 May 2010).
55 Peter Cunningham, 'Progressivism, Decentralisation and Recentralisation: Local Education Authorities and the Primary Curriculum, 1902–2002', *Oxford Review of Education*, 28:2–3 (2002), 218–20.
56 F. Smith, *History of English Elementary Education*, 313–15.
57 J. Lawson and H. Silver, *A Social History of Education in England* (London: Methuen, 1973), 332–3; Smith, *History of English Elementary Education*, 315.
58 Smith, *History of English Elementary Education*, 334. In chronological order, dedicated centres were opened in London, Birmingham, Durham, Manchester, Nottingham, Cardiff, Cambridge, Leeds, Liverpool, Sheffield, Glasgow, Oxford, Aberystwyth, Bangor, Reading and Southampton. See M. Hyndman, *Schools and Schooling: A Documentary History* (London: Harper and Row, 1978), 175.
59 B. Porter, *The Absent-Minded Imperialists: What the British Really Thought about Empire* (Oxford: Oxford University Press, 2004), 202–4. Research into teachers and teachers' professional identities is a growing field, at the forefront of which is Philip Gardner and Peter Cunningham's recent work. P. Gardner, 'Classroom Teachers and Educational Change 1876–1996', *Journal of Education for Teaching*, 24:1 (1998), 33–49; P. Gardner, 'Reconstructing the Classroom Teacher, 1903–1945', in Ian Grosvenor, Martin Lawn and Kate Rousmaniere (eds), *Silences and Images: The Social History of the Classroom* (New York: Peter Lang, 1999), 123–44.
60 Oscar Browning, *An Introduction to the History of Educational Theories* (London: Kegan Paul, Trench and Co., 1881), 1–2.
61 See, for instance, David Rubinstein, 'The Socialisation of the London School Board, 1870–1904', in P. McCann (ed.), *Popular Education and Socialization in the Nineteenth Century* (London: Methuen, 1977), 231–64.
62 D. Lawton and P. Gordon, *HMI* (London: Routledge, 1987), 30–2.
63 J. Landon, *The Principles and Practice of Class Teaching and School Management* (London: Alfred M. Holden, 1894), 394.
64 There is insufficient space here to develop analysis of teachers' identities specifically. After all, some teachers may have taught in a manner which was pro-imperial; others, however, may not. Dina Copelman's study of London's women teachers, for instance, indicates that teachers, the large majority of whom in London were women, might have resisted masculinist notions of nationality that they considered endemic within schooling. Wendy Robinson has emphasised that female teachers, as trainees, were subject to as many attempts at socialisation as the children they would be teaching. Dina Copelman, *Class Acts: London's Women Teachers* (London and New York: Routledge, 1996), 124; W. Robinson, 'The "Problem" of the Female Pupil Teacher: Constructions, Conflict and Control, 1860–1910', *Cambridge Journal of Education*, 27:3 (1997), 365–78.
65 Wendy Robinson, 'The Pupil-Teacher Centre in England and Wales in the Late Nineteenth and Early Twentieth Centuries' (Unpublished PhD thesis, University of Cambridge, 1997), 116–18.
66 Browning, *Introduction to the History of Educational Theories*, 172.

67 Selleck, *The New Education*, 227–72. Despite being written in 1968, this text remains the most recent comprehensive reference work on the importance of Herbart on English education.
68 E.A.G. Holmes, *In Defence of What Might Be* (London: Constable, 1914), 1.
69 Findlay, *Principles of Class Teaching* (London: Macmillan, 1911 edn), 333. This was part of the rewrite of the new edition, not present in the original of 1899.
70 Raymont, *The Principles of Education*, 14.
71 Withers, *The Teaching of History*, 102.
72 F.J.C. Hearnshaw, 'The Place of History in Education', *History*, 1 (1913), 35.
73 On technical education, see Eric Evans and Penny Summerfield (eds), *Technical Education and the State since 1850: Historical and Contemporary Perspectives* (Manchester: Manchester University Press, 1990).
74 G.R. Searle, *The Quest for National Efficiency: A Study in British Politics and Political Thought, 1899–1914* (Oxford: Blackwell, 1971), 207–16. Linda Simpson, 'Imperialism, National Efficiency and Education, 1900–1905', *Journal of Educational Administration and History*, 16:1 (1984), 28–36; Anna Davin, *Growing Up Poor: Home, School and Street in London, 1870–1914* (London: Rivers Oram Press, 1996), 208–14; Lionel Rose, *The Erosion of Childhood: Child Oppression in Britain, 1860–1918* (London: Routledge, 1991), 19–35.
75 J.S. Hurt, 'Drill, Discipline and the Elementary School Ethos', in P. McCann (ed.), *Popular Education and Socialisation in the Nineteenth Century* (London: Methuen, 1977), 167–91; P. McIntosh, *Physical Education in England since 1800* (London: G. Bell and Sons, 1952), 109–21; Anna Davin, 'Imperialism and Motherhood', in Raphael Samuel (ed.), *Patriotism: The Making and Unmaking of British National Identity* (London: Routledge, 1989); Anne Colquhoun, Phil Lyon and Emily Alexander, 'Feeding Minds and Bodies: The Edwardian Context of School Meals', *Nutrition and Food Science*, 31:3 (2001), 117–25.
76 Stephen Humphries, *Hooligans or Rebels? An Oral History of Working-class Childhood and Youth, 1889–1939* (Oxford: Blackwell, 1981), 40–2.
77 Withers, *The Teaching of History*, 200.
78 For overview, see Graham Goodlad, *British Foreign and Imperial Policy* (London: Routledge, 1999), 29–53. See, also, Simon Potter, *News and the British World: The Emergence of an Imperial Press System, 1876–1922* (Oxford: Oxford University Press, 2003).
79 Andrew Thompson, *Imperial Britain: The Empire in British Politics, 1880–1932* (Harlow: Longman, 2000).
80 See Simpson, 'Imperialism, National Efficiency and Education', 28–36; Kenneth Morgan, 'The Boer War and the Media', *Twentieth Century British History*, 13:1 (2002), 1–16.
81 Penny Tinkler, *Constructing Girlhood: Popular Magazines for Girls Growing Up in England, 1920–50* (London: Taylor and Francis, 1995); Jeffrey Richards (ed.), *Imperialism and Juvenile Literature* (Manchester: Manchester University Press, 1989); Kathryn Castle, *Britannia's Children: Reading Colonialism through Children's Books and Magazines* (Manchester: Manchester University Press, 1996); Michael Paris, *Warrior Nation: Images of War in British Popular Culture, 1850–2000* (London: Reaktion Books, 2000), 49–82. J.S. Bratton, '"Of England, Home and Duty": The Image of England in Victorian and Edwardian Juvenile Fiction', in J.M. MacKenzie (ed.), *Imperialism and Popular Culture* (Manchester: Manchester University Press, 1986), 73–93; Kelly Boyd, *Manliness and the Boys' Story Paper in Britain: A Cultural History, 1855–1940* (Basingstoke: Palgrave, 2003); Michele Smith, *Empire in British Girls' Literature and Culture: Imperial Girls, 1880–1915* (New York: Palgrave, 2011); M. Kutzer, *Empire's Children: Empire and Imperialism in Classic British Children's Books* (London: Garland, 2000).
82 John Springhall, *Youth, Empire and Society: British Youth Movements, 1883–1940* (London: Croom Helm, 1977), 23–52; Tammy Proctor, *Scouting for Girls: A Century of Girl Guides and Girl Scouts* (Santa Barbara, CA: Praeger, 2009).

83 On these (and others), see J. MacKenzie, *Propaganda and Empire: The Manipulation of British Public Opinion* (Manchester: Manchester University Press, 1984), chapter 6; J.G. Greenlee, *Education and Imperial Unity, 1901–1926* (New York and London: Garland, 1987); Eliza Riedi, 'Women, Gender and the Promotion of Empire: The Victoria League, 1901–14', *The Historical Journal*, 45:3 (2002), 569–99.
84 J. Springhall, 'Building Character in the British Boy: The Attempt to Extend Christian Manliness to Working-class Adolescents, 1880 to 1914', in J.A. Mangan and J. Walvin (eds), *Manliness and Morality. Middle-Class Masculinity in Britain and America, 1800–1940* (Manchester: Manchester University Press 1987), 52–74.
85 Cited in Porter, *Absent-Minded Imperialists*, 203.
86 Cited in J.H. Grainger, *Patriotisms: Britain 1900–1939* (London: Routledge and Kegan Paul, 1986), 54.
87 'J.R.C.', letter to *The Times* (28 December 1903), 9.
88 David Cannadine, Jenny Keating and Nicola Sheldon, *The Right Kind of History: Teaching the Past in Twentieth-Century England* (Basingstoke: Palgrave, 2011), 43.
89 MacKenzie, *Propaganda and Empire*, 175.
90 Withers, 'Memorandum on the Teaching of History', 186–90.
91 The Oxford and Cambridge Schools Examinations Board was established in 1873 for public schools, soon followed by London Matriculation, the College of Preceptors and the Northern Universities Matriculation Board (1903). In 1890, 75,000 candidates sat the London Modern History examination. See John Roach, *Public Exams in England, 1850–1900* (Cambridge: Cambridge University Press, 1971), 93; 172.
92 C.H. Spence, *History and Geography Examination Papers* (London: George Bell and Sons, 1888), 45, 62, 66, 72.
93 MacKenzie, *Propaganda and Empire*, 177–97. See, also: K. Castle, 'India in British History Textbooks for Schools, 1890–1914', in J.A. Mangan (ed.), *The Imperial Curriculum: Racial Images and Education in the British Colonial Experience* (London: Routledge, 1993), 23–39; P. Horn, 'English Elementary Education and the Growth of the Imperial Ideal', 39–55.
94 Pitman's *King Edward History Readers*, cited in Valerie Chancellor, *History for their Masters*, 26–7.
95 C.H.K. Marten, 'Some General Reflections on the Teaching of History', *History*, 2 (1913), 98.
96 P. Mantoux, 'The Effect of the War on the Teaching of History', *History*, (1918), 16.
97 Joseph Cowham, *A New School Method: For Pupil-Teachers and Students* (London: Westminster School Book Depot, 1894), 348.
98 T. Cox and R.F. Macdonald, *The Suggestive Handbook of Practical School Method* (London: Blackie and Son, 1896), 357–8.
99 J.W. Adamson, *The Practice of Instruction: A Manual of Method General and Special*, second edition (London: National Society's Depository, 1912), 79, 258–9.
100 C.R.L. Fletcher and R. Kipling, *A School History of England* (Oxford: Clarendon, 1911).
101 Horn, 'English Elementary Education and the Growth of the Imperial Ideal', 39–55.
102 Porter, *Absent-Minded Imperialists*, 239.
103 E.H. Blakeney, letter to *The Times* (29 November 1915), 9. Blakeney taught at King's School, Cambridge.
104 *Educational Times* (1 March 1912), 136.
105 Quoted in Porter, *Absent-Minded Imperialists*, 239.
106 Cited in Cannadine, Keating and Sheldon, *The Right Kind of History*, 57.
107 R. Bray, 'Patriotism and Education', in Lucian Oldershaw (ed.), *England: A Nation* (London: Brimley and Johnson, 1904), 217, 201, 207.
108 Earl of Meath, 'Duty and Discipline in the Training of Children' (1910), cited in Heathorn, *For Home, Country and Race*, 27.

109 Jim English, 'Empire Day in Britain, 1904–58', *The Historical Journal*, 49:1 (2006), 247–76.
110 Cited in Heathorn, *For Home, Country and Race*, 28.
111 J.A. Mangan, '"The Grit of Our Forefathers": Invented Traditions, Propaganda and Imperialism', in J.M. MacKenzie (ed.), *Imperialism and Popular Culture* (Manchester: Manchester University Press, 1986), 129.
112 Porter, *Absent-Minded Imperialists*, 186–7.
113 Robin Betts, 'A Campaign for Patriotism in the Elementary School Curriculum: Lord Meath, 1892–1916', *History of Education Society Bulletin*, 46 (1990), 38–45; J. Springhall, 'Lord Meath, Youth and Empire', *Journal of Contemporary History*, 5:4 (1970), 107.
114 Nathan Roberts, 'Character in the Mind: Citizenship, Education and Psychology in Britain, 1880–1914', *History of Education*, 33:2 (2004), 179.
115 E. Low, 'The Concept of Citizenship in Twentieth-century Britain', in P. Catterall, W. Kaiser and U. Walton-Jordan (eds), *Reforming the Constitution: Debates in Twentieth-century Britain* (London: Cass, 2000), 186.
116 B. Beaven and J. Griffiths, 'Creating the Exemplary Citizen: The Changing Notion of Citizenship in Britain, 1870–1939', *Contemporary British History*, 22:2 (2008), 203–25. On education, specifically, see Beaven, *Visions of Empire: Patriotism, Popular Culture and the City, 1870–1939* (Manchester: Manchester University Press, 2012), 125–49.
117 David Salmon, *The Art of Teaching* (London: Longmans and Co., 1898), 213.
118 Cowham, *A New School Method*, 343.
119 Adamson, *The Practice of Instruction*, 258–9.
120 Withers, 'Memorandum on the Teaching of History', 200. This is an adaptation of J.R. Seeley's comment that politics without history has no root, and that history without politics lacks fruit. For more on Seeley's influence, see Chapter Three.
121 Oscar Browning, *The Citizen: His Rights and Responsibilities* (London: Blackie and Son, 1893), 10–11.
122 A.J. Waldegrave, *Lessons in Citizenship* (London: Thomas Nelson and Sons, 1912), 3–4.
123 Waldegrave, *Lessons in Citizenship*, 60. In order to elaborate upon the *immediate* lessons to be learned, this extract speaks for itself: 'now pass to the consideration of questions of *work* and *character* in this connection. Does it make any difference to the nation if there are large classes of the population engaged in unhealthy occupations and living in slums? Does it matter if some citizens are ignorant and unable to vote intelligently? Can a nation be healthy if large numbers of people are addicted to drinking or gambling? Suppose shopkeepers are dishonest, or workmen scamp their work, does the nation as a whole suffer? ... Is it good for the nation that there should be schools and diligent scholars? Indeed, yes' (Waldegrave's emphases, 62).
124 Browning, *The Citizen*, 13.
125 Richard Aldrich and Denis Dean, 'The Historical Dimension', in R. Aldrich (ed.), *History in the National Curriculum* (London: Institute of Education, 1991), 102.
126 Julia Stapleton, 'Citizenship Versus Patriotism in Twentieth Century England', *The Historical Journal*, 48 (2005), 151–78.
127 Welton, *Principles and Methods of Teaching*, 228.
128 J. Gunn, *Class Teaching and Management* (London: T. Nelson and Sons, 1895), 136, emphasis in original.
129 Gunn, *Class Teaching and Management*, 136–7.
130 Raymont, *The Principles of Education*, 141.
131 E. Pascoe-Williams, letter to *The Times* (4 September 1884), 3.
132 A.F. Pollard, *On the Educational Value of the Study of History* (London: Historical Association, leaflet no. 26, 1911), 7.
133 Landon, *Principles and Practice*, 401.
134 Cowham, *New School Method*, 342.

135 G. Collar and C.W. Crook, *School Management and Methods of Instruction with Special Reference to Elementary Schools* (London: Macmillan and Co., 1900), 181–2.
136 *The English Homeland* (n.d.), cited in Stephen Heathorn, ' "Let Us Remember that We, Too, Are English": Constructions of Citizenship and National Identity in English Elementary School Reading Books, 1880–1914', *Victorian Studies*, 38:4 (1995), 415.
137 John Finnemore, *Black's School Series: Black's Story of the English People*, I (London: A. & C. Black, 1905), 143–6.
138 Charles de Garmo, *Herbart and the Herbartians* (London: Sonnenschein, 1895), 53–6.
139 Victor H. Allemandy, 'The Herbartian Principles of Education', *Parent's Review*, 12:9 (1901), 888–9.
140 Selleck, *The New Education*, 250.
141 F.H. Hayward, *An Educational Failure: A School Inspector's Story* (London: Duckworth, 1938), 255–6.
142 Peter Gordon, 'Hayward, Frank Herbert (1872–1954)', *Oxford Dictionary of National Biography* (Oxford: Oxford University Press, 2004). Available at: www.oxforddnb.com/view/article/38808 (accessed 30 November 2007).

CHAPTER TWO

The renaissance of the child: educational theory and the teaching of history

Reading books should be chosen with great care. Poor children read few other books, and no children read any other books so slowly, so minutely, or so repeatedly. We cannot expect children to love books which are not worth loving; hence, whether the lessons of the reading book be continuous or detached, whether they be selected because they contain certain words, convey certain information, inculcate certain moral truths, or stimulate certain emotions, they should invariably be interesting.[1]

Give an analysis of the notion of character, bringing out (a) the psychologically distinct factors in it, (b) the more general and important phases through which the formation of character proceeds.

In what does character consist? How would you cultivate it?

Character has been described as 'a completely fashioned will'. What does this mean?

(Examples of examination questions put to teachers in training in 1901)[2]

In 1904 Terence Raymont wrote that the 'most important item in the programme of "the New Education" – the one that implies many of the rest – is that the educator should keep in view not only what sort of person he wishes the child to *become* in later life, but also what manner of person the child *is*, here and now'.[3] There had been, he observed, a noticeable 'renaissance of the child'.[4] Developments in the field of child psychology played a significant role in the rapidly changing nature of state provision of education in late Victorian and Edwardian England. It might be argued that this was especially so in the case in history teaching. Cutting-edge developments in child psychology emphasised that education needed to appeal to the child's imagination and evoke an emotional response: it is this which helps explain why historical reading lessons were afforded such a prominent place in the timetables of elementary schools. Indeed, if recent criticism of history education has emphasised the deleterious impact of educational theory since the 1960s, then it is a delicious irony – as this chapter demonstrates – that in its perceived 'golden age', history was far from divorced from developments in child psychology. Historical stories were uniquely positioned to teach values and, as a result, assist in shaping the child's world-view and its moral conduct. As is argued in the final section of this chapter, these developments which were geared towards promoting civic *and* national pride bore close resemblance to both the language and intentions which underpinned reforms in the 1960s and 1970s and became commonplace in the much maligned School's History Project of the 1980s.

In order to investigate further the educational theories which underpinned the teaching of history, especially through stories, this chapter explores five main factors. In the first section, detailed explanation is made of the dominant theoretical underpinnings of this 'new' education. In particular, the principles of Herbartianism which dominated recommended approaches to history education are studied along with its emphasis upon the perceived potential of history teaching to act as a site for the transmission of moral and civic values. Educationists generally asserted the need to incorporate pedagogical developments, and it was in this period that the names of 'great educators' became widely known to English audiences: Pestalozzi, Montessori, Froebel, and Herbart were frequently cited.[5] Herbartians, however, concentrated especially on the need to invoke the child's 'will' to be a good citizen by appealing to its emotions. 'Will' was defined by Dexter and Garlick in their textbook on educational psychology as 'the all important factor' of education which 'moulds and fashions the character' of the individual.[6] The second section analyses how history teaching was geared towards the perceived capabilities of the child, in particular explaining the educational value of an emotions-oriented education. Third, the influence of the Herbartian method is demonstrated by the ways it influenced history syllabus design – that is, the selection, arrangement and sequencing of subject content deemed likeliest to invoke the child's sympathies. Fourth, focus is placed upon how national 'time', depicted as an uncontested continuous narrative, was represented to children in the deliberate belief that, if they were to judge and appreciate values evident in the past, they needed not only to be able to compare the past with their present, but also to appreciate the scale of national progress over time. Lastly, a brief note is made about the persistence of Herbartian language and ideas across the twentieth century.

Herbartians exercised the most significant influence on the development of historical education at the turn of the twentieth century.

Catherine Dodd, for instance, was central to the reorganisation of elementary schooling and teacher training in Manchester.[7] Joseph Findlay, Dodd's colleague in Manchester from 1903, claimed his first manual was written from 'the workshop instead of the lecture room'.[8] John Adams, Professor at London, and described by Richard Selleck as one of the most widely-read educational theorists of the period, spent more time lecturing to teachers-in-post than he did to those in the training college.[9] Findlay, like Dodd, had studied Herbartianism in Germany (more on this soon). Michael Sadler was a close friend and ally of Findlay's: it is no surprise that when Sadler's tenure in the civil service had expired (and following his research trip to Germany mentioned in the previous chapter), he was appointed to a Chair in Comparative Education in Manchester at Findlay's behest.[10] Both men, alongside Dodd and Adams, were pronounced enthusiasts of Herbartian pedagogy; they were drawn to its emphases on moral education.[11] School inspector Dr Frank Hayward sang loudly from the Herbartian hymn sheet.[12] So, too, did a large number of writers of method manuals. Simply put, Herbartianism prioritised a moral curriculum in which the teaching of knowledge was secondary to an education in civic values. As a consequence, Herbartianism was crucial to the transformation of the teaching of history because it conceived that lessons to be learnt from historical stories were central to civics education, and thus – as adapted to the English context – central to the promotion of enlightened patriotism. Therefore, more needs to be known about its methods and the far-reaching impact of its determining principles. This is especially so since most studies of the history of history teaching either fail to make mention of pedagogical systems or, if they do, seriously underestimate both the significance of developments in child psychology and the far-reaching authority of educational theorists. Rather, as demonstrated below, it was precisely the identification of the reading lesson as a site for the teaching of values which gave historical primers such a prominent place in turn of the century educational culture: so much so that when history became compulsory in 1902 (for two hours a week), it was the reading book which became the commonplace classroom resource for the vast majority of the nation's schools.

Herbartianism and the moral dimension of historical education

If little has been written on the relationship between educational psychology and the teaching of history, even less has been made of Herbartianism and its exponents. In his 1970 study of the dissemination of Herbartian ideas in North America, Harold Dunkel observed that 'little more than 50 years ago his doctrines, or at least views passing as his, were a major force in educational theory and practice'.[13] The omission of Herbartianism has been a major oversight: it was the pedagogical method used in almost all teaching manuals; it gave history its educational function; it was approved and endorsed by the state; and, crucially, promised a science of education which could instil community, national and imperial values.

Within a decade of its first *translation* into English in 1892,[14] Herbartianism had spawned a revolution in the printing of texts on the theory and psychology of education.[15] 'Herbartianism' is a term used to describe the system of an influential group of educational theorists who shared the common objective to make common practice teaching methods derived from Johann Friedrich Herbart's (1776–1841) psychology of education. Often, Herbartianism was constituted of ideas Herbart himself would not have recognised. Instead, it refers to the development and interpretation of his ideas adapted to fit late nineteenth-century English needs.[16] Dodd, Findlay and Hayward had studied in Jena under Tuiskon Ziller, a firm advocate of Herbart, in the 1870s and 1880s. 'In 1890 scarcely any English teacher knew of Herbart's existence', Findlay reflected, but by 1896, however, 'almost everyone in the Training Colleges was talking and teaching this new pedagogics'.[17] In reviewing John Adams's *The Herbartian Psychology Applied to Education* (1897), the *Journal of Education* reported that Herbartian ideas 'now occupy a unique position in educational theory'.[18] Herbartian methods had formed something akin to a new orthodoxy in methodologies for teaching children their moral and civic values. This level of consensus in objectives and methods explains why there was relatively little variation within manuals on why and how to teach history. This consensus, moreover, indicates why reading books were largely uniform in content and layout. Herbartian methods were recommended by the Department of Education in 1905 in its influential pamphlet *Handbook of Suggestions*.[19] Indeed, Professor of Education John Adamson reflected back in 1912 that, over the course of the previous two decades, the Herbartian system had come to 'constitute the best-known and most comprehensive norm of instruction'.[20]

If Herbartianism was not always referenced explicitly in training manuals, then this was because authors perceived that one of their responsibilities was to explain complex educational theories in everyday language. Teaching Centres, Wendy Robinson writes, 'frequently recommended and made use of the growing range of books available to teachers and pupil-teachers on the subject of practical school method'.[21] Terence Raymont, David Salmon, John Adamson and John Gunn all taught Herbartian techniques in their manuals, as did Thomas Cox, R.F. Macdonald, J.A. Green and C. Birchenough in their jointly authored texts.[22] Others, such as Joseph Landon and M.A. Howard, adopted Herbartian language without acknowledging its source. Arthur Garlick, by no means an advocate of progressivist education, directed those of his readers interested in the theoretical underpinnings of the 'new' orthodoxy in history teaching to John Gunn's manual.[23] Gunn's development of the 'concentric system', as will be seen in the third section of this chapter, became manifest in practice and was important since it imparted structure and coherence to the overall syllabus. As Findlay commented: 'Most of the books on Method written in recent years reveal their obligations to the Herbartian pedagogy, even where they make no direct reference to it'.[24]

An understanding of the significance of Herbartianism is particularly relevant since contemporaries held that its emphasis on the child's internalisation of moral and civic values could provide guaranteed solutions to the social problems discussed in the previous chapter. 'The children of today are the men and women of tomorrow', wrote Cox and Macdonald in their manual of 1896. 'To them', they continued, 'will be presented for solution the social and political problems of their time'.[25] This short statement was not atypical, and does not surprise. What might seem surprising, however, is that manual authors held the conviction that education *would* enable children to confront and overcome these challenges. Indeed, the very appeal of Herbartianism, in Hayward's explanation, was that it provided a 'definite standpoint', 'principle of unity', 'coherence' and 'clearness of purpose'.[26] To this, Findlay added that it 'gave us a clear-cut, detailed scheme by which means and ends could be related'.[27] In short, Herbartians proposed a *science* of education, justified by cutting-edge educational psychology which, should the curriculum be tailored to their proposals, was expected to produce certain results.[28] This is one reason why Herbartianism was held in such high esteem by educationists.

Those who campaigned rigorously for the systematic use of Herbartian methods championed the special qualities of the historical reading lesson. History teaching was 'pre-eminent among school studies', according to Dodd, because it assisted 'in moulding the character and in stimulating interest'.[29] The development of 'character', she continued, was 'of more importance than knowledge',[30] since the promotion of moral values would assist the creation of engaged citizens: 'Herbartians consider that History is real character-forming material, and place it as the centre of all subjects to be studied; the other subjects ... are subordinate to it'.[31] The use of public elementary education to develop 'character' had already been established in educational discourse. The importance of these notions – 'character', 'values', 'experience', 'interests' – may seem obvious, but they were all innovative in the context of late nineteenth-century schooling. Miss M.A. Howard lauded the contribution of history teaching to 'moral education': it 'increased veneration for truth, in the acquisition of noble ideals of conduct, in the development of intelligent [enlightened] patriotism'.[32] Moral education was loosely synonymous with enlightened patriotism. Cox and Macdonald's classification of six explicit objectives for the teaching of history, clearly designed with Herbartian principles in mind, indicate this conjoining of moral education and enlightened patriotism:

1. 'to trace the progress of the nation in political and personal liberty';
2. 'to trace the development of the social condition of the people';
3. 'to teach the love of all that is noble';
4. 'to lay the foundation for a knowledge of the rights and duties of citizenship';
5. 'to foster love of country';
6. and, 'to exercise the powers of judgement, comparison and imagination'.[33]

These are indicative of how the majority of manual authors explained the objectives of history teaching.[34] In order to produce moral citizens out of schooling, Herbartians insisted that the *interest* of the child had to be invoked in order that his or her 'character' develops. This included six types of 'interest', which in combination formed the 'many-sided interest' believed to inculcate in the child not only knowledge of what civic values were, but also the desire to behave according to them: thus making the child moral (labelled 'application').

The six Herbartian 'interests', according to Dodd in 1901, had become required learning for all teachers in training.[35] The following is a summary: arising from 'experience' with the 'social world', teachers should appeal to the 'empirical interest' (the child should want to 'know' things), the 'speculative interest' (the child should want to ask questions about things) and the 'aesthetic interest' (the child should want to creatively engage with topics being taught). This tallied with interest derived from 'social intercourse' with other humans, including 'sympathetic interest' (a desire to understand motivations and to empathise with others), 'social interest' (the subsequent development of interest and participation in community life) and 'religious interest' (the ultimate objective in realising that 'one's power is not necessarily one's own').[36] The fifth and sixth of these 'interests' constituted the desired end-result, while interests one to four constituted the method. The ultimate objective was an education in civic responsibilities and community participation achieved through the development of the child's moral faculty. These six interests constituted the core tenets of how to produce enlightened patriots. As Cox and Macdonald emphasised under their heading on citizenship, history 'teaches the value of men co-operating to accomplish some social object which one alone could not do'.[37] If Herbartianism was deemed essential because it proposed a collective state education which sought to transform all of the nation's young children into moral and obedient citizens, the teaching of history – through stories – was consequently declared the curricular vehicle best suited to delivering its message.

Historical stories were judged best suited because of their emphases on the stories of individuals: this was not the fawning, militaristic, adulation of soldiers, sailors and generals which Valerie Chancellor identifies as symptomatic of a shift to a nationalistic curriculum,[38] but rather a series of lessons grounded in moral biography. Herbartians considered stories about role models to be the link between the child as an individual and the child as part of a community. Telling history as a series of human beings 'doing things' was believed the best method to hook the child's imagination, thus prompting an emotional reaction. Appeal to the 'sympathetic interest' would activate other interests: exciting stories appealed to the child's empirical, speculative and aesthetic interests. 'Human beings as they appear in history', Frank Hayward wrote in 1902, are moral (or immoral); and if 'a child is led to observe the relations of these persons and hears the judgement favourable or unfavourable passed by the teacher upon them, its moral sense develops'.[39] Stories which would *interest* the child would likelier invoke her or his sympathetic interest since they would provide examples of ideal characteristics and values deemed appropriate for emulation. In the first of Cox and Macdonald's tasks for history (tracing the progress of liberty), they urged teachers to bear in mind that 'heroic deeds that saved a nation's freedom shine forth as bright examples for emulation'; in the third (to teach the love of all that is noble) they specify how history provides stories of heroes and heroines whose deeds 'stimulate others to the nobility of character, quickening the pulse of both old and young'.[40] In their sixth task, they inform their readers that 'History is a subject which, whilst exciting many influences, affects character most; for from it moral influences emanate spontaneously, and affect and mould the character'.[41] As was explained some years later in 1919 by Hayward, in a book co-authored with Arnold Freeman, fellow of the Royal Historical Society:

It is, I hold, only by emotional appeal that the moral law which is our heritage from thousands of generations of by-gone men, can be handed on and implanted in the youth of to-day. It is necessary that this emotional appeal should be deliberately and systematically made. It is of the highest importance that it should be a chief duty of the school and schoolmaster. The recitation of noble stories, the singing of noble songs and the crowning of heroes, not as exceptional or accidental occurrences, but as a regular and ordered part of the life of each week in a school, are undoubtedly methods of implanting moral law.[42]

It was via the child's emotional reaction to stories that the process of converting what children read into their internalisation, and subsequent performance, of values was believed to be met. Developing Karl Lange's interpretation of Herbart's texts,[43] this transmogrification of learning into the creation of values was known at the time as the process of 'apperception'.[44] Defined by Findlay as 'the vivid, lively assimilation of new ideas', apperception was described as the link between 'knowledge and will' brought about by 'feeling, or emotion'.[45] The stimulation of emotional responses was fundamental to history's task.

Hence, the essential value of storytelling and moral biography was prioritised at all opportunities. Dodd, for example, suggested stories about Jack the Giant Killer were of greater intrinsic educational value than those about Gladstone. 'Nobody but a Gradgrind would hesitate' to differ, she asserted, since to be effective, material taught had to meet the child's 'interest and capability [because] true interest is awakened only when the appetite is created'.[46] Findlay insisted that reading 'sentimental' stories would simultaneously invoke all of these interests and, thus, transform *all* children into dutiful citizens.[47] Manual authors articulated this pedagogy by explaining that historical stories were especially valuable because they would more successfully 'eliminate drudgery' and take on moral meaning if the child's imagination and empathetic capacity was invoked.[48] Salmon urged teachers to reflect that 'History has a powerful ethical influence. Conduct springs from feelings rather than intellect and the effect of History upon them can hardly be overestimated'.[49] Gunn emphasised the significance of 'imagination and sympathy' as pre-requisites for the development of 'reasoning and reflection'.[50] Garlick insisted 'the *chief* uses of a reading book' were not only to 'promote interest' in reading and thus 'cultivate affections and moral feelings', but also to invoke the 'sympathies' and thus the child's own moral development.[51] The methods employed by educationists to make these historical stories as appetising as possible will be discussed in the next section; their manifestation in reading books in Chapters Three, Four and Five.

Knowing the child

It was acknowledged that the period of schooling was short for the children of the working class. Consequently, the need was not to instil in them a colossal compendium of information, but to make the most of this brief opportunity to mould their world-view. This meant traversing the national story from beginning to end in the small time-span available.

In particular, method manuals reveal the concern to teach stories which held relevance to the child. Complicated content was to be avoided. 'Care must be taken that we do not attempt to deal with causes and motives which are beyond the power of the child's imagination', wrote Joseph Cowham.[52] 'In planning a series of lessons', Salmon advised, 'one has to think of more than the logical and chronological sequence of the facts, – one has to think of the mental growth of the pupil. What would be impossible to a child of ten would be easy to a boy of fifteen and puerile to a youth of eighteen'.[53] The child's *will* to want to become a proud citizen had to be seized from the earliest age possible. Howard's comments on what was perceived interesting to children is important since it emphasises the appeal to emotional responses:

> They like to hear of people who *do* things, whether they be heroes or villains [. . .] they like to hear about soldiers and sailors; girls like to hear about the women of history, and the children of history are always a source of interest to present-day children [. . .] Anything with plenty of story appeals to children, anything dramatic, anything moral. They like to have their feelings stirred, and are interested by whatever arouses laughter, admiration, pity, wonder, or horror [. . .] Anything connected with their own lives or experiences is interesting.[54]

Raymont added that children have 'a strong dramatic instinct, a keen interest in stories of all kinds, and perhaps a growing preference for stories that are true'.[55] According to Salmon's manual, 'when little ones have been told a story they generally ask, "Is it true?" and if the narrator can answer "Yes", their interest is greatly increased'. He concluded: 'History is a succession of stories all true'.[56] James Welton's explanation of the value of history as storytelling is of particular significance. He maintained that in the historical reading book, fiction and truth could be intertwined in order to both promote curiosity and, hence, inspire the historical imagination. Although not adopting explicitly Herbartian terminology, Welton was talking about combining the empirical, speculative, aesthetic and sympathetic interests. In doing so, he informed his readers that fiction could be used to produce fixed moral meanings:

> If the term 'reading book' be confined to those books which are used mainly for oral reading, then we see that the contents should be of value as literature rather than as information. The attempt to combine the two, like most endeavours to kill two birds with one stone, usually hinders the attainment of the result which should be sought from each. The chief exception is the history reader, which, if well chosen, is at once literature and the medium of conveying definite information.[57]

This has profound implications: despite telling stories designed to appeal to the emotions, and which 'rest upon very weak authority',[58] it was believed these lessons could convey truths about the past and henceforth make examples of moral conduct far more compelling.

Hence, in order to influence children, manual authors were resolute that if children were to learn values, then they needed first to be provided with examples of these values in action. This explains why reading books were organised around simple, chronologically told biographies of past actors, while simultaneously encouraging children to pass moral judgement upon the values and actions played out in the stories which they read. But how were children to formulate these judgements? The answer to that resides in how theorists recommended the teaching of chronology.

'Cultivating the Historical Sense':[59] the concentric system

This section describes the dominant approach to history syllabus design which had been adopted by late nineteenth-century elementary schools. Iain Steele has found that some schools used the 'regressive' approach to history teaching, which included working backwards from the present.[60] However, this was a limited practice and was far from commonplace. Indeed, Cowham was adamant that in order to teach values, history teaching would be far more effective if it 'begin with the remote past'.[61] 'There is no need from the teacher's point of view to adopt an order which a historian would call topsy-turvy', Joseph Landon averred.[62]

The 'concentric system', which was designed to meet the requirement that the child would receive the fullest possible exposure to the full chronological span of the English national past in the short amount of time available, drew heavily from Herbartian notions of how to present chronology to children. Gunn's application of the concentric system became the standard model. Here, he explains how it should operate:

> The whole history of the country is first gone over in outline, the leading events only being referred to. The character or critical points receive all

the attention of the class, and the subsidiary and intermediate events which are connected with these are left over for future study. Next year, the class goes over the same ground, but in more detail. The important landmarks are now known, and form the centres round which a circle of less important but still great events is grouped. Next year the same plan is followed, most of the time being spent on the fuller details, and less prominent events, always referring, however, to those formerly known as the centres of the various periods. In this way the unity and the march of events are never lost sight of in the details.[63]

This model served to meet Herbartian recommendations in two ways. First, it ensured that connections were made, within a coherent whole, between one lesson and the next which, second, encouraged the child to engage in recapitulation. Recapitulation, later adopted and adapted by Piaget (and thus, ironically, playing a role in reformulations to history teaching in the 1960s),[64] was of crucial importance since it was believed that for the child to form moral judgements, they should be able to contrast different historical periods. Through recapitulation, they could be taught about moral progress over time. This was especially significant, as we will see below, in the representation of the evolution of national values across the longer story of the English people.

To elaborate upon content and structure of reading books, introductory texts surveyed English history in broad sweeps. Volume I usually told the 'Simple Story' of English history from beginning to end. Volume II spanned from the days of Roman Britain to the early sixteenth century (Wars of the Roses or the death of Elizabeth seem to be the most frequently selected half-way points of English history) and followed the 'Simple Stories' formula; Volume III meanwhile continued the story from the sixteenth century through to the most recent event of note (more often than not the death of General Gordon at Khartoum, Baden Powell's heroics at Mafeking, or a eulogy for Victoria, Edward's coronation and so on). Volumes IV through to VII covered the history in greater detail, concurrently revisiting old ground while filling in further details to basic stories and introducing new content. Books varied on what constituted the content of these later volumes. Some like *The Britannia History Readers* (1901), had an *Introductory Book* which replaced Volume I, so its Volumes I and II told the story in separate parts and Volume III focused on events in the reign of Victoria. First reading books did not introduce children to complex events such as the Henrician Reformation; lessons such these came later once the child had a grasp of basic, core, Christian ethics, such as those learnt in stories about Alfred, Canute or Sir Philip Sidney. The Reformation might occur by Volume V (told usually through the lens of Wolsey or Thomas More), as might other more complicated topics such as the loss of the American colonies, imperial trade, foreign policy or nineteenth-century franchise reforms. Of course, this is a snapshot of the majority practice: some texts differed, though that they were seriously few in number is suggestive. As stories progressed to the early modern and subsequent periods, the progress of the English was made clear: examples abounded of Christianity, sacrifice, heroism, innovation, fair-play, courage, a predisposition towards seafaring, settlement and Christianity. These provide the key foci for analysis in the next three chapters.

Chapters Three, Four and Five draw on examples from Volumes I through to III (including introductory texts) for three reasons. First, as outlined earlier, the history of history teaching has been skewed towards the study of textbooks which, unlike early years reading books, were not used by all children. Initial volumes were most likely read by all children attending school. Second, by Volumes V, VI and VII it was assumed the child could read, and these texts included much depth but this was only because preliminary reading books had already established the groundwork chronology. Third, this was the period of the child's development in which educationists believed she or he was most susceptible to influence. Adamson wrote that 'the aims of history as a school study must vary with the ages of the pupils, and with the type of school as determined by length of school life [. . .] [J]ust as the intellectual and emotional differences between mature and immature minds impose differences of aim and method, so there must be variety in the historical instruction, corresponding to the varieties of immaturity in the pupils'.[65] Findlay was more precise and classified 'childhood' to be between the ages of three and nine, and as such, reminded teachers that it was their 'professional responsibility' to capture the child's sympathetic interest at the earliest stage possible.[66] I am interested here in those 'immature minds': those children receiving their lessons in the elementary schools; those reading historical stories 'before the pupil can read easily, or at all'; children whose minds, however immature, were subject to socialisation.[67]

There were two further, but more specific, reasons for why the concentric system was so widely endorsed and practiced: first, *recapitulation* was deemed a vital ingredient in the formation of moral sentiments; second, stories from the chronological beginnings of the national story were believed more intelligible to the child. In conjunction, these shaped the way content was presented in texts (to be seen in subsequent chapters). Manual authors demanded use of the concentric system, in which events from the past would be revisited in later years, because the presentation of the past as straightforwardly continuous provided opportunities to encourage recapitulation and hence encourage children to form judgements about progress over time. In particular, the concentric system added educational value since it would contribute to the creation of historical *distance*. The theory ran that the further back in time the story, the more appealing – and therefore comprehensible – it might be to the child. As Adamson explained: 'the story of our own country unfolds as we pass down the stream of time [...] the simpler types of society existing in earlier days are more easily made known to him'.[68] 'Whereas the present is more or less commonplace, and is certainly less attractive', wrote Joseph Landon, 'about old times there is an air of strangeness and romance which adds greatly to their interest for children'.[69] According to Christian Üfer, the leading living Herbartian whose works were translated in English, historical stories must be written in a style which is 'truly child-like, that is, simple without being trivial' while simultaneously being 'full of imagination'. Stories from the remote past were believed:

> morally formative in the sense that they contain characters and relations; they are instructive, for they offer occasions for appropriate discussions concerning nature and society; they are of enduring value; they invite a constant return; they form a unit and thus make a deep impression, and they are sources of a possible many-sided interest.[70]

It was crucial to begin the child's introduction to history with stories from the deep past since Herbartians believed the child's intellectual and emotional faculties were closer to those of 'our ancestors'. Thus, it would be easier for the child to identify with stories of civilisation when civilisation itself was in its child-like stage.

This approach, developed out of Tuiskon Ziller's interpretation of Herbart's works and integrated into English Herbartianism by Dodd, Findlay and Hayward in particular (all three of whom had studied under him at Jena), was labelled at the time as the 'historical culture epochs' theory, or 'race recapitulation' theory.[71] This was no accident of language. It was believed that the child developed in stages which mirrored the different stages of civilisation. The inculcation of values required matching the child to a chronological period similar in intellectual and emotional capability. In Adamson's words, this approach held particular appeal because 'the pupil is made to retrace the path of development followed by his race, and thus *ex hypothesi* his own development is fostered in the most natural manner'.[72] He summarised by quoting Findlay: this approach 'recapitulates in a few short years the progress which it has taken the race slow centuries to work out'.[73] Thus, for Dodd, 'the little child possesses the same circle of ideas as those of our remote ancestors'.[74] And, as Findlay elaborated, 'not only do these early days provide the necessary introduction to what comes later, they are in themselves easier to understand, the characters and motivations are simpler – Canute is easier to handle than Napoleon; Simon de Montfort easier than Gladstone'.[75]

Use of recapitulation was intended to invoke the many-sided interest of the child and encourage a sense of collective belonging. Salmon urged that children should be trained in the habit of 'contrasting and comparing the past with the present' in order that they come to witness, historically, how rights and responsibilities had been inherited across time.[76] Cowham insisted that, in order to understand the demands of citizenship, 'contrasts between the conditions of life *now* and *then* should be drawn at each stage of the lesson, and the scholars should take a prominent part in the effort'.[77] As Cox and Macdonald put it, 'the past leads up to and makes the present intelligible [...] Under the influence of the teacher, the scholar is taught to judge of present needs from the successes or failures of the past; to compare the past with the present and the present with the past, so that by the aid of imagination the one may illustrate and make clear the other'.[78] Recapitulation would better enhance the child's appreciation of progress over time. 'This method would make use of the knowledge [they] have of the present', Cowham wrote: 'It would picture the Briton in his half-savage condition, with his rude home, his warlike disposition, and his ignorant and heathenish forms of worship'.[79] Children should be grateful for what they had. 'Half-savage', 'ignorant' and 'heathen' were the characteristics that children should identify as historical – that is, remote, and firmly relegated to the past. Such a study, Cowham continued, would ensure that the child reader 'would contrast this Briton, living entirely almost and by and for himself, with the Englishman of the present; with his appearance, his home, his knowledge, and his employment; with his social, civil and religious privileges – the citizens of a grand Empire, and sharing in national life'.[80]

Pedagogical emphasis, then, was placed on historical transformation and evolution. The strategy of showing historical distance sharpened the textual demonstration of historical progress. Contrasting current life with the past was a technique suggested by all manuals and the obvious implications are twofold. First, the implicit lesson was that children should be grateful for what they have now, and would draw 'conclusions about the consequences of dutiful behaviour'.[81] The second implication was that the story of the English was ongoing. Stories have their beginnings: this is why so much attention was focused on promoting historical distance. Children were to be made aware of how much progress the nation, collectively, had made. To illustrate: 'Many hundreds of years have passed between the time of the poor Britons, who lived wild in the forests', Oscar Browning informed in a reading book he wrote, 'and the time of the last battle which ended the Wars of the Roses, but through all these years, England has been slowly turning herself into one of the greatest countries of the world'.[82] The actions of individuals in these stories were intended to make children aware of characteristics worthy of emulation (or condemnation). It was the duty of these children to emulate the best of the past in order to contribute to ongoing national greatness. This was a story not only of the evolution of the English race, but also the expansion of the English character, over time: imperial values were stitched into national origins so as to tell how the story of the enlargement of English civic values went hand-in-hand with the acquisition of empire. Historical stories appealed to the emotions, triggered the senses and provided lessons which accorded to the Herbartian blueprint for the creation of active citizens.

A community of interests and values

The final two ingredients in the establishment of a many-sided interest, social and religious, were considered more difficult to attain. These constituted the desired outcomes of converting the child's learning about values: if successful, these lessons in enlightened patriotism would shape the child's moral code and affect how he or she conducted his or her civic life. 'Social interest', defined as a desire to understand and share community values, was part of the project of elementary education generally. So too was 'religious interest', which was not necessarily related to shared Christian values (though they featured) but the development of the child's sense that it was part of a community and that its duty was to the community, not to itself. 'So far as school-boys and school-girls are concerned', wrote Adamson, 'the chief immediate purpose of the study of History is to widen their horizon by anticipating and supplementing their intercourse with men'.[83] That was the first step, but how to connect that sense of 'intercourse' to the child's understanding of its civic obligations? On the one hand, the school was given as an example of a collective. That 'the child should see in school life a foretaste of real social life is important', wrote Cox and Macdonald, who continued:

> All in the school, as in the community, have equal rights and privileges; the school is an epitome of society under a paternal government; hence the civic virtues – forbearance, justice, and obedience to authority – should be as the breath of school life, and the social graces – kindness, courtesy, etc – should accompany them.[84]

Dodd maintained that 'in school the child must feel himself a part of a community, and must realise his responsibility to others'.[85] On the other hand, lessons learned from past examples validated the need for the child's own performance of enlightened patriotic values. These become clear in the conclusions of reading books, and two are reproduced here:

> We have now read the story of the English people during their life in England. We have seen them land on our shores, a race of rude, savage warriors. We have seen them grow in strength and in knowledge until they have become a leading nation of the world. And let us remember that we, too, are English. In our hands lies the future of our great race. Let us resolve to do all we can to uphold the fame of our country, so that fresh honours may yet be added to the story of the English People.[86]

The child was obliged to identify with the values of past actors, to respect, revere and even emulate them. Upon their commitment to the national cause – the community writ-large – depended the national future. This was the social and religious interests in operation. The community for participation could be local, yet the power of history's example meant that the community could also be represented as national. This extract from a reading book of 1884 indicates the extent to which reverence was intended to constitute a significant factor in children's behavioural performance of their citizenship:

> Thus has Britain been changed into modern England, and the great English nation formed out of the German and British barbarians of the past, by the manliness, the wisdom, and the piety of our forefathers. At every moment of our lives, in the food we eat, in the clothes we wear, in the towns and villages we inhabit, in the books we read, in the laws we live under, in the very thoughts and principles which guide us onwards, each of us reaps the fruits of their labours. Them we cannot repay, but we reverence them, and in return we must labour for the good of those who will come after us [...] It is the duty of Englishmen and Englishwomen to do their best to make England great in the future also. The first thing necessary is that they should live worthy and honourable lives themselves; for a country can only be great when its people are temperate, truthful, orderly, reverent, industrious, merciful and courageous. It may happen, as it has happened to Englishmen before, that we shall be called on to make great sacrifices, and overcome great difficulties, in doing our duty to our country and our fellow-men; but we have to bear them patiently and courageously, remembering that it is through the toils and the sacrifices of our forefathers in days gone by that England had become the noble and prosperous country in which it is our happiness to live.[87]

This passage makes explicit how historical stories could combine the six key Herbartian interests. Note how both concluding statements recapitulate past stories and are written in accessible conversational prose style. They emphasise the relationship between individual values and national characteristics; both urge the child into action. It is interesting to note that the second of the extracts predated the Herbartian invasion of English pedagogical thinking. This is significant since reading books, designed as we know to meet the requirements of literacy lessons, were highlighted by Herbartian theorists as examples of existing good practice. The aim in the 1880s had been to promote the child's civic values. Throughout the course of the 1890s and 1900s this approach became validated by educational psychology to the extent that, by 1902 when the subject-specific history lesson had become compulsory, it was the historical reading lesson which was the model recommended for emulation.

These lengthy extracts are reproduced since they typify the concluding comments of many reading books. They also exemplify how paying reverence to past Englishmen and women became a civic obligation for present-day children. For children to *want* to emulate their forefathers, however, they must surely have come to admire, respect, laud, be proud of and even love these figures. This is why the following chapters analyse in further detail the roles played by heroes and heroines in how the English past was taught. These historical actors told a history of progress: they helped to break down the national past into small, easy to digest and fascinating chunks, yet they also gave coherency to the story as a whole. Through them, children learned lessons about the development and the absorption of national values: children could be instructed in what *they* should do in order to belong. It is here that we witness how, through stories of enlightened patriotism in action, that lessons in civic and moral values reinforced locality, nation and empire as sites for collective belonging and identification. As such, if stories were to promote imperial ideals it was not through the teaching of content but through the teaching of values. As will be seen in the next few chapters, nowhere is this pedagogical reasoning more pronounced than in the contrast between reading books for younger children and textbooks for older scholars.

Legacies

It is a delicious irony that New Right critics in the 1980s inveighed not only against the content selected by 'new' history, but also against the idea that children should be taught historical 'skills'. These skills included the reconstruction of the historical past (essentially, empathy) and identification of historical 'interpretations'. In Stewart Deuchar's denunciation, for instance, 'new history' was made up of no more than 'six paragraphs of gobbledegook'.[88] However, this chapter has demonstrated that previous attempts to use the teaching of history to influence children's sensations of national identity primarily required the appeal to the imagination (empathy?), rather than the intellect alone. As educationists knew in the 1890s, knowledge of factual content alone was insufficient: it was of secondary pedagogical significance to the need to encourage an emotional response to stories in order to prompt the will to act on lessons learnt. Thus, it might be argued – albeit playfully – that should the principles of Herbartian pedagogy be adapted to the current context, national identity teaching (which the political right demands) would require an education in sympathetic engagement (which it rejects as anti-patriotic). This would, however, constitute a primacy for educational theory antipathetic to the New Right formulation of a fact-led ideal curriculum.

This irony can be probed a little further. In the 1970s the rationale of history teaching was reorganised in order to make history an inquiry-led system.[89] The development and large uptake of Schools Council History Project modules (SCHP) – the so-called 'new history' – signified that emphasis was being placed on teaching key skills and historical thinking.[90] In doing so, educationists mobilised recent advances in educational theory. It is in these recommendations that one witnesses the persistence of a language of educational objectives connecting the 'new' education of the 1890s to the 'new history' teaching of the 1970s and 1980s. Piagetian theories of learning, for instance, sought to demonstrate that to teach children chronological understanding required the systematic use of processes of recapitulation.[91] Jerome Bruner wrote that history teaching should seek to activate the cognitive interaction of 'many-sided complex interests'.[92] F. Musgrove reminded those who would plan history curricula that lessons based on the remote past would appeal more to the child: not only would these lessons better match the child's understanding of human nature to those past humans under study, but they would also teach them skills of understanding chronological change.[93] E.A. Peel emphasised the absolute requirement that history lessons should begin with an appeal to the imagination, from which the child could be taught how to draw meanings by contrasting past and present.[94] Jeanette Coltham and John Fines, similarly, insisted that history appeal to the emotions and imagination because it was out of a sympathetic understanding of the motivations of past characters that the child's historical understanding would develop.[95] On this, Peter Lee comments that for Coltham and Fines the 'imagination' meant the teaching of empathy, sympathy and emotional identification.[96] Denis Shemilt, author of the original SCHP document, lauded the importance of teaching empathy in order that children would better understand the motivations of historical actors.[97]

Thus, one can witness a corollary running from the doctrines of a Herbartian-oriented education of the 1890s and changes to history teaching in the 1970s. Of course, these suggested connections are tentatively made, since other traditions of educational theory had inevitably gained dominance. However, one might assert that it is significant that ideas central to reformulations of history teaching in the 1970s were so similar in language and intent to those of the Herbartians at the turn of the twentieth century. In the above examples, key Herbartian notions of recapitulation, 'many-sided interests', the teaching of medieval history to young children and teaching to the imagination took central place. This is a topic for further detailed study of course, but this brief survey serves to underline just how little we know about the historical relationship between educational theory and the teaching of history. That the New Right constructed the 'traditional' teaching of history as divorced from educational psychology is clearly a misrepresentation. In attacking the foundations of new history, critics were in fact lambasting pedagogical methodologies which had developed from essentially similar educational principles of the 1890s and early 1900s. In doing so, they undermined history's potential contribution to a values-oriented curriculum.

Late Victorian concerns that insufficient imperial content was taught is not too dissimilar to recent calls for control over the raw bones and flesh of the curriculum. Given that modern critics bemoan the paucity of the teaching of national chronology, and openly campaign for the inclusion of national heroes, it makes sense to now move on and explore the teaching of key biographies in the earlier period. In particular, what moral lessons were children expected to learn? What messages about locality, nation and empire were transmitted via such stories, and how were these intended to serve as vehicles for the transmission of enlightened patriotism? How were children expected to enact their civic values? How, precisely, did educationists stitch these values into the fabric of the national story? How were these intentions, and theoretical principles, brought to bear in reading books?

Notes

1 David Salmon, *The Art of Teaching* (London: Longmans, Green and Co., 1898), 115.
2 T.F.G. Dexter and A.H. Garlick, *Psychology in the Schoolroom* (London: Longmans, Green and Co., 1901), 360.

3 T. Raymont, *The Principles of Education* (London: Longmans, Green and Co., 1904), 65, emphasis in original.
4 Raymont, *Principles of Education*, 67.
5 John Lawson and Harold Silver, *A Social History of Education in England* (London: Methuen, 1973), 353–6. Generally, on the development of educational psychology, see A. Wooldridge, *Measuring the Mind* (Cambridge: Cambridge University Press, 1994).
6 Dexter and Garlick, *Psychology in the Schoolroom*, 335.
7 Alex Robertson, 'Schools and Universities in the Training of Teachers: The Demonstration School Experiment, 1890 to 1926', *British Journal of Educational Studies*, 40:4 (1992), 361–78.
8 He had previously been elected to a Lectureship at the College of Preceptors in London (1895–98). In the five years between academic appointments he had set up experimental schools in Hampstead and Letchworth and had been working in Cardiff and south Wales spreading the Herbartian gospel. Ron Brooks, 'Findlay, Joseph John (1860–1940)', *Oxford Dictionary of National Biography* (Oxford: Oxford University Press, 2004). Available at: www.oxforddnb.com/view/article/46690 (accessed 13 January 2014).
9 R.J.W. Selleck, *The New Education: The English Background, 1870–1914* (London: Isaac Pitman, 1968), 243–4; P.B. Ballard, 'Adams, Sir John (1857–1934)', rev. M.C. Curthoys, *Oxford Dictionary of National Biography* (Oxford: Oxford University Press, 2004). Available at: www.oxforddnb.com/view/article/30334 (accessed 13 January 2014).
10 'Administrative History', John Rylands Library Archives website. Available at: http://archives.li.man.ac.uk/ead/html/gb-0133-fed-p1.shtml (accessed 12 January 2007).
11 Alex Robertson, '"Between the Devil and the Deep Blue Sea": Ambiguities in the Development of Professorships of Education, 1899–1932', *British Journal of Educational Studies*, 38:2 (1990), 144–59.
12 Two of Hayward's most frequently cited works are: *The Reform of Moral and Biblical Education in the Lines of Herbartianism, Critical Thought and the Ethical Needs of the Present Day* (London: Sonnenschein, 1902); and his bombastic defence of pedagogics against its doubters in *The Critics of Herbartianism* (London: Sonnenschein, 1903). For summary of his career, see: Peter Gordon, 'Hayward, Frank Herbert (1872–1954)', *Oxford Dictionary of National Biography* (Oxford: Oxford University Press, 2004). Available at: www.oxforddnb.com/view/article/38808 (accessed 13 January 2014).
13 H. Dunkel, *Herbart and Herbartianism: An Educational Ghost Story* (Chicago: Chicago University Press, 1970), 3.
14 J.F. Herbart, *The Science of Education*, trans. H.M. and E. Felkin (London: Sonnenschein, 1892).
15 Selleck, *The New Education*, 243. John Adams, *The Herbartian Psychology Applied to Education* (London: Isbister and Company, 1897); Catherine Dodd, *Introduction to Herbartian Principles of Teaching* (London: Sonnenschein, 1901); T.G. Rooper, 'A Pot of Green Feathers', *Parent's Review*, 4 (1893–94), 8–16; Charles de Garmo, *Herbart and the Herbartians* (London: Sonnenschein, 1895); H.M. and E. Felkin, *An Introduction to Herbart's Science and Practice of Education* (London: Sonnenschein, 1895); M. Fennell, *Notes of Lessons on the Herbartian Method* (London: Longmans, Green and Co., 1902); R.E. Hughes, *Schools at Home and Abroad* (London: Sonnenschein, 1902); A. Darrock, *Herbart and the Herbartian Theory of Education* (London: Longmans, Green and Co., 1903).
16 As a result, it is no surprise that there were some differences of opinion on how to interpret and apply 'Herbart*ian*' ideas. However, there was relative consensus, on which I concentrate here, about underlying principles, predominant methods and intended outcomes. The use of the term 'Herbartian' to describe a group of theorists with common purpose is therefore appropriate. For a fuller discussion of

the *variations within* Herbartian educational theory, see Selleck, *The New Education*, 227–72.
17 J.J. Findlay, *Educational Essays*, 6–7, cited in Selleck, *The New Education*, 244.
18 *Journal of Education*, 343 (1898), 109, cited in Selleck, *The New Education*, 243.
19 Peter Cunningham, 'Progressivism, Decentralisation and Recentralisation: Local Education Authorities and the Primary Curriculum, 1902–2002', *Oxford Review of Education*, 28:2–3 (2002), 218.
20 J.W. Adamson, *The Practice of Instruction: A Manual of Method General and Special*, second edition (London: National Society's Depository, 1912), 49.
21 W. Robinson, 'The Pupil-Teacher Centre in England and Wales in the Late Nineteenth and Early Twentieth-Centuries: Policy, Practice and Promise' (unpublished PhD thesis, University of Cambridge, 1997), 136.
22 Selleck, *The New Education*, 242–4, 267–8.
23 A. Garlick, *A New Manual of Method*, sixth edition (London: Longmans, Green and Co., 1904), 291.
24 J.J. Findlay, *Principles of Class Teaching* (London: Macmillan, 1911 edition), 333.
25 T. Cox and R.F. Macdonald, *The Suggestive Handbook of Practical School Method* (London: Blackie and Son, 1896), 355–6.
26 F.H. Hayward, *Three Historical Educators: Pestalozzi, Froebel, Herbart* (London: Ralph, Holland and Co., 1905), 20.
27 Cited in Selleck, *The New Education*, 262.
28 Selleck, *The New Education*, 261–2.
29 Dodd, *Introduction to Herbartian Principles*, 35–6.
30 Dodd, *Introduction to Herbartian Principles*, 37.
31 Dodd, *Introduction to Herbartian Principles*, 42.
32 M.A. Howard, 'History', in J.W. Adamson (ed.), *The Practice of Instruction: A Manual of Method General and Special* (London: National Society Repository, 1907), 251.
33 Cox and Macdonald, *Suggestive Handbook*, 357–9.
34 See, for examples of similar categorisations, J. Welton, *Principles and Methods of Teaching*, second edition (London: University Tutorial Press, 1909), 222–8; John Gunn, *Class Teaching and Management* (London: T. Nelson and Sons, 1895), 136–42; J. Landon, *The Principles and Practice of Class Teaching and School Management* (London: Alfred M. Holden, 1894), 394–6; Raymont, *The Principles of Education*, 394–8; J. Cowham, *A New School Method: For Pupil-teachers and Students* (London: Westminster School Book Depot, 1894), 340–4; Howard, 'History', 250–4.
35 Dodd, *Introduction to Herbartian Principles*, 19.
36 Adapted from Christian Üfer, *Introduction to Herbart*, trans. J.C. Zinser (London: Isbister and Co., 1895), 60–3; Dodd, *Introduction to Herbartian Principles*, 19–22.
37 Cox and Macdonald, *Suggestive Handbook*, 358.
38 V. Chancellor, *History for their Masters: Opinion in the English History Textbook, 1800–1914* (London: Adams and Dart, 1970), 137.
39 Hayward, *Reform of Moral and Biblical Education*, 165–6.
40 Cox and Macdonald, *Suggestive Handbook*, 357.
41 Cox and Macdonald, *Suggestive Handbook*, 358.
42 F.H. Hayward and A. Freeman, *The Spiritual Foundations of Reconstruction* (1919), cited in Anna-Katherina Mayer, 'Moralizing Science: The Uses of Science's Past in National Education in the 1920s', *The British Journal for the History of Science*, 30:1 (1997), 64–5.
43 Karl Lange, *Apperception: A Monograph on the Psychology and Pedagogy of Education*, trans. Elmer E. Brown. (Boston: D.C. Heath and Co., [1879] 1894).
44 This is a necessarily simplified account of 'apperception'. For fuller contemporary analysis of it, see Adams, *The Herbartian Psychology*, 51–4; Adamson, *Practice of Instruction*, 24, 72; Findlay, *Principles of Class Teaching*, 270–2; de Garmo, *Herbart and the Herbartians*, 166–79.
45 Findlay, *Principles of Class Teaching*, 270.

46 Dodd, *Introduction to Herbartian Principles*, 39.
47 Findlay, *Principles of Class Teaching*, 271.
48 Raymont, *Principles of Education*, 253.
49 Salmon, *Art of Teaching*, 214.
50 Gunn, *Class Teaching and Management*, 136.
51 Garlick, *A New Manual of Method*, 178, 258.
52 Cowham, *New School Method*, 344
53 Salmon, *Art of Teaching*, 214–15.
54 Howard, 'History', 269–70.
55 Raymont, *Principles of Education*, 167.
56 Salmon, *Art of Teaching*, 212.
57 Welton, *Principles and Methods of Teaching*, 136.
58 As was explained in the preface to one reading book. *Britannia History Readers*, I (London: Edward Arnold, 1901), preface.
59 This is Howard's phrase, 'History', 251.
60 I. Steele, *Developments in History Teaching* (London: Open Books, 1976), 48–61. For an example, see Dorothea Beale, 'The Teaching of Chronology', *Parent's Review*, 2 (1891–92), 81–91.
61 Cowham tentatively suggested that the regressive approach could be effective with much older scholars, in subject specific lessons, but was steadfast in his belief that it would be an erroneous ploy with younger children. Cowham, *New School Method*, 340–1.
62 Landon, *Principles and Practice*, 195
63 Gunn, *Class Teaching and Management*, 139–40
64 R. Hallam, 'Piaget and Thinking in History', R. Hallam (ed.) *New Movements in the Study and Teaching of History* (London: Temple Smith 1970), 162–78.
65 Adamson, *Practice of Instruction*, 260
66 Findlay, *Principles of Class Teaching*, 96–7, 3.
67 Adamson, *Practice of Instruction*, 268
68 Adamson, *Practice of Instruction*, 261–2.
69 Landon, *Principles and Practice*, 397.
70 Üfer, *Introduction to Herbart*, 68.
71 Selleck, *The New History*, 239–41.
72 Adamson, *Practice of Education*, 109–11.
73 Adamson, *Practice of Instruction*, 111.
74 Dodd, *Introduction to Herbartian Principles*, 7.
75 Findlay, *Principles of Education*, 179.
76 Salmon, *Art of Teaching*, 216.
77 Cowham, *New School Method*, 345.
78 Cox and Macdonald, *Suggestive Handbook*, 358–9.
79 Cowham, *New School Method*, 341.
80 Cowham, *New School Method*, 341.
81 Cowham, *New School Method*, 343.
82 *The Newbery Historical Readers* (Oscar Browning), I (London: Griffith, Farran and Co., 1893), 101.
83 Adamson, *Practice of Instruction*, 260–1.
84 Cox and Macdonald, *Suggestive Handbook*, 5–6.
85 Dodd, *Introduction to Herbartian Principles*, 21.
86 J. Finnemore, *Black's School Series: Black's Story of the English People*, I (London: A. & C. Black, 1905), 154.
87 *Cassell's Historical Course for Schools*, I (London: Cassell and Co., 1884), 181–2.
88 S. Deuchar, *History and GCSE History* (London: Centre for Policy Studies, 1987), 6.
89 Richard Aldrich, 'New History: An Historical Perspective', in A.K. Dickinson, P.J. Lee and P.J. Rogers (eds), *Learning History* (London: Heinemann Educational, 1984), 210–24.

90 Schools Council 13–16 Project, *A New Look at History* (Edinburgh: Holmes MacDougal, 1976).
91 Hallam, 'Piaget and Thinking in History', 166–7.
92 Cited in D. Gunning, *The Teaching of History* (London: Croom Helm, 1978), 12.
93 F. Musgrove, 'Five Scales of Attitude to History', cited in Hallam, 'Piaget and Thinking in History', 167.
94 E.A. Peel, 'Some Problems in the Psychology of History Teaching', in W.H. Burston and D. Thompson (eds), *Studies in the Nature and Teaching of History* (London: Routledge and Kegan Paul, 1967), 173–90.
95 J. Coltham and J. Fines, *Educational Objectives for the Study of History: A Suggested Framework* (London: Historical Association, Teaching of History Series 35, 1971), 7–9.
96 A. Gard and P.J. Lee, '"Educational Objectives for the Study of History" Reconsidered', in A. Dickinson and P.J. Lee (eds), *Historical Teaching and Historical Understanding* (London: Heinemann, 1978), 32.
97 D. Shemilt, 'Beauty and the Philosopher: Empathy and History in the Classroom', in A. Dickinson, P. Lee and P. Rogers (eds), *Learning History* (London: Heinemann, 1984), 39–83.

PART II

Imperial values and enlightened patriotism in the teaching of history, c. 1880–1930

IMPERIAL VALUES AND ENLIGHTENED PATRIOTISM

The use of the term 'English' as a synonym for 'British' is more than just a slovenly application of the word. It represents a series of assumptions about the natural right of England to speak for Britain and, by the imposed silence, the inability of the Welsh, Irish and Scottish voices to challenge effectively those assumptions. It reproduces the imperial philosophy in which the mother country represented the greater whole.[1]

In order to inculcate values of enlightened patriotism, it is no surprise that educational theorists concentrated on the teaching of young working-class children. As seen, the majority of children would have gained their historical education through stories read in compulsory reading lessons, and only a small minority would have stayed in school long enough to take the subject-specific examination lesson. When one compares the representation of British imperial history in reading books and subject-specific textbooks, a number of interesting differences become self-evident. Prioritisation in reading books of the longer narrative of English history, with particular focus on stories of national origins, was intended to provide children with a long, albeit basic, chronology. This served a number of pedagogical functions: it allowed recapitulation; and, in doing so, enabled simple contrasts between past and present to be drawn out by demonstrating the progress of English values over time. Collective identity was to be represented through the promotion of a historically entrenched national story.

The argument that proceeds over the following chapters is that reading books depicted a two-fold process of nation-building. First, the contemporaneous present – especially the British imperial present – was increasingly explained by reference to the longevity of established English character traits. Given educationists' insistence that young children would be likelier to internalise lessons about the values of enlightened patriotism from stories of medieval history, it is little wonder that we find in reading books stories of national (and consequently imperial) origins, the innate English love for freedom and their predisposition towards seafaring and colonisation (Chapter Three). Second, it is yet to be made clear why the 'nation' to which these young citizens should devote their loyalty and national pride was designated to be English, not British.[2] Those civic obligations inherent within the composition of 'enlightened patriotism' were explained by reference to the racial composition of the English people. Stories explaining who actually constituted the English 'race' drew on the full time-span of 'English' history. Together, as argued in Chapter Four, these added weight to representations of the national present as an accumulation of characteristics over time. Focus on the early period enabled contrasts between 'now' and 'then', but also encouraged the narrative depiction of the evolution of the national character. Moreover, the space within formulations of the 'nation' – the English nation – excluded those non-English Britons who refused to commit themselves to English dominance.³ Maintenance and administration of empire was a collectively British endeavour.⁴ However, although texts addressed that some of their audience were Irish, Scottish or Welsh, they paid no attention to the fact that a fair proportion of pupils in elementary schooling, especially in large urban centres, were likely to be of Jewish or other immigrant origin.⁵ Explanations in reading texts of imperial origins reveal much about the intra-British power relations in the later nineteenth and early twentieth centuries. If Linda Colley is correct in her assertion that Britishness was constructed through shared identifications to the institutions of the British state, then did this model remain valid in representations of an imperial identity which drew both from Anglo-Saxon origins and depicted English progress against negative images of the Welsh, Scottish and Irish? Moreover, how did reading books and textbooks represent colonial subjects and what messages did these depict about the English and their empire?

Chapter Five scrutinises the teaching of moral biography and the pedagogical function of role models. Although Herbartian principles are clearly evident in the use of recapitulation and the drawing of racial contrasts, it is in the teaching of moral biography that these principles are at their most explicit. Chapter Six, which focuses on how the experience of war and its aftermath affected the teaching of history, demonstrates the persistence of pre-war methods. A shift in policy and content is identified: internationalist calls for peace education and the Europe-wide harmonisation of history curricula in the aftermath of war met with resistance in England. The English had grown accustomed to the way history was taught. English history was global history and any demand to teach internationalism was contested on the grounds that the British empire constituted the noblest of international alliances.

Notes

1 Ken Lunn, 'Reconsidering "Britishness": The Construction and Significance of National Identity in Twentieth Century Britain', in B. Jenkins and S. Sofos (eds), *Nation and Identity in Contemporary Europe* (London: Routledge, 1996), 87.
2 The study here is of texts used in English schools, and hence of how 'other' races were represented to children being taught in English elementary schools. An intriguing project for future research would be to undertake a comparative analysis of how imperial history was taught in England, Scotland, Wales and Ireland.
3 Colin Kidd, 'Race, Empire and the Limits of Nineteenth-Century Scottish Nationhood', *Historical Journal*, 46:4 (2003), 873–92.

4 P. Ward, *Britishness since 1870* (London: Routledge, 2004), 22–8; John MacKenzie, 'Empire and National Identities: The Case of Scotland', *Transactions of the Royal Historical Society*, 6th series, 8 (1998), 215–32.
5 Benjamin J. Lammers, '"The Citizens of the Future": Educating children of the Jewish East End', *Twentieth Century British History*, 19:4 (2008), 393–418; Tony Kushner, 'New Narratives, Old Exclusions? British Historiography and Minority Studies', *Immigrants and Minorities*, 24:2 (2006), 47–51.

CHAPTER THREE

Imperial values in the teaching of history I: national origins, seafaring and the Christian impulse

In the late nineteenth century, Britain defined itself as not only an imperial nation, but also the pre-eminent imperial nation in history. What did people mean by 'imperial'? Many emphasised territorial acquisition and settlement which included the export of democracy, economic expansion, maritime supremacy and the conduct of a decidedly Christian mission to civilise 'backward' races.[1] British imperial power was explained not as a result of economic exploitation and brutality – though plenty at the time posited such arguments – but as power divinely ordained: present-day Britain was understood to be the logical culmination of centuries of English, specifically Anglo-Saxon, progress. As Joseph Chamberlain, then Secretary of State for the Colonies, declared in 1895:

> In the first place, I believe in the British Empire and in second place I believe in the British race [. . .] in this Anglo-Saxon race, so proud reaching, self-confident and determined, this race, which neither climate nor change can degenerate, which will infallibly be the predominant force of future history and universal civilisation [. . .] We are all prepared to admire the great Englishmen of the past. We speak of the men who made our Empire, and we speak of them as heroes as great as any that have lived in the pages of history.[2]

It is not surprising to find that reading books for young children identified the origins of the British empire in the deep history of the English race. In keeping with what Asa Briggs labelled 'the Anglo-Saxon infatuation', propagandists and politicians alike emphasised the Anglo-Saxon origins of the imperial present.[3] Stephanie Barczewski has shown how, as the nineteenth century progressed, myth was intermixed with science in order to create a distinctively Anglo-Saxon definition of English nationhood. It was in this context of a fusion of race and biology that intellectual culture could recast the Celtic Arthur as a Saxon hero, for instance.[4]

Herbartians emphasised the teaching of medieval history on the grounds that, pedagogically, it was sensible to instruct children in moral lessons from periods of time in which civilisation was, like them, in its infancy. The teaching of national origins, however, served the additional purpose of locating imperial roots not only in the remote past in general, but in the Anglo-Saxon settlement of Britain in particular. If the designated task for historical reading lessons was to impart imperial values, then stories of Anglo-Saxon settlement provided plenty of examples of the English nation's predisposition towards seafaring, colonisation, settlement and fair rule. Moreover, emphases on the Anglo-Saxon 'love' for liberty and their conversion to Christianity also highlighted those traits which defined modern, imperial Britain. Reading books were intended to teach children that England's right to possess the empire was sanctioned by the uninterrupted arrow of national time. Textbooks, on the other hand, did not emphasise medieval origins. Instead, they tended to locate imperial origins in the Elizabethan age. Fletcher and Kipling's text, for instance, first makes explicit mention of the 'Empire' in its account of Walter Raleigh whose success was to 'create a piece of "England-beyond-the sea", a piece, in fact, of an English Empire'.[5] Whereas reading books emphasised that imperial values were embedded in the English genetic code, textbooks tended to concentrate on trade and geographical expansion.

On national and imperial origins: 'Thus has Britain been changed into modern England'

Chapter One identified that the history practised in schools was, in part, influenced by the changing nature of history in the academies. Some further comment is necessary. There were two distinct approaches to the study and teaching of academic history within this period: the emergence of modern history as a discipline in its own right tussled for attention with the established and apparent dominance of medieval history.[6] 'By 1890', David Newsome has written, the practice of academic history had 'virtually passed into the hands of the medievalists: William Stubbs, Edward Augustus Freeman, F.W. Maitland, J.H. Round, Mandell Creighton, Frederick Seebohm, Mary Bateson'.[7] In effect, however, both modernists and medievalists enjoyed greater public awareness of their works because of a culture of increasing public zeal for the past as a leisure form, and the opening up of new opportunities for the dissemination of their ideas.[8]

Increased public exposure to history was significant since both modernists and medievalists sought to use the study of the past to explain the unfolding of the present. Whiggism was melded to the Rankean scientific approach to history as the search for identifiable truths. Peter Mandler has suggested that English historians, in contrast to their continental colleagues, had long been able to admire the histories of their national institutions from the vantage point of the present since 'time' itself sanctioned the English way.[9] By the last third of the nineteenth century, however, this self-confidence took voice in exclamations of the glory of English history. This dovetailed neatly with the approach to history as storytelling, recommended as we have seen by authors of method manuals. Although a term they themselves might not have employed, one topic for study – whether medievalist or modernist – was the Englishness of the empire's origins. For medievalists, the constitutional origins of the English parliamentary tradition could be traced back to times of Anglo-Saxon settlement. So too, given 'colonisation' by the English of Anjou, Aquitaine, Gascony, Calais, Ireland, the Isle of Man and Wales, could pre-'British empire' examples of the governance and administration of a colonial polity from London be similarly traced. In short, these medieval experiences provided 'traditions and usages' that 'passed into British colonial practice in the modern period'.[10]

Emphasis upon understanding the English historical origins of the imperial present was also a concern for modern historians. School reading books met face-on Hugh Egerton's advice that 'the history of England should be identified with the British Empire'.[11] Egerton was the First Beit Professor of Colonial History at Oxford, appointed in 1905, and is widely recognised to have followed fast in the footsteps of John Robert Seeley, Regius Chair at Cambridge.[12] Seeley's lecture course on the British empire, delivered in 1881–82, was subsequently published as the *Expansion of England* in 1883. According to Richard Aldrich, this text 'established imperialism as a central theme of modern British history' in schools as well as 'in the public mind'.[13] The study of history, Seeley emphasised, should be an uplifting moral source rather than an avenue for sating curiosities; history should not be so much the account of the machinations of state power as the story of the expansion of the English race.[14] Seeley had argued for the synonymy of 'Greater Britain' and 'a vast English nation'. Indeed, he averred that 'if Greater Britain in the full sense of the phrase really existed, Canada and Australia would be to us as Kent and Cornwall'.[15] His intention was to position the Anglo-Saxon race firmly at the hub of this Greater Britain. In his vision, it did not matter so much that Britain had lost colonial control of the thirteen American colonies in the eighteenth century: what mattered more was the unity and onward and outward expansion of the Anglo-Saxon race. Thus, Robert Colls is right to observe that 1588, rather than 1688, was the key date for

Seeley: imperial expansion – in this instance, gaining maritime supremacy following the defeat of the Spanish Armada – mattered more to the evolution of the English story than constitutional revolution.[16] As Seeley wrote, 'liberty is not so much an end to which we have been tending as a possession which *we have long* enjoyed'.[17]

Seeley's call to place race and culture above constitutionalism is indeed evident in the contrasting treatment of 1588 and 1688: the Glorious Revolution was a staple of textbooks for older children but nowhere to be seen in historical reading books. The story of the Armada, on the other hand, was everywhere. This made sense in pedagogical terms. Political history was too complicated for young minds. The defeat of the Armada was exciting, confirmed England's historical relationship to the sea and asserted 'traditional' English liberties (as opposed to the despotic Philip I) as intrinsic to the English race (more on the Armada later in this chapter). J.H. Grainger suggests Seeley had 'prescribed a conscious national morality' which constituted a 'practical idealisation of England through the teaching of her history'.[18] It is no accident, therefore, that many studies of the later nineteenth-century expansion of history teaching take Seeley's writings as their point for departure.[19] Bernard Porter suggests that over-attention to the impact of Seeley is misleading since he had little immediate influence on university curricula.[20] Irrespective of Seeley's direct impact, one cannot underestimate the influence of the first generation of university academics that both took the history of the British empire as their topic for research *and* contributed to debates about history in schools. Indeed, it was not so much Seeley who mattered to the dissemination of the imperial gospel as those who embellished and then sung loudly from his hymn sheet.[21]

The three most indicative examples of historians to disseminate this gospel are Egerton, A.P. Newton and Sir Charles Lucas.[22] All three promoted the study of imperialism in the universities as well as schools.[23] The empire was depicted as the logical culmination of long histories of the accumulation of liberties, seafaring and colonisation. 'By more clearly associating the expansion of liberty with the English "race"', Mark Lee observes, Egerton, Newton and Lucas 'infused British and imperial history with Anglocentric whiggism'.[24] This dovetailed neatly with the approach to history as storytelling. As Andrew Thompson notes, 'the Whig interpretation of history was fundamental to constructions of British national identity, so it occupied a privileged place in thinking about the British Empire'.[25] Late nineteenth-century scientific and cultural languages of race suffused both the histories of Anglo-Saxon and Teutonic origins, and encapsulated the evolution of these English forbearers over time (about which we will hear more in the next chapter).[26] Thus, it was within a dominant Whiggish discourse of history that increased attention was paid to questions of national origins by both medievalists and modernists.

This view found popular expression in school reading books. J.R. Green, in his celebrated *Short History of the English People* (1874), which became something of a reference guide for historical reading books, wrote that:[27]

> It is with a reverence such as is stirred by the sight of the headwaters of some mighty river that one looks back to these tiny moots, where the men of the village met to order the village life and the village industry, as their descendants, the men of later England, meet in Parliament at Westminster, to frame laws and do justice for the great empire which has sprung from this little body of farmer-commonwealths in Sleswick.[28]

How, specifically, did reading books narrate the beginnings of the story of the English people? Texts were keen to emphasise the Englishness of English origins; that is, to associate the origins of modern Britain – including imperialism – in the earliest stories of Anglo-Saxon settlement. One reading book began with cavemen.[29] Others began with the Roman departure. Some started their story with accounts of ancient Britons. They were unanimous, however, in locating the beginning of the *national* story in stories of Anglo-Saxon settlement of what became 'English' territory. Most reading books began with passages such as: 'the English people have lived so long in our island that it seems hard to believe they have not always been here'.[30] Another claimed: 'When we go back to the beginnings of our history we see how great is the difference between the condition of England and Englishmen in past times and in our own'.[31] In 1901, Lady Katie Magnus, in the preface to her school book, *First Makers of England*, wrote that 'the seeds of our national character are sought in the lives and heroes of early England, from whom we trace the beginnings of our best habits and institutions'.[32] The English came, they conquered and, in the words of the same text, 'thus has Britain changed into modern England'.[33]

Emphasis upon Anglo-Saxon settlement helped depict an English propensity towards colonial expansion. Under a chapter heading, 'The English Settle in England', John Finnemore informed his child readers that 'the homelands of the Old English grew too small for them'.[34] 'Most likely', according to another author, 'they had always felt at home on the sea, but they had only taken to being sea-robbers because there was not enough room for them in the old country, and they were obliged to find new homes'.[35] The Old English had no natural homeland. They chose 'our' territory because of its many advantages. Another text began by telling children that 'in old times, England – or Britain, as it was then called – was a very wild country'.[36] Under the stewardship of the 'wild' indigenous Britons, the territory was being put to waste, the *Ship Historical Reader* told children, 'but when the Saxons saw what a good country this was, they made up their minds to stay here'.[37] Britain was depicted as a pleasant country ripe for settlement. In this text, the matter of the indigenous Britons with whom battle was fought was easily bypassed. Emphasis was on the agreeableness of the British landscape: 'Britain was a pleasant country, with fine meadows and cornfields, rich herds of cattle and sheep, gardens and orchards. Being much better than their own country, the Jutes determined to stay, and asked their kinsmen at home, the Jutes, the Saxons and the Angles, to come and share this pleasant country with them'.[38] And as the *Britannia History Readers* explained, 'these Angles, Saxons and Jutes were the forefathers of the English. It took them a great number of years to turn Britain into Angle-land, or England'.[39] The earliest English identified with the national landscape. The explicit message was that, so too, should present-day children.

The beginnings of the history of the British empire were melded to these stories of English national origin. Newton, in a pamphlet for teachers, advised that 'colonial history is but a continuation of the history of folk wanderings'.[40] This was true of geography as well as history texts – a correlation which Stephen Heathorn argues made early years geographical and historical reading lessons occasionally indistinguishable.[41] John Meiklejohn, who held the Chair in Education at St Andrews, wrote in his geography primer: 'the story of the growth of the British Empire is the story of the expansion of the Anglo-Saxon race'.[42] History texts were identical in their message of national and imperial origins: one of 1896 claimed that 'no race could have built up this Empire unless it possessed the qualities of honesty, courage and endurance'; another noted that it was because of Anglo-Saxon qualities that the Englishman had 'the energy and perseverance' that enabled him to 'face the difficulties of opening up a new country', as well as the 'independence of character [that] drives him to new lands'.[43] The *Britannia History Readers* explained the empire's origins as English:

> England is only part of the island called Great Britain, the other parts of which are Scotland and Wales. To the west of Great Britain is another island, called Ireland. The two together are known as the British Isles. From the first, Englishmen have had much to do with the inhabitants of the other parts of the British Isles, that it is impossible to write about them quite separately. And they are all now under one sovereign, and

form the kingdom of Great Britain and Ireland. The British Isles are only a small part of the dominions of the British Sovereign, to whom new lands belong all over the world. It is said that upon the British Empire the Sun never sets [...] English history has to tell, among other things, how it is that we have come to possess such a large part of the world.[44]

'We greatly owe the freedom we now enjoy to our forefathers': Christianity and the love for English liberties

In terms of identity teaching, pronounced emphases on stories of national origins served two purposes. First, stories showed that the English character was predisposed towards colonisation, settlement, love for liberty and industriousness. Second, in asking children to identify what their English ancestors used to be like, the pedagogical method of recapitulation could be used to draw contrasts against less salutary moments in the development of the national character, thus highlighting progress over time.

If texts for younger scholars painted a romantic picture of national origins, texts for older children were not reluctant to point out some of the less appetising Anglo-Saxon characteristics; nor were they so interested in making the material appealing. Most textbooks rushed through the medieval period, but those which did make comment painted Anglo-Saxons in a negative light. Fletcher and Kipling described the 'Saxon Englishman' as 'a savage with the vices and cruelties of an overgrown schoolboy, a drunkard, a gambler and very stupid'. Despite the negativity, they still concluded that the Saxon was 'a truth-teller, a brave, patient and cool-headed fellow'.[45] Arthur Innes' textbook merely listed dates of conquest and provided complicated explanations of the geographical distribution of territory and the operation of Heptarchy.[46] G.W. Cox informed his readers that Saxons demonstrated 'many of the worst faults of youth'; they were 'rash, headstrong, quarrelsome, greedy, violent and cruel' and should be considered 'strangers' to the modern schoolchild.[47]

Attention to negative character traits did not matter because the recapitulation method required demonstration of how the English had progressed. For young children, the message was simple: 'you must not think the English, at the time we are talking of, were foolish . . . [they] were good sailors and brave soldiers, hardworking farmers and skilful smiths and carpenters; and they could take care of themselves, and hold their own whether at work or play'.[48] In words appropriate for an elementary-school audience, the *Britannia History Readers* informed children that 'at first the English were heathens [...] their religion made them fierce and cruel to their enemies, instead of teaching them to be merciful and gentle'. The implication was that Christianity had added immeasurably to the national character. Despite their pre-Christian ferocity, the text continued, the English 'were kind to their own wives and children, and they were also very truthful people'.[49] Readers of the *Young Student's English History Reading Book* were informed (one assumes that, because of the complicated language, this text was designed for older scholars): 'in the hearts of these uncultured sons of German soil [were] noble qualities of character and disposition [...]; an earnestness of feeling, a love of independence, a fidelity to engagements, and a national sense of honour, all of which fitted them to be the progenitors of a nation of law-abiding Englishmen, self-respecting, self-governed, and delighting in an ordered freedom'.[50] That was progress of which children should be proud. Archibald Dick, in his *First Historical Reader* (1881) explained that 'the Saxons [...] loved freedom, and loved justice, in a rough but true way, and they were only heathens because no one had ever taught them better'.[51] This love of freedom formed a recurrent theme in these texts. *Blackie's New Series* (1904) stated that the 'love of freedom which these Old English felt is still felt by their descendants. And this love of freedom and wish to manage their own affairs has certainly helped to make England the great country she is'.[52] Another text explained that all 'Englishmen are now agreed that we greatly owe the freedom we now enjoy to our forefathers, who resolved to bleed and die on the battlefield rather than submit to the arbitrary will of misguided kings'.[53]

Building on this foundation of a love for freedom, 'civilisation' arrived in the form of Christianity. As Dick commented, 'there came a time when they [the English], too, learnt about Christ, and then their love of freedom and justice was of more worth than ever, when it was backed up by the truth that maketh free'.[54] The English were imbued with proselytising properties even prior to their own Christianisation. Given the frequency with which this story occurs over a range of reading books, it is worth reproducing at length – especially so since its clear link to contemporaneous justifications for imperial conquest as Christian missionary activity are obvious:

> Some fair headed children had been carried off as slaves from England to Rome, the largest city in the world. They were standing in the market place watching the faces of all who passed by to see who was most likely to buy them, when a good man, named Gregory, came along. He looked at their sweet faces, their blue eyes, and their golden hair, and he felt full of sorrow. The owner was standing by, so Gregory asked to what country such dear children belonged. 'They are Angles', said the dealer. 'No, not Angles', said Gregory, 'from their faces I think they must be

Angels. Who is the King of their Country?' he asked? 'Ella' said the dealer. 'Alleluia shall be sung in his land', replied Gregory.[55]

Gregory went on to become Pope and returned the children to England, with Augustine, thus beginning the process of Christianising the English. 'Christianity made the English less fierce and barbarous in their wars, and less cruel to the enemies they conquered', one text explained, continuing that '[t]hey became a kindlier and gentler people, and more civilised in many ways'.[56] The widely told story of Edmund, medieval King of East Anglia, was included to indicate the extent to which the English absorbed their new faith. When threatened with execution lest he give up his faith, Edmund was almost universally reported in these texts to have replied that his death 'may teach Danes that an Englishman can be true to his country and his God'.[57]

Furthermore, although the seventeenth-century civil wars were only reported occasionally in texts for younger children, when they were mentioned they concentrated on the poor kingship of Charles I. In no longer representing the will of his people, Charles was 'not a good king' because he would challenge 'the rights of Englishmen to be free'.[58] He had to go since 'if a man could not speak his mind freely in Parliament, then freedom was dead in England'.[59] The message must have been that the English would and should fight to defend their freedoms. Accounts of developments in English democratic history tended, instead, to focus on Magna Carta. This, Stephen Heathorn demonstrates, served two functions: first, it enabled children to judge the wickedness of 'Bad' King John, by far 'the most reviled of all domestic monarchs in school readers', and second, it confirmed the legal reinstatement of specifically English freedoms.[60] Magna Carta was 'dear to the hearts of all Britons'. That it was on display in the British Museum was also used to encourage admiration: 'all Englishmen who love their country should try to see it at least once in their lives'.[61] Love of 'freedom' was thus cemented as a central component of Englishness and was melded to stories of imperial origins. This will be further underlined in the next chapter regarding the way in which children were taught about slavery.

Case study: Sir Philip Sidney

At a recent public lecture, I asked an audience of approximately thirty people ranging in age from children to pensioners to raise their hands if they had heard of Grace Darling; only about half did (more on Grace in a subsequent chapter in which the gendered dynamics of history teaching are subjected to analysis). When asked about Sir Philip Sidney and the Zutphen sacrifice (of 1586), only eight responded affirmatively

– four of whom had been taught history in schools in the 1960s or earlier.[62] This is indicative: although Grace was not always ever present in readers, she was included in texts with increasing consistency after the 1890s and remains frequently taught in schools. Philip Sidney's story was consistently taught and only slipped out of curricula in the 1970s. A closer analysis of these two characters reveals much, since attention to those considered unexceptional by our modern mind, but heroic to the late Victorians, more emphatically indicates the fears and concerns of the period out of which these heroes were selected. That Sidney's story was popular content, especially in reading books for the young, owed entirely to the way in which his life could be used to demonstrate the fusion of religious and imperial values in the sixteenth century. He embodied the characteristics of the imperial race before the geographical empire had been accumulated.

Sidney's story indicates how the development of Christianity was linked into the long-standing English love for freedom. His then famous words, as he rejected the offer of water while he lay dying on the battlefield, lest someone else might use it to survive, were frequently invoked: 'Thy Necessity is far greater than mine'. As the story concluded, children were reminded: 'We shall always remember him as the man who could forget himself and think of others even in the hour of death'.[63] His courage was his humility, his self-sacrifice and his service. His sacrifice was of great significance since, as a role model, he articulated the ideal characteristics suitable for social absorption. 'When the need arose', Sir Philip Sidney, otherwise a 'poet and a man of a very gentle and loving nature', chose to fight 'as bravely as the best of his queen's brave men'.[64] Another text commented that 'he had always been kind, and even when he was in the greatest pain himself, he could think of others in their trouble [. . .] such a noble man can never be forgotten'.[65]

At the time of the second Boer War, the Bishop of Durham had waxed that '[W]e hold our Empire in the name of Christ'.[66] Keith Robbins has observed that one of the idiosyncrasies of late nineteenth-century England was that 'at a time when British Christianity was making its biggest impact overseas its domestic differences were still only too apparent'.[67] The problem for those who devised curricula was that the power of the churches was not only in steady decline, but that the power of the church as an organising pillar for British national identity was waning. Stories of contemporary missionaries filled public media. The missionary par excellence was David Livingstone who, according to John MacKenzie, was promptly elevated to hero status precisely because in him were welded the twin tenets of British Protestantism and a beneficent face of the imperial project.[68] However, missionaries did not feature much in reading books.[69] This may also have been because of the much-disputed effects of the Cowper-Temple Clause, written into the 1870 Education Act, which allowed parents to remove children from religious education. Given religion remained a socially divisive issue, Sidney's story could be used to teach moral lessons – as the Herbartians would wish – which corresponded to Christian doctrines of service and goodwill. Sidney's story implied the important lesson that Christianity could be reconciled to war, so long as the cause was justified. As a story of progress, it masked the religious turmoil of the sixteenth century, while enabling focus on early modern Protestantism as a foundation stone of empire (he died in 1586). What Sidney's story indicates is the Christian ethic of service: his service is mobilised to represent sacrifice for the greater good. Veneration of Sidney placed him on an equal footing with medieval saints. Sidney's celebrated characteristics – service, duty, heroism, sacrifice, love of learning and commitment to the greater cause – contributed to a narrative trope of heroism which transcended national time and was used to frame later stories of specifically imperial heroes such as Nelson, Clive, Wellington and Gordon (see Chapter Five).

The island race and seamanship

It was noted in the introduction that descriptions of British history as an 'island story' characterise recent critiques of the teaching of history. First used by Tennyson in stanza eight of his *Ode to the Duke of Wellington* ('[N]ot once or twice in our rough island story/The path to duty was the way to glory'), the phrase found its way into common English usage by the end of the nineteenth century to denote the story of the expansion of England (rather than Britain) into an imperial power.[70] It did not take long to filter into school history books. Henrietta Marshall's celebrated *Our Island Story* (1905) became a popular bestseller, though it was purchased less for use in schools and more in the home. In the same year, the London educational publishers T.C. and E.C. Jack produced an eight-volume set of reading books entitled *Jack's Concentric Histories: Our Island's Story* (1905) for use in primary schools. In Arthur Mee's popular school book, *Little Treasure Island* (1920), the national past was the story of the growth of 'the Island in the Middle of World'.[71] Emphases on Britain (England) as an island race with a natural, innate mastery of the seas endured, not least because of the preponderance of the navy as emblematic of identity. The island story trope was given sustenance by tales of Britain's maritime supremacy during the Second World War and became folklore as part of Churchill's rhetoric of an obdurate race that would fight on the seas, the oceans, in the air and on the beaches, never surrendering, in defence of our island. It was shaken by media anxiety about the opening of the Channel Tunnel in 1992.[72] It was the title of a 1980s school textbook and a publication made to accompany the popular BBC television series *Coast* in 2010.[73] It is little surprise that the phrase, modified to expunge explicit racial overtones typical of the Victorians, remains readily available as a means to depict narrative British history. But how did reading books depict seafaring as a core component of both British national identity and as central to this longer narrative of English imperial history?

Anthony D. Smith suggests modern preoccupation with the 'island story' phrase denotes ambivalence regarding the ever-increasing likelihood of European political integration.[74] There is certainly some merit to the argument that in times of perceived identity crisis, history is mobilised to reinforce English insularity. Turn of the twentieth century Britain celebrated and hence defined itself as a seaborne nation.[75] Such a calling card of nationalism is not so readily available now. Much recent scholarly interest in the maritime essence of British national identity might be explained by the bicentenary of Nelson's death.[76] That such a historiographical interest is only recent is indeed surprising, since John MacKenzie was surely right to emphasise that, in the late nineteenth and early twentieth centuries, the British 'spent much energy seeking the nautical roots of world greatness'.[77] It was crucial for a nation, which in the late Victorian period defined itself as an 'island race', to demonstrate its longstanding mastery of the seas: the Royal Navy served as a source of propaganda for promoting empire, monarchy *and* state.[78] In the context of a nation that felt its empire stretched, and felt pronounced fear in the rise of German sea-power,[79] it is not surprising that children were taught comforting stories about England's inherent right, and inveterate duty, to rule the waves.

Famous stories of naval victories, such as the defeat of the Spanish Armada and the Battle of Trafalgar, provided awe-inspiring tales of derring-do and heroism (additional analysis of the Armada and Trafalgar follows in Chapter Five). Textbooks, paying little attention to Anglo-Saxon origins, tended to present the sailing skills of early Saxon settlers in negative language. Morris's *Class Book of English History* (1902) explained the earliest English as 'pirates', drawing no connections between Saxon seafarers and the development of English imperial attributes. For Morris, it was only following Drake's defeat of the Spanish that England demonstrated she was 'mistress of the sea'.[80] Ince and Gilbert's *Outlines of English History* (1906) dealt with the period pre-dating 1066 in a measly ten pages, arguing that 'the supremacy of Britain on the seas' was achieved only 'by their success over the

Spanish Armada'.[81] Fletcher and Kipling were damning in their assessment: with a polemical statement about contemporaneous military and naval apathy they bemoaned that the Saxon 'forgot his noble trade as a sailor, which had brought him to Britain, so completely that within two centuries his coasts were at the mercy of every sea thief in Europe'.[82]

Stories for younger children, however, demonstrated the presence of Herbartian pedagogy: they celebrated mastery of the seas – as with the love for freedom and predisposition towards colonisation – as intrinsic character traits of the very first English. For Finnemore, contemporary British maritime supremacy was explained as a positive legacy of the 'restlessness' felt by 'our' Anglo-Saxon forefathers who 'loved the sea, and feared nothing they could meet upon it'.[83] As one text for older scholars stated, 'love of the sea' was 'inherent in the breasts of a people sprung from a race whose greatest exploits of conquest and adventure have been intimately associated with seamanship'.[84] The defeat of the Spanish Armada, Berry's text for younger scholars declared, was possible because 'Britannia had already begun to rule the waves';[85] Berry had earlier explained that the sea had a mystical quality for the English since it 'really tempts the English to sail on its waters'.[86] The *Britannia History Readers* presented the same message. Although it was only since the sixteenth century 'that English sailors first became famous both as fighters and for the long voyages they made', the adventures of Raleigh, the Mayflower expedition and other stories of maritime exploration were only conceivable because 'Englishmen have always felt at home on the sea'.[87] The storytelling prose style is evident in the accounts of Sir Richard Grenville – this is the Grenville who was a veteran of the Armada and died at the naval Battle of Flores in 1591– who was far more interesting to authors of reading books than his more famous son who gained notoriety during the civil wars. When captured by the Spanish three years after the failure of their Armada, following his ship's resilient fight when significantly outnumbered, the Spaniards spared him from execution since 'they loved a brave man when they met one'.[88] As one text triumphantly summarised Grenville's story: 'English men might be killed and English ships burnt, but England's courage was invincible'.[89] Grenville's bravery was thus depicted, in simple language, as representative of a trait of the national character and enforced the heroic relationship between the English and the sea. 'As long as there is an English navy, the story of Richard Grenville's fight in the *Revenge* will be told as one of its bravest deeds'.[90] Grenville thus joined Edmund and Sidney in the national pantheon as an imperial martyr, later to be joined (as analysed in the fifth chapter) by Nelson and Gordon.

Lighthouse keepers, even, made a signal appearance in one text! They were described as 'brave fellows always willing to risk their own lives to save the lives of their brothers in peril'. The text followed this with the emphatic statement: 'so long as such is the case, England need have no fear that she will be able to beat off any foe that cares to meet her on the sea'.[91]

Reading books explained explicit continuities between the Anglo-Saxons and the nineteenth-century Royal Navy. In particular, authors were keen to celebrate the role of Alfred the Great in establishing a national navy: 'the idea of a navy to protect the country from invasion' was Alfred's, and for that posterity owed him a debt.[92] Having discussed Alfred's battle with the Danes, his imprisonment and his decision to construct a navy, the *Patriotic Historical Reader* notes: 'The King never used his ships to attack his neighbours. He only wanted them to protect our own shores, so he stationed them round the coast, ready to drive off any enemies who might try to land'. 'Since Alfred's time', the text continued, the English 'have always kept up *their* love for the sea, and many of the most famous British victories have been won by *our* navy' (note the intonation in the original on 'our' navy, which positions the medieval as part of the modern and reinforces historical permanence).[93] Bisecting the text is a photograph of a modern battleship, thus rendering this imperial continuity explicit. John Finnemore also emphasised Alfred's significance to the story of the English people: it is 'fitting', he wrote, that Alfred should demand a sizeable role in the national story, since he showed to 'the full every quality which has marked the greatness of our race'.[94] In particular, Finnemore continued, Alfred was the 'first to build a fleet, which was the beginning of the British Navy, the navy which now has ships on every sea, and flies the Union Jack in every corner of the world'.[95] Another reported, again drawing on historical permanence, that 'Alfred saw, what our kings and his ministers see today, that England's bulwark is her navy'. Alfred deserves the utmost adulation, the *Tower History Readers* elaborated, because the English now have 'the most powerful navy in the world, and for centuries no foreign foe has set foot on English soil'.[96] Reading books for older children were keen to emphasise the civilised Alfred, distancing him from the barbarism of the first Anglo-Saxon settlers. One reader for children in the senior standards declared: 'as a warrior, his wars were conducted in self-defence and his victories were never stained by cruelty', whereas another emphasised that he 'was always thinking and working for his people's welfare [because he was] ... religious before God'.[97] Thus, stories of medieval history set the scene both for the acquisition of the empire and maritime supremacy, but united progress with wisdom, compassionate leadership and religion. Little wonder that reading books encouraged children to adore Alfred: 'And although it is a thousand years since he lived, we still love him, as a king who did nobly, and always loved that which was good'.[98] The Reverend Dr Brewer lauded 'one of the most amiable and virtuous men that ever lived'.[99]

Once these outline stories of English maritime dominance were presented to children, texts for older students placed emphasis on the child's obligation to support the navy as part of their duties as enlightened patriots. Past Englishmen had supported the navy and contributed to its greatness: the message, then, was that it was essential that the contemporary generation do the same. In a geography text for older children, stark warnings about the potential calamity of an unsupported navy were made explicit:

> The fleet is England's right arm. But for her fleet England would be a cipher in the councils of Europe, might be stripped of her colonies, and could not hold her Indian Empire a year. But for the fleet, the working-man might, any day, find his daily work gone, and the price of his children's bread half-a-crown a loaf.[100]

A further geography text, again intended for older children, worried: 'the teeming millions of our people would be starved to submit to any foe who could so block our ports as to prevent stores of food coming to us from other lands; hence the navy of England should be strong enough, not only to defend our coast, but to protect our merchant ships against all comers'.[101] Clearly, in these partisan extracts, the perpetuation of national greatness was connected to the standard of living for the majority. By this method children were urged to venerate the navy and hence the empire and home life it supported. For all the gains made by past generations, the onus was on the children reading these stories to work hard, learn their lessons, and in doing so, do their bit for the endurance of this national greatness.

Summary

The use of 'island story' connotes a relationship between the sea and national identity on the one hand, and the notion of 'homeland' on the other. There is no doubt that late Victorian England understood itself as a maritime nation and that this was reflected in stories taught. Indeed Jan Rüger convincingly argues that scholars of Britishness have for too long overlooked the navy and the way its history has been told (concentrating instead on warfare, state formation and religion). 'It was', he argues, 'one of the most important agencies of Britishness in the Victorian and Edwardian era [. . .] on the mental map of the Empire, the fleet provided a symbolic link between far-flung colonies and the four nations of the mother country'.[102] In the late nineteenth century, the Royal Navy served symbolically to represent Scotland, Ireland and Wales as well as England: one of its functions was to promote intra-British unity. Rüger analyses pageants, jubilees and newspapers and finds genuine enthusiasm for the *British* fleet – especially since the land army drew heavily from provincial and regional identities.[103] However, attention to histories taught to young children indicates that the origins of the navy were depicted as quintessentially English. This tallied with late Victorian enthusiasm for all things Anglo-Saxon and established the predisposition towards seafaring and colonisation, as well as democracy and religion, as part of the genetic code of the imperial race. This is but one example of the contemporary slippage between English and British. Moreover, Heathorn argues that the navy was afforded a significant place in texts since it both 'associated the empire with notions of racial destiny' and served as the 'material as well as the symbolic link between the mother country and the colonies'.[104] It is on the subject of the representation of the historical relationship between England and the other nations of the empire, including constituent British nations, that the next chapter focuses.

Notes

1 John Wolffe, *God and Greater Britain: Religion and National Life in Britain and Ireland, 1843–1945* (London: Routledge, 1994), 222–5; Andrew Porter, 'Religion and Empire: British Expansion in the Long Nineteenth Century', *Journal of Imperial and Commonwealth History*, 20:3 (1992), 370–90.
2 Quoted, initially, from Valerie Chancellor, *History for their Masters: Opinion in the English History Textbook, 1800–1914* (London: Adam and Dart, 1970), 115; extended quotation from *The Times*, 12 November 1895.
3 A. Briggs, 'Saxons, Normans, Vikings', in *Collected Essays of Asa Briggs*, II (London: Harvester, 1985), 215–35. See also Reginald Horsman, 'Origins of Racial Anglo-Saxonism in Great Britain Before 1850', *Journal of the History of Ideas*, 37:3 (1976), 387–410; and Billie Melman, 'Claiming the Nation's Past: The Invention of an Anglo-Saxon Tradition', *Journal of Contemporary History*, 26 (1991), 575–95.
4 Stephanie Barczewski engages specifically with the relationship between 'scientific racism' and literary and other cultural productions: *Myth and National Identity in Nineteenth Century Britain: The Legends of King Arthur and Robin Hood* (Oxford: Oxford University Press, 2000), 124–61.
5 C.R.L. Fletcher and R. Kipling, *A School History of England* (Oxford: Clarendon, 1911), 166.
6 The question of the 'modernism' of this 'modern' history, as well as the modernism of novels and other art forms of the nineteenth century, are considered in the essays in Gary Day (ed.), *Varieties of Victorianism: The Uses of the Past* (Basingstoke: Macmillan, 1998).
7 See David Newsome, *The Victorian World Picture* (London: Fontana, 1998), 187.
8 On the increase, generally, of public infatuation with history-as-leisure, see Peter Mandler's fascinating survey, *History and National Life* (London: Profile, 2002);

see also Paul Readman, 'The Place of the Past in English Culture, c. 1890–1914', *Past and Present*, 186:1 (2005), 147–99. For further analysis of the relationship between empire and the writing of history, see Joanna de Groot's *Empire and History Writing in Britain c. 1750–2012* (Manchester: Manchester University Press), 2013.
9. Peter Mandler, '"In the Olden Time": Romantic History and English National Identity, 1820–50', in L. Brockliss and D. Eastwood (eds), *A Union of Multiple Identities: The British Isles, c. 1750–1850* (Manchester: Manchester University Press, 1997), 78–92.
10. See A.F.M. Madden, '1066, 1776 and All That: The Relevance of the English Medieval Experience of "Empire" to Later Imperial Constitutional Issues', in John Flint and Glyndwr Williams (eds), *Perspectives of Empire: Essays Presented to Gerald S. Graham* (London: Longman, 1973), 10.
11. Quoted in James Greenlee, *Education and Imperial Unity, 1901–26* (New York and London: Garland, 1987), 29.
12. See Mark Lee, 'The Story of Greater Britain: What Lessons Does it Teach?' *National Identities*, 6:2 (2004), 123–42; Peter Burroughs, 'John Robert Seeley and British Imperial History', *Journal of Imperial and Commonwealth History*, 1:2 (1973), 191–212; J. Greenlee, '"A Succession of Seeleys": The "Old School" Re-examined', *Journal of Imperial and Commonwealth History*, 4:3 (1976), 266–82; Richard Aldrich, 'Imperialism in the Study and Teaching of School History', in J.A. Mangan (ed.), *Benefits Bestowed? Education and British Imperialism* (Manchester: Manchester University Press, 1988), 23–38.
13. Aldrich, 'Imperialism in the Study and Teaching of School History', 25.
14. Michael Bentley, *Modernizing England's Past: English Historiography in the Age of Modernism, 1870–1970* (New York: Cambridge University Press, 2006), 72. See also D. Wormall, *Sir John Robert Seeley and the Uses of History* (Cambridge: Cambridge University Press, 1980).
15. Extracts cited in Krishan Kumar, *The Making of English National Identity* (Cambridge: Cambridge University Press, 2003), 189.
16. Robert Colls, *The Identity of England* (Oxford: Oxford University Press, 2002), 134.
17. J.R. Seeley, *The Expansion of England* (London: Macmillan and Co., [1883] 1914), 8–9 (emphasis added).
18. J.H. Grainger, *Patriotisms: Britain 1900–1939* (London: Routledge and Kegan Paul, 1986), 46.
19. See, for instance, J.M. MacKenzie, *Propaganda and Empire: The Manipulation of British Public Opinion* (Manchester: Manchester University Press, 1984), 179; Aldrich, 'Imperialism in the Study and Teaching of School History', 25.
20. Bernard Porter, *The Absent-Minded Imperialists: What the British Really Thought about Empire* (Oxford: Oxford University Press, 2004), 49–50.
21. See Mark Lee, 'The Story of Greater Britain', 126–8. Porter's argument runs adrift since he draws only from anecdotal evidence on Seeley's reputation at Cambridge, and not on Seeley's influence beyond elite academia.
22. Egerton was appointed in 1905 as the first Beit Professor of Colonial History at Oxford. Newton was appointed in 1919 as the first Rhodes Professor of Imperial History at King's, University of London and Lucas went on to become Chairman of the Royal Colonial Institute from 1915.
23. MacKenzie, *Propaganda and Empire*, 169.
24. Mark Lee, 'The Story of Greater Britain', 127.
25. Andrew Thompson, *Imperial Britain: The Empire in British Politics* (Harlow: Longman, 2000), 18.
26. Paul Rich, *Race and Empire in British Politics*, second edition (Cambridge: Cambridge University Press, 1990) – especially chapter 1; Christine Bolt, *Victorian Attitudes to Race* (London: Routledge and Kegan Paul, 1971), 13–21.
27. See G.M.D. Howat, 'The Nineteenth-Century History Textbook', *British Journal of Educational Studies*, 13 (1965), 147–59. See also Anthony Brundage, *The*

People's Historian: John Richard Green and the Writing of History in Victorian England (London: Greenwood, 1994), 73–100.
28 J.R. Green, *A Short History of the English People*, I, illustrated edition (London: Macmillan and Co., [1874] 1902), 7. 'Sleswick' (Schleswig now) was one of the German territories from where some of the original settlers originated.
29 A.J. Berry, *England and the English* (Glasgow: Blackie and Son, 1910).
30 John Finnemore, *Black's School Series: Black's Story of the English People*, I (London: A. & C. Black, 1905), 1.
31 *Cassell's Historical Course for Schools*, II (London: Cassell and Co., 1884), 11.
32 Lady Katie Magnus, *First Makers of England: Julius Caesar, King Arthur, Alfred the Great* (1901), vii, cited by Stephanie Barczewski, *Myth and National Identity in Nineteenth Century Britain*, 12.
33 *Cassell's Historical Readers*, I (London: Cassell and Co., 1882), 181.
34 Finnemore, *Black's Story of the English People*, I, 8.
35 *Britannia History Readers*, II (London: Edward Arnold, 1901), 29.
36 *Cassell's Historical Readers*, I, 1.
37 *Longman's Ship Historical Readers*, I (London: Longmans, Green and Co., 1893), 24.
38 *King Edward History Readers*, IV, *The Evolutionary History of England* (London: Isaac Pitman and Sons, 1902), 224.
39 *Britannia History Readers, Introductory Book*, 12.
40 A.P. Newton, *An Introduction to Colonial History* (London: SPCK, 1919), 6.
41 S.J. Heathorn, ' "Let Us Remember that We, Too, Are English": Constructions of Citizenship and National Identity in English Elementary School Reading Books, 1880–1914', *Victorian Studies*, 38:4 (1995), 395–427.
42 J. Meiklejohn, *The British Empire: Its Geography, Resources, Commerce, Landways and Waterways* (1891), cited in Stephen Heathorn, ' "Let Us Remember that We, Too, Are English" ', 408.
43 Both of these texts were aimed at older schoolchildren. The first is extracted from the seventh book of the *Warwick History Readers*, and the second from the fifth book of the *King Edward History Readers*. Both cited by Stephen Heathorn, ' "Let Us Remember that We, Too, Are English", 408–9.
44 *Britannia History Readers*, II, 9–10.
45 Fletcher and Kipling, *A School History of England*, 29.
46 A.D. Innes, *History of England: For Use in Schools* (Cambridge: Cambridge University Press, 1907), 1–6.
47 G.W. Cox, *England and the English People* (London: Joseph Hughes, 1887), 14, 23.
48 *English History Reading Books: Old Stories from English History* (1882), cited in Heathorn, *For Home, Country and Race: Constructing Gender, Class and Englishness in the Elementary School, 1880–1914* (Toronto: Toronto University Press, 2000), 105.
49 *Britannia History Readers*, I, 31.
50 *The Young Students English History Reading Book* (1881), cited in Heathorn, *For Home, Country and Race*, 105.
51 A.H. Dick, *First Historical Reader for Standard II: English History, Roman and Saxon Period* (London: Gall and Inglis, 1881), 20.
52 *British History in Periods: A New Series of Historical Readers*, IV (London: Blackie and Son, 1904), 25.
53 *Chambers' Historical Readers*, III (London and Edinburgh: Chambers, 1882), 134.
54 Dick, *First Historical Reader*, 20.
55 Berry, *England and the English*, 31–2.
56 *Cassell's Historical Readers*, I, 28.
57 *Royal School Series, Stories from English History Simply Told*, I (London: T. Nelson and Sons, 1884), 28.
58 *Britannia History Readers, Introductory Book*, 102.
59 Finnemore, *Black's Story of the English People*, II, 99.
60 Heathorn, *For Home, Country and Race*, 63.

61 Examples taken from texts for older children, and cited in Heathorn, *For Home, Country and Race*, 63.
62 Peter Yeandle, 'Victoria, Queen of Wessex: Heroes and Heroines in the Teaching of History in Nineteenth-Century England', Lancaster Unlocked History Festival, 4 June 2012.
63 *Britannia History Readers, Introductory Book*, 85.
64 *Britannia History Readers, Introductory Book*, 84.
65 *King Edward History Readers*, III, 48.
66 Cited in Newsome, *The Victorian World Picture*, 139.
67 Keith Robbins, *Nineteenth-Century Britain: Integration and Diversity* (Oxford: Clarendon, 1988), 96.
68 John MacKenzie, 'The Iconography of the Exemplary Life: the Case of David Livingstone', in G. Cubitt and A. Warren (eds), *Heroic Reputations and Exemplary Lives* (Manchester: Manchester University Press, 2000), 84–104.
69 This is quite surprising given the need to contrast the civilisation of the English against the barbarity of others. The absence is less noticeable in textbooks.
70 See Robert MacDonald, *The Language of Empire: Myth and Metaphors of Popular Imperialism* (Manchester: Manchester University Press, 1994), 48–79.
71 A. Mee, *Little Treasure Island: Her Story and Her Glory* (London: Smith and Elders, 1920), preface.
72 Richard Rogers, ' "Do You Want to Go for a Ride on the Chunnel"? The British Public Understandings of the Channel Tunnel Meet the Eurotunnel Exhibition Centre', *Public Understanding of Science*, 4:4 (1995), 363–96.
73 P. Larkin, *Island Story: Georgian and Victorian Britain* (Amersham: Hulton Educational, 1985); Nicholas Crane, *Coast: Our Island Story* (London: BBC, 2010).
74 Anthony D. Smith, ' "Set in the Silver Sea": English national identity and European integration', *Nations and Nationalism*, 12:3 (2006), 433–52.
75 Jan Rüger, 'Nation, Empire and Navy: Identity Politics in the United Kingdom 1887–1914', *Past and Present*, 185:1 (2004), 159–87; Mary Conlon, *From Jack Tar to Union Jack: Representing Naval Manhood in the British Empire, 1870–1918* (Manchester: Manchester University Press, 2009).
76 For an analysis of Trafalgar, see Marianne Czisnik, 'Admiral Nelson's Tactics at the Battle of Trafalgar', *History*, 89:296 (2004), 549–59. See also recent biographies: Christopher Hibbert, *Nelson: A Personal History* (London: Penguin, 1995); Brian Lavery, *Horatio Admiral Nelson* (London and New York: British Library and New York University Press, 2003); D. Cannadine (ed.), *Admiral Lord Nelson: Context and Legacy* (Basingstoke: Palgrave, 2005).
77 MacKenzie, *Propaganda and Empire*, 47. Though not explicitly focused on questions of nationhood, Christopher Bell's research is useful for analysis of the variety of naval propaganda, especially in light of the increasing public fascination with the aerial wing of the armed forces. Christopher M. Bell, *The Royal Navy, Seapower and Strategy Between the Wars* (Basingstoke: Macmillan, 2000), chapter 8, ' "Something Very Sordid": Naval Propaganda and the British Public', 162–79.
78 Indicative articles include K. Lunn and A. Day, 'Britain as Island: National Identity and the Sea', in R. Phillips and H. Brocklehurst (eds), *History, Identity and the Question of Britain* (Basingstoke: Palgrave, 2004), 124–36; developed and extended in, 'British Maritime Heritage: Carried Along by the Currents?', *International Journal of Heritage Studies*, 9:4 (2003), 289–305. See also R. Harrington, ' "The Mighty Hood": Navy, Empire, War at Sea and the British National Imagination, 1920–60', *Journal of Contemporary History*, 38:2 (2003), 171–85.
79 See Paul Kennedy, *The Rise of the Anglo-German Antagonism, 1860–1914* (London: G. Allen and Unwin, 1980).
80 D. Morris, *Class Book of English History* (London: Longmans, Green and Co., 1902), 10, 250.
81 H. Ince and J. Gilbert, *Outlines of English History* (London: W.B. Clive, 1906), 78.
82 Fletcher and Kipling, *A School History of England*, 29.
83 Finnemore, *Black's Story of the English People*, I, 7.

84 C.H. Wyatt, *The English Citizen: His Life and Duty* (1894), cited in Heathorn, *For Home, Country and Race*, 182.
85 Berry, *England and the English*, 103.
86 Berry, *England and the English*, 6.
87 *Britannia History Readers*, I, 186.
88 *Britannia History Readers*, I, 89–92.
89 Collins' School Series, *Patriotic Historical Readers*, IV (London: Collins, 1894), 179.
90 *Longman's Ship Historical Readers*, II, 39.
91 Berry, *England and the English*, 155.
92 *The Catholic Child's History of England* (1890), cited in Heathorn, *For Home, Country and Race*, 181.
93 *Patriotic Historical Readers*, III, 37–9.
94 J. Finnemore, *Famous Englishmen*, I (London: A. & C. Black, 1901), 7.
95 Finnemore, *Famous Englishmen*, I, 13.
96 *Tower History Readers*, III (London: Pitman, 1907), 61.
97 Morris, *Senior Standard Readers* (1883), cited in Chancellor, *History for their Masters*, 71.
98 *Longman's Ship Historical Readers*, I, 48–9.
99 *Allison's Guide to English History* (1880), 79, cited in Chancellor, *History for their Masters*, 104. For more on the Victorian cult of Alfred, especially how he was reinvented as founder of the empire in high culture, see Joanne Parker, *England's Darling: The Victorian Cult of Alfred the Great* (Manchester: Manchester University Press, 2007), 146–60.
100 *Avon Geographical Readers*, VI (1895), cited in Heathorn, *For Home, Country and Race*, 180.
101 *Raleigh History Readers*, VII (1896), cited in Heathorn, *For Home, Country and Race*, 180.
102 Rüger, 'Nation, Empire and Navy', 161–2.
103 This is an argument carried forward, and enhanced, by Mary Conley's study of masculinity and the navy between 1870 and 1914, *From Jack Tar to Union Jack*.
104 Heathorn, *For Home, Country and Race*, 184.

CHAPTER FOUR

Imperial values in the teaching of history II: the English 'race'

> The British Empire at the beginning of the twentieth century includes lands in every part of the globe, some gained by the valour of our soldiers, or by the patient toil or steady enterprise of colonists from the mother country. It embraces people of almost every race, colour and religion, all living peacefully and prospering under the British flag, and content with the knowledge that the strong arm and brave spirit that gained freedom for them will always be ready to defend the precious gift.[1]

Just as it was deemed pedagogically important to demonstrate to young children that British imperial characteristics were embedded in the English medieval past, so too was it essential to depict the origins of the imperial relationship between the British nations in such a way that explained English historical dominance. Recapitulation required the child to draw contrasts between past and present and, in doing so, become aware of progress over time. For Herbartians, race recapitulation theory was the method to provide for the child a means of measuring progress. Progress was identified not only by comparison to the history of the English at various moments in their historical development, but also by contrast to other races.

Late Victorian and Edwardian scientific constructions of racial difference stipulated that the strength of races which inter-mixed was likely to weaken as blood became diluted.[2] Stories presented in reading books, however, were not so clear cut: indeed, for some authors, emphasis was placed on those historical moments in which cultures merged. Paul Rich argues that 'racial Anglo-Saxonism became [...] a natural accompaniment of British overseas imperialism since it was an ideology that both embodied a view of the historical past as well as stressing the common racial make-up of the white British colonies of settlement'.[3] It was in this sense that pedagogy and scientific context were aligned. In order to highlight progress over time, reading books held the mirror of identity up against the old English and their intra-

British others. Textbooks, on the other hand, were decidedly more jingoistic and xenophobic in emphasising English superiorities by drawing contrast against recently colonised subjects, especially Indians, Africans and Chinese.

The means by which reading books and textbooks differed in their stories of the English and other races is significant. Frances Mannsaker, in discussion of the representation of subject races in literature, observed a telling dichotomy: texts either emphasised the 'savage and uncivilised' characteristics of the colonised, or depicted them as 'childlike and unsophisticated'.[4] As Douglas Lorimer explains, '[r]acial stereotypes derived their power and utility from their ambiguous and even contradictory character, as in the common depiction of colonised peoples as having the attributes of children and of savages'.[5] It appears to be the case that reading books, when they did tell stories about English adventures in colonial climes, treated Africans and Asians as immature, that is, akin to the early English at the onset of their path towards 'civilisation'. Textbooks, however, invoked the language of irredeemable barbarism and savagery. It is my argument that this dichotomy was no accident, but was deeply reflective of different pedagogical approaches and was indicative of the *age* differences of children. Nowhere, as will be seen in the final section of this chapter, was this more explicit than in explanations of slavery.

Separation and assimilation: the English and the non-English British

Even though the Irish, Welsh and Scots had been – and were – central to the British imperial project, space within reading books was generally only made for them as yardsticks against which the English could measure their own national progress. This was similarly the case in textbooks for older children. However, the representation of English people, and their history, as racially homogeneous presented numerous complications. The story of the English demonstrated, among other things, that England had been a country which had experienced multifarious stages of settlement and mixing. A curious child might well have assumed that the original English settlers must have mixed with indigenous Britons (a blanket term used here to include Picts and Celts, as well as Britons and Gaelic Scots), for instance, or that the Normans must have been assimilated into the English, and so on. If the English progressed rapidly and teleologically towards civilisation as these foundation stones of empire – the increments of Englishness – were laid, what of their immediate neighbours and territorial cohabitants who, when politically united with England, lent their name to the British empire? The answer to this conundrum was two-fold. First, Herbartian emphasis on teaching historical distance and chronology for purposes of recapitulation meant that these stories contrasted advances to the English character against the stases of indigenous Britons. Second, stories presented England's path to its contemporary (self-given) status as the most civilised and progressive nation as a model to which other races should aspire. If other races accepted and subsumed themselves within the dominant English narrative, they were welcomed into the imperial fold. Englishness was presented as biologically determined by virtue of Anglo-Saxon origins: however, reading books reflect contemporary notions that citizenship could be shared by those who absorbed salient English characteristics. As J.H. Grainger explains, 'English patriotism was assimilative rather than exclusive'.[6]

The progression of the English race was measured against the barbarism once identified as part of the English genealogical fabric, yet firmly relegated to the past. The English 'people of those times had not the advantages that we have', the author of *Chambers' Historical Readers* (1882) explained, continuing that 'we need not wonder, then, that they were so ignorant and loved fighting so much'.[7] Furthermore, texts demonstrated the propensity of the English towards racial assimilation which was brought into bold relief by comparison with the inflexible character traits of the non-English British. This was not an admission of racial weakness, but a celebration of strengthening of the English race over time. As the *King Edward History Readers* (1902) informed its audience: 'we', by which the author meant the English, 'have the power of absorbing new people into ourselves'.[8] This was a consistent and powerful message. Reflecting race-thinking of the time, the progress of the English character was represented – in words suitable for its intended audience of course – as a Darwinian struggle: the English were equipped to absorb the best characteristics, values and aptitudes of those other races with whom they came into contact, while concomitantly rejecting the worst. Although its foundation was laid deep in the English past, this was how the empire could be both modern and British. Obligation was placed upon the non-English British to buy into this narrative: accept it, and then they could belong; reject it, and then they were 'other'.

How were these contrasts represented in historical reading books? In discussing the enemies of Roman Britain, the *Britannia History Reader* explained: 'The Picts and Scots belonged to somewhat the same race as the Britons [who become the Welsh]. But the third set of foes who came to Britain from the east over the North Sea [that is, the English] belonged to quite a different race, and spoke a different language . . .'.⁹ The Picts were 'fierce', according to Browning, forming 'a race of very cruel men'.¹⁰ This racial difference was not only marked by language, but by explicit contrast against the intrinsic English love for freedom.¹¹ The Welsh, Irish and Scots were described as living in clans or tribes with a 'Chief' who 'was very powerful' to the extent that 'his word was law [. . .] he could put anyone to death who disobeyed him'. This was in direct contrast to the English who 'lived in quite a different way [. . .] there were some chiefs and nobles, but they might not oppress freedom'.¹² Unlike lessons shown to have been learnt by the English, native Britons could neither fend off Picts nor Saxons, since they 'quarrelled among themselves, and were not true to one another'.¹³

Histories of Ireland and Scotland (and this is echoed in geography texts, on which more in a moment) were tagged on to later books for older children which dealt with the different countries of the empire. Wales all but ceased to be mentioned after Edward bestowed on them the title of his son the Prince of Wales. Indeed, prior to his reign the Welsh were not only castigated for being speakers of 'the old British language',¹⁴ but they were 'wild' and:

> loved nothing better than to rush down from their hills, plunder the country around the castles, then escape to their mountainous homes with the booty they had gathered. Every time, too, that there was trouble in England the Welsh took advantage of it [. . .] burning and destroying all before them.¹⁵

The human dimensions of this story were brought to the fore in the popular *Cassell's Historical Course for Schools*: Edward had 'made good laws for the Welsh, but for a long time they hated their conqueror'. The intervention of Queen Eleanor and the birth of the future Prince of Wales meant that there was no bar to assimilation:

> However, Queen Eleanor had a little son, who was born at Carnavon [sic], in Wales; and when the Welsh had submitted to the King, Edward made them the most gracious speech, and said that he was going to present them with a prince who was born in their own country and could not speak a word of any other language; who had never offended them, or indeed done anything that was wrong or cruel; and that this prince could be called the Prince of Wales. The people wondered very much who this prince could be; but soon the King went away and came back carrying his baby-son in his arms.¹⁶

Following the investiture of the infant Prince (1282), all was simple and relations became unproblematic. In summarising the Anglo-Welsh relationship, Finnemore emphasised the triumph of harmony and cooperation: the 'Welsh settled down in peace, and have ever since been regarded as part of the Kingdom, and fellow-countrymen of the English'.[17] This was a representation of an unproblematic assimilation: the problem of Edward I's Norman heritage was easily overcome. The Welsh had become aligned with civilisation as a result of their union with the English.

A similar model was applied to Scotland. According to these texts, once England had allied politically with their neighbours, all was fruitful and happy. England brought stability to Britain. For instance, the first volume of *Cassell's Union Jack Series*, rare in that it was specially commissioned for Scottish and Irish as well as English schools, introduced its story of British history with a portrait of the monarch, an image of the Union Jack and a description of British unity:

> At the foot of the picture of the king, you will see the rose, the thistle and the shamrock [note, no leek]. Which of these three do you like best? If you are an English boy or girl you will like the rose best, because the sweet rose is the flower of England. If you are a Scotch boy or girl, you will like the thistle best, for the thistle is the flower of Scotland. But if you are a little Irish boy or girl, you will know that the sweet little shamrock is loved best in your country. Let us say, the rose for England, the thistle for Scotland, the shamrock for Ireland, and the Union Jack and 'God Save the King' for us all.[18]

The *Britannia History Reader* stated of the Union flag (with a telling mix of past and present tense): '[u]nder that flag Englishmen, Scotsmen and Irishmen fight gallantly side by side, and forgot old quarrels in upholding the common cause of justice and right'.[19] Another stated that, as a result of the Act of Union of 1707, 'all the quarrels and disputes between England and Scotland came happily to an end, and the two countries have ever since formed one united nation, under the name of Great Britain'.[20] In these texts, the story of Britain coming together was unproblematic. Sites of conflict effortlessly became sites of unity.[21] The Welsh and Scots, now united with England, prospered because of their increased contact with English values. In David McCrone's words, the financial rewards and resultant increase in international status meant that the empire, although explained as English in origin, contributed to an ongoing 'marriage of convenience'.[22] This was part of a process, in Keith Robbins' phrase, of an 'assimilation into England' which many Welsh and Scottish were prepared to undergo.[23]

Englishness did not always, however, slide effortlessly into Britishness and some Britons, likewise, did not always eagerly comply with the dominant English pitch in the British voice. Earlier constructions of racial difference were not to be overcome by mere gestures of political (or economic) assimilation. It was explained that the Union with

Scotland, for instance, was 'a great blessing to both countries'. However, this particular text continued with a typically English understatement: this was true for all but a few of the Highlanders who 'felt as though they had lost their independence, and were rather sore about it'.[24] They were represented as backward and barbaric, which stood in stark contrast to the enlightened and civilised English who had progressed over time. This was how the Jacobite uprisings were explained. These Highlanders, some several centuries later, were described in language akin to that used to describe the Picts. Both were 'thieves', 'robbers', 'warlike', 'savages' and 'barbarians'.[25] On themes closer to the contemporary, nineteenth-century ill-relations with Ireland could be contextualised 'if we remember that the Irish people are a different race from the English'. The Irish were said to be 'unhappy' and, by paying little or no attention to food deprivation, starvation and the policies of the English government, the Irish were shown to be responsible for their own plight because they had not endeavoured to learn, and therefore 'cannot speak English'.[26] Another text observed that 'the real Irish [. . .] were still very rough and uncultured, and behind the rest of the world'.[27] In contrast to English heroes who loved their education (see the next chapter), the Irish example was used to extol the dangers of not doing one's best in school. This is not surprising given that reading books generally waxed that 'everyone who speaks English as his mother tongue has a right to be called English'.[28] Fletcher and Kipling declared that Ireland was 'incapable of ruling herself and impatient of rule by others'.[29] The implication was that those 'peripheral' Britons who rejected England as the dominant force of Britishness – both linguistically and culturally – were excluded and marginalised as the internal other: they were analogous to the earliest English, but unlike them, had failed to emulate the English and thus achieve civilisation.

Therefore, a degree of strategic distancing was in operation; distance both between the historically positioned English self but more noticeably against non-English Britons who shared empire, time and territory. Although the parameters of national belonging were sharpened along lines of race, this need not have equated to an insurmountable barrier since Englishness was depicted as flexible enough to readily absorb others. In this regard, emphasis was not only upon differences between races but on shared or compatible characteristics. The *Britannia History Reader*, for instance, made the benefits of racial blending explicit: 'The English were very different from the other three peoples, who were all a good deal alike, and some of the differences between them continue to this day'. In describing each of these races, the text moves on to suggest how their attributes might be mutually complimentary:

THE ENGLISH 'RACE'

> The Irish, Welsh and Scots are generally quicker-witted than the English, and more excitable. They are merrier when they are gay, and sadder when they are in trouble; hotter-tempered and more ready to show their love or hatred. The English are slower and steadier in everything, and more ready to work patiently and with perseverance [...] It is a good thing for a country to have people of different characters in it, for what one lacks the other can supply.[30]

Highlighting the positive racial characteristics of others was one method to invite non-English Britons into the English story. Even in this extract, however, the Irish, Welsh and Scots are shown to be overemotional, which implied a calmness and determination for the English. Other examples of racial blending often involved the literal mixing of bloodlines. For instance, one text told how 'many Englishmen married Welsh women'.[31] Another method was to accentuate similarities in racial make-up. If the Welsh and Irish had been portrayed as of a different 'race' entirely from the English, then the Vikings and the Normans were marked for their similarities. That the Vikings 'belonged to the same race as the English, but they were still heathens' was a common statement.[32] The story of Bishop Dunstan was often told as an epilogue to stories about Alfred the Great. Alfred may have contained the Danish threat, but by their mere existence on English territory, the Danes still challenged the assimilation narrative. Dunstan's 'great wish was to make the English and the Danes live peacefully side by side'. The Danes had been merciless, irreligious and cruel. However, their racial proximity to the English meant that Dunstan's task 'was not so difficult to bring about as might have been thought. After all, they were very much alike. They spoke so much the same language that they could understand each other, and now that most of the Danes in England had become Christians, they spoke the same language'.[33] In another example, the Simon de Montfort's (senior) Norman family could be overlooked because he extolled English values in standing up to the tyrannical King John.[34]

Reflecting that this was an era where discussion of social Darwinism was pushed to the fore, these reading books told a story of the race coming together, growing stronger together, absorbing the best and rejecting the worst of those 'races' with which it came into contact.[35] The Danes not only became anglicised, but crucially, the English obtained something in return. The *Young Student's English History Reader* confirmed the inability of 'Britons' to fend for themselves, but noted how the English had profited from Teutonic and Viking strength:

> The conquest of Britain was indeed partly wrought out after two centuries of bitter warfare. At its close, Britain had become England, a land

that is, not of Britons, but of Englishmen [...] [t]he Britons, abandoned to themselves, were destined to be driven out, or extinguished, or absorbed, according to that apparently inevitable law of nature by which the weaker race disappears before the stronger. We are of that stronger race, the race of the Teutons and Scandinavian Vikings.[36]

Such strength, when coupled with the religiosity, innate maritime dominance and the humility of the English, was a sure indicator of the advantages of racial assimilation. In similar vein, the Norman Conquest was rationalised as a good thing. The Normans may have been a 'new race of people',[37] according to one text, but their geographical origins – they were Norsemen – meant that their racial code was close enough to that of the English to enable intermixing. Even though the Normans were able to win the Battle of Hastings, in the longer-term battle of the races, there was likely to only ever be one winner: ultimately, the Normans became anglicised. This is how it was explained by Finnemore (note the comments on the English-speaking world and its connotations for Edwardian imperialism):

> The Normans soon mixed with the English, and the two races became one nation. It was easy for them to mix, for English and Norman were really brothers in blood. The Norman was a Northman, just as Saxons and Danes were. When the races were joined, a very mighty nation was the result. The spirit and charm of the Norman, together with the solid strength of the Saxon, have formed the English speaking world of today, the people who rule so much of the earth, and whose language is spreading so widely.[38]

The Normans brought a number of valuable qualities to the racial mix. From the Normans, the English gained 'knowledge of building cathedrals, castles, and other fine buildings' as well as an enhanced appreciation for 'books', fashion, and a better sense of hygiene when cooking.[39]

These examples demonstrate how English national character was flexible enough to absorb characteristics of other races. They also provide instances wherein the English homeland was under threat. As a result, English racial strength was shown to matter more than mere battles. Ultimately, the English gained: not only since a raft of new attributes were fused with the English character, but because the English came to appreciate the importance of unity. Of the Norman alterations to the distribution of power across society, texts universally averred that a shared enemy gave the English reason to recognise one another as kin. Josiah Turner was perhaps the most explicit: 'these changes in laws and customs', he argued, 'made England, for the first time in its history, a united nation'.[40] Another text informed its readers that although 'it was a hard time for the poor English', they nonetheless learnt 'one great lesson. From this time [...] they began to feel that they were all Englishmen'.[41] Arabella Buckley wrote in her text that those who resisted the Normans were 'English patriots'.[42] As was the case with the Irish, language was given as an example to demonstrate not only the strength of the English but as an opportunity for integration. Although the 'English soon learnt to do as the Normans did', a text of 1893 stated, they never gave up their own speech, and in time the Normans also 'learnt to speak English'.[43] 'In the end the English won the day', this is Finnemore again, 'and Norman French died out'.[44]

Absorption, therefore, was not shown to weaken the Englishness of the English race. The Danish invasions and Norman Conquest were shown, ultimately, to have strengthened the English. Reading books thus explained the British empire as a result of the evolution of the English national character, core characteristics of which were flexibility and adaptability. Texts depicted a story not only of English history, but the development over time of Englishness in which non-English Britons – and others – were required to accept English dominance of both political union and British empire. Those who wished to call themselves British needed to subscribe to English values: this entailed, if not the tacit acknowledgement of English dominance, then the acceptance of England's right to speak for Britain and English proprietorship of the imperial story. One must be careful, of course, not to assume that children absorbed these messages. I am, after all, reading these narratives in the context of Celtic recrudescence and vocal campaigns for political devolution. Clearly there were some quite complicated issues at stake. However, stories presented to children reflected contemporary ideas about the historical relationship between the English past and the imperial origins.

Ethnicity: textbooks, readers and the representation of race difference

The codification of the national 'us' as flexible, adaptable and historically entrenched brings to mind Linda Colley's assertion that a nation's identity is defined not only by recognition of what a collective has in common, but in shared awareness of those values and characteristics defined as definitively *not* belonging to that group. Her notion of 'otherness' requires further comment. In her invaluable book, *Britons: Forging the Nation*, Colley convincingly demonstrates that Britishness was invented in the eighteenth century. This, she argues, was the direct result of a century and a half of conflict between the British and the French. It was a sentiment 'forged above all by war'. The British were able to celebrate what they had in common, by means of collectively identifying their sameness against how they, together, defined the French. The French were 'superstitious, militarist, decadent and unfree'.[45] Her original thesis is compelling, yet it is problematic since it is less persuasive in the context of the later nineteenth century. Simply put, after 1815 and the Battle of Waterloo, the French were no longer the military threat they once were. Protestantism had long given the British a sense of their sameness, but the incorporation of Ireland into the Union in 1800 and the Catholic Emancipation of 1829 required that these common assumptions be rethought.[46] 'Freedom' had defined British patriotism because it could be measured against French absolutism: the power of that message came to carry less sway. Indeed, following the British signature on the *Entente Cordial*, one reading book called the French 'our bright and witty neighbours' and texts concentrated on the evils of Napoleon as an individual rather than berate the French people in general.[47] The Germans, instead, became Britain's contemporary European competitor. That the English and the Germans shared a historically proven racial heritage posed questions about racial proximity – especially since English history was intimately connected to Saxon heritage. Moreover, Britain itself was subject to all sorts of questions about how 'free' its people were. Should the vote, for instance, extend to all classes and all people, including women?[48] Did the franchise reforms of 1884–85 go far enough (or too far)? And what about self-governance for the Irish? Colley, hence, extended the argument of *Britons* to maintain that, in the late nineteenth-century climate, 'Otherness' still functioned as the core principle of British identity. If not against the French, she argues, Britons increasingly came to identify themselves against those they had colonised.[49] For Colley, the British empire, collectively forged, collectively maintained, and collectively celebrated, was the hub for continued sensations of Britishness.[50]

In considering the evidence of narrated identity in history lessons, Colley's argument is both persuasive and problematic. By the 1880s, 'Englishness' – as seen – had emerged as a competing populist designation for national identity based predominantly on ethnic – Anglo-Saxon – sameness. Stories in reading books, as demonstrated, reflected historiographical, scientific and literary emphases on Anglo-Saxon traditions: if they held a 'mirror' up to an 'other' by which to define identity, it was against the 'old' English and the non-English Britons. On the other hand, however, Colley's argument can be substantiated by analysis of the content of resources designed for older children and those in fee-paying schools. Here, we need a quick reminder: reading books were produced in series, each volume corresponding to the age and, consequently, the intellectual capabilities of the student. By the upper standards, reading books incorporated more detailed historical coverage and ranged closer to the present day; they became increasingly similar, in content, to subject-specific textbooks. Unlike readers, textbooks made explicitly derogatory reference to racial difference, drawing contrast between the whiteness of Europeans and the colour of those they colonised.[51]

The work of Avril Maddrell and Teresa Ploszajska reveals a much more explicit place for teaching about the empire in geography lessons, which included far greater attention to colonial subjects and territorial expansion.[52] Stephen Heathorn confirms that for younger children, 'the presentation of the "racial" other [...] was most often found in geography readers' rather than in texts about English history.[53] This does not surprise for a number of diverse reasons. First, those advocating more geographical education were less likely to encounter debates with educational psychologists when they pressed for greater emphasis on the empire in the curriculum. Indeed, when the Royal Geographical Society claimed in 1886 that if 'the fate of a nation may depend on a battle, a battle may depend on knowledge of geography', their campaign for more teaching about the colonies met with near universal approval.[54] Second, in the late nineteenth century, geography lessons were partly intended to encourage emigration. That put no small premium on teaching about settler societies and the justification, in schools, of the empire as a civilising mission.[55] The third reason is the most significant: as noted in the first chapter, geography was a much more popular optional subject than history because it was believed less abstract, and it was therefore easier to gear teaching to the examination. Such was the prevalence of geography that a number of educationists insisted that history and geography should be taught as a sequential pair. Joseph Cowham, for example, explained that the subject-specific geography lesson was more immediately valuable for younger scholars since it was the 'easier intellectual exercise'. Geography, he elaborated 'exercises powers of observation, memory and imagination – powers which one achieves in early school-life'. History, alternatively, 'affords scarcely any opportunity for sense-effort, but it demands the exercise of considerable powers of comparison, of judgement, and of reasoning'.[56] Subject-specific geography classes and historical reading lessons were seen as an ideal marriage for the education of enlightened patriots. The government issued its 'official' advice in the form of the *Suggestions for the Consideration of Teacher and Others* in 1905, stipulating that:

> From geography they learn how Great Britain is but one country amongst many. It is therefore important that from the history lessons they should learn something about their nationality that distinguishes them from the people of other countries. They cannot understand this, however, unless they are taught how the British nation grew up and how the mother country in her turn has founded daughter countries beyond the seas. The broad facts of this growth when properly handled ought to form a stirring theme full of interest to even young citizens of the British Empire.[57]

The logistics of age and timetabling, however, determined that younger children would not receive much coverage of nineteenth-century imperial history in historical reading lessons. In her report on the teaching of history in England, Olive Shropshire noted the state first recommended the explicit teaching of empire after the Code of 1904 and this was for children in the upper standards: that is, at the age by which most children had left school.[58] Teresa Ploszajska's meticulous research reveals that geography lessons made use of reading texts too, many of which incorporated similar content to historical readers in that imperial content did not feature until the child was older.[59] There was palpably more imperial content in geography lessons for older children, yet it remained history's task to explain the origins of empire and to lay the foundations of an emotional attachment to nation.

Kathryn Castle and Frank Glendenning have traced the representations of Africans, Indians and Chinese in schools, both analysing reading books and textbooks. Both are concerned with the history of racism and multiculturalism. Glendenning, writing in the early 1970s, was concerned with the pressing issue of British race relations, especially since he noticed that 'British schoolbooks today still carry, as a hangover, the nineteenth-century approach to the world'.[60] Castle, writing in the context of the National Curriculum debates of the 1990s, feared the ways 'the past may be activated to ends which "abuse" the discipline [of history], and that the dangers of nationalist bias examined in this study remain to be challenged'.[61] The desire to unearth past practice which contributed to the formation of racist attitudes is honourable, and in many ways, my motivations are no different: I am seeking to explore the history of history teaching partly to expose mythmaking and am particularly concerned by proposals to reassert a 'positive' teaching of British imperial history, especially since these myths of a 'golden age' are grounded in serious historical misunderstanding. Together, Glendenning and Castle's analyses suggest that both reading books and textbooks perpetuated dangerous jingoism through negative portrayals of colonial subjects.

My analysis of texts leads to a more intricate conclusion. Given educationists' emphasis on 'enlightened patriotism' as the key objective underpinning primary school history lessons, the narration of explicit histories on the relationship between coloniser and colonised signify a sometimes subtle, but quite suggestive, difference of agenda. Reading books, given limited timetable space, were particularly selective. When they engaged with British imperial activity in India, (older) children would only have read the stories of the 'Black Hole of Calcutta', Plassey and the 'Mutiny'. Stories of the British in Africa would include the Boer Wars, occasionally battles with the Asante tribes, and always the death of General Gordon. Chinese history was reduced to the Opium Wars and the Boxer rebellion. Textbooks, on the other hand, covered more chronology in significantly more detail. Arthur Innes' text included dry details of decidedly dull legal, technical and economic history including 'The Franco-British Struggle in Southern India' (361–4); 'The Nile, the Second Coalition, and the Peace of Amiens' (420–4); and a summary of 'Foreign, Indian and Colonial Affairs (463–4), among others.[62]

Both Castle and Glendenning oversimplify matters. Glendenning conflates readers and textbooks; Castle acknowledges the age of the child as a factor for different tone, yet fails to comment on the pedagogical principles which underscored this variance. Neither sufficiently acknowledges that textual differences accounted for very different audiences, nor do they explore why this may explain differences in ways Africans and Asians were represented. Reading books were likely to present other races as naive and childlike. To be sure, the narrow selection of stories would have enhanced praise for the British by drawing comparison to the colonised: that was one of the key components of race recapitulation theory. As Glendenning and Castle more than amply demonstrate, there was persistence across genre of derogative epithets: the Chinese were 'crafty', 'perfidious', 'ruthless', 'scheming' and 'cunning';[63] Africans 'warlike', 'savage', a 'host of barbarians', 'kaffirs' (for those on the south of the continent), 'intransigent', 'untrustworthy' and ungrateful;[64] Indians 'weak', 'cruel', 'effeminate', 'debauched', 'despotic', 'treacherous', 'cold-blooded'.[65] The volume of the *Patriotic Historical Reader* for older children commented that 'history teaches us that white men are more inclined to travel and enterprise than black and yellow races are; and this is especially true of those races that live near the sea'.[66] However, the way stories made use of these adjectives requires analysis.

Castle cites J.F. Bright's, *A History of England for Public Schools* (1887–1901), on the Asante Prempeh and the war of the 'Golden Stool' of 1896: 'he had fallen out with the British authorities [...] by his slave trading, human sacrifices and refusal to pay indemnities and vexatious interference with trade [...] The British called for remonstrance which he disregarded and defied'. The complicated, accusatory tone of the textbook was at odds with the storytelling mode of the reading book. Castle quotes from Lady Maria Callcott's *Little Arthur's History of Britain* (1913 edition): 'the King was treating his people so cruelly that the Queen felt she must interfere'.[67] Both texts laid blame at the door of the Asante, justifying British military intervention as necessary action because of the cruelty of a leader against those for whom he was responsible. Whereas textbook language is derogatory, reading books deployed the same prose techniques used to describe the medieval English and Britons: as uncivilised. In textbooks, the African is presented as barbaric and beyond help. R.S. Pringle, in his text to help older scholars cram for their exam, explained that the British had always to be on their guard in Africa because of a 'desire for plunder and bloodshed inextinguishable in savage tribes'.[68] The Chinese were 'treacherous' and 'insulted the British flag'; Indians became 'half-niggers' after the Mutiny.[69] Although reading books used languages of racial difference – with a nod to race recapitulation theory – they did not tend to depict colonised people as irredeemably uncivilised: indeed, readers depicted subject races as on the path towards civilisation and hence concentrated on telling tales of how English values had helped the colonised overcome their animalism. As one reading book explained, the manners and characteristics of the Indians, as with the Irish, were similar to early English: thus they 'were stuck at the ABC of civilisation'.[70] However, by the end of the century, the Indians – as had the Welsh and Scottish – become assimilated into the imperial project through their shared love for the monarchy and submission to English dominance. Upon the coronation of Edward VII, 'the people of India were very sorry when Victoria died' and celebrated the Delhi Durbar of 1903 thus: 'then, one by one, the native princes came up to the Viceroy and said they would always be true to their Emperor. And we hope that the people of India will ever be our friends' (compare this to the how the Welsh became similarly assimilated following the investiture of the first Prince of Wales).[71] 'Thus, little by little', wrote Arabella Buckley in her *History of England for Beginners* (1904), 'this great country of the East, which was full of ancient learning when Britain was inhabited by savages, is becoming more and more closely linked to the little island of the West, which is the centre of the British Empire'.[72] Distinctions are made obvious when considering that most controversial of topics: slavery.

Slavery

Fletcher and Kipling's textbook, as discussed in an earlier chapter, was roundly lambasted for its crude nationalism: it is not hard to understand why when one reads their description of liberated West Indians:

> The prosperity of the West Indies, once our richest possession, has very largely declined since slavery was abolished in 1833. The population is mainly black, descended from slaves imported in previous centuries, or of mixed black and white race; lazy, vicious and incapable of any serious improvement, or of work except under compulsion. In such a climate a few bananas will sustain the life of a negro quite sufficiently; why should he work to get more than this? He is quite happy and quite useless, and spends any extra wages he may earn upon finery.[73]

We know this text did not enjoy a particularly wide circulation in schools, but Bright's text – cited above – was in common usage in upper standards of the elementary school. Bright neglects the British part in any slave trade to concentrate upon Africans as self-slavers. The message within textbooks was that Africans were predisposed towards becoming slaves because theirs was a slave culture, and that they needed the civilising hand of the British – for which they should be grateful – to lift them from their feckless state. This image remained strong in textbooks into the twentieth century.[74] G.W. Cox retained negative language in describing abolition as 'the liberation of an idle and improvident people'.[75] Few reading books engaged the topic of the slave trade, but when they did, they took a completely different approach. In explaining the trade, the *Patriotic Historical Reader* (Volume II so for children in compulsory education) was blunt and straightforward: the West Indies 'is very hot. It is so hot that white men cannot work there, as they do in this country. So the work had to be done by Negroes [who had been] stolen from their homes in Africa and carried across the Atlantic Ocean. This was called the Slave Trade'. The text continued:

> We are very proud that there are no slaves in any part of the world which belong to us. We often say, that no slave can breathe on British soil. That means that every person, black or white, no matter where they come from, are free as soon as they reach any part of our Empire.[76]

Accompanying the account was a picture of well-dressed smiling former slaves, chatting with their previous master as if now friends. Other reading books, rather than echo textbooks and bemoan the laziness of the free slave, celebrated English humanitarianism and condemned past atrocities. Pitman's *King Edward History Readers* (1902) evoked sympathy for 'poor negroes' who had been 'made to work hard', 'treated very much like horses or dogs' and 'often beaten with whips, if they did not please their masters. Even little boys and girls were taken from their mothers, who perhaps would never be able to see them again'.[77] The *Royal Story Book* chose to concentrate on the slaves' reaction to their freedom: when first told of their liberty, they immediately 'praised God', then were 'sombre' and 'quiet', and then:

> They could no longer keep down their strong feelings. Some shouted for joy. Some groaned as the load of a lifetime passed away. Some tossed up their arms to show they were free [...] On Monday morning all went to work – work which now seemed noble in their eyes, because it was given by free men to buy the means of living for themselves and their families.[78]

Heathorn makes the valid argument that 'the slave trade only ever appeared in comments about its abolition'.[79] However, much more can be drawn from these significant differences between textbook and reading book content. Accounts of other races and slavery reveal diverging attitudes towards intended audiences across textual genres. Naturally, texts for younger children were written in an accessible and conversational prose style. Textbooks for older scholars, on the other hand, were thickly descriptive and tended towards negative representations of other races. As J.A. Mangan explains, textbooks worked in conjunction with juvenile literature, to create a world populated by different 'types' of people distinguishable by race: for older scholars, using textbooks, Africans existed in school books only 'to demonstrate the heroism of the white hero'.[80] In this context, it could be argued that Colley's (and Castle's) argument that history (textbooks) served to hold a mirror up against Africans and Asians for the British so that they might know their identity makes some sense. Stories about slavery in reading books, however, complemented lessons from earlier in the national story: freedom, when attached to religious devotion and hard work, was something to cherish; an Englishman who defends freedom is to be a celebrated and one who denies it to be frowned upon. Moreover, although primers would have extended a language of difference through shared use of derisory labels, they nonetheless posited the perfectibility of all humankind along the lines of the English route towards civilisation: like the 'old' English, and the non-English Britons, colonised subjects – if they absorbed English values – could form part of the collective team dubbed 'British empire'. Whereas textbooks adapted overtly negative stereotypes which reinforced the superiority of the British, reading books tapped into an English identity discourse which used English history as the roadmap towards civilisation.

THE ENGLISH 'RACE'

Summary

The formation of such a template for collective racial identity had profound implications for the construction of codes of citizenship. This was the organic representation of belonging: each had to do their bit for the collective good. This model for civic belonging was enhanced by the application of ideas of 'race' to history. As the Oxford historian and textbook author, F.J.C. Hearnshaw, informed the Historical Association:

> No individual man ever finds himself twice in precisely the same situation, nor can one discover unvarying sequences of cause and effect in the relations between himself and his fellows; yet, notwithstanding this, every man in his mature years is guided and governed by his experiences as recorded in his memory, and by the principles of conduct which his judgement has derived from them. As with the individual so with the race; but subject to this important difference, that the race lacks the personality, that continuity of self-consciousness which marks the individual. It has no natural memory, and in order that it may not lose the vast accumulated wealth of the experiences of the past, a memory has to be created for it. That race-memory is History.[81]

In this exposition, ethnic heritage was merged with cultural and biological determinism, proposing shared history as a link not only between individuals in the now, but between those alive and those passed. That may explain why, for the purpose of representing English national identity, the attention of young children was focused more upon the longer history of the English race as measured against their own progress across time. Rather than forge imperial patriotism through crude depictions of the colonial 'other', young children were encouraged to take pride in English improvement and reflect on the accumulation of imperial values.

History teaching often avoided contentious material, encouraged empathetic engagement and was shaped, in pedagogical intent at least, by the rapidly growing influence and professionalisation of educational psychology. The imperial possession was thus depicted as the logical future for the forefathers of the child audience. This simplistic narrative connected the children of present days to original English settlers, linking them not only to innately imperial English characteristics, but forging racial homogeneity. Colley's conception of 'othering' works, therefore, but reading books for a predominantly working-class audience chose people other than colonial subjects for the reflective gaze. By drawing comparison against historical bookmarks in the evolution of English imperial race, texts contributed to the tangential operation of otherness and 'sameness', promoting distance while simultaneously

IMPERIAL VALUES AND ENLIGHTENED PATRIOTISM

celebrating continuity. For the purpose of fostering enlightened patriotism, this twofold process reinforced ideas of collective heritage and shared bloodlines spanning the ages.

This chapter has concentrated mainly upon the pedagogical device of recapitulation. In the language of Herbartianism, the next chapter investigates how texts engaged the 'sympathetic' interest of the child in order to achieve the 'social' and the 'religious': that is, more specifically, how were moral biographies used in order to forge an emotional connection between individual and the whole? Furthermore, how were stories deployed to motivate the child to 'want' to be a good, useful, enlightened patriot?

Notes

1 *King Edward History Readers*, III (London: Isaac Pitman and Sons, 1902), 5–6.
2 On the manifestation of 'scientific racism' in education, see Marika Sherwood, 'Educating Racism', *Race and Class*, 42:3 (2001), 1–28; W. Marsden, 'Rooting Racism into the Educational Experience of Childhood and Youth in the Nineteenth and Twentieth Centuries', *History of Education*, 19:4 (1990), 333–53.
3 Paul Rich, *Race and Empire in British Politics*, second edition (Cambridge: Cambridge University Press, 1990), 13. See also M. Biddiss, 'Racial Ideas and the Politics of Prejudice, 1850–1914', *Historical Journal*, 15:3 (1972), 570–82.
4 Frances M. Mannsaker, 'The Dog that Didn't Bark: The Subject Races in Imperial Fiction at the Turn of the Century', in David Dabydeen (ed.), *The Black Presence in English Literature* (Manchester: Manchester University Press, 1985), 121.
5 Douglas A. Lorimer, 'Science and the Secularisation of Victorian Images of Race', in B. Lightman (ed.), *Victorian Science in Context* (Chicago: Chicago University Press, 1997), 213.
6 J.H. Grainger, *Patriotisms: Britain 1900–1939* (London: Routledge and Kegan Paul, 1986), 54.
7 *Chambers' Historical Readers*, I (London and Edinburgh: Chambers, 1882), 149.
8 *King Edward History Readers*, IV, *The Evolutionary History of England* (London: Isaac Pitman and Sons, 1902), 212.
9 *Britannia History Readers*, I (London: Edward Arnold, 1901), 24.
10 *The Newbery Historical Readers* (Oscar Browning), I (London: Griffith, Farran and Co., 1893), 25.
11 On the development in the nineteenth century of *intra*-British linguistic imperialism, see Keith Robbins, *Nineteenth-Century Britain: Integration and Diversity* (Oxford: Clarendon, 1988), 131–61; and Victor Kiernan, 'The British Isles: Celt and Saxon', in Mikulas Teich and Roy Porter (eds), *The National Question in Europe in Historical Context* (Cambridge: Cambridge University Press, 1993), 1–34.
12 *Britannia History Readers*, I, 29.
13 *British History in Periods: A New Series of Historical Readers*, IV (London: Blackie and Son, 1904), 21.
14 *Cassell's Historical Course for Schools*, I (London: Cassell and Co., 1882), 73.
15 J. Finnemore, *Men of Renown: King Alfred to Lord Roberts* (London: A. & C. Black, 1902), 62–3.
16 *Cassell's Historical Course for Schools*, I, 73–5.
17 Finnemore, *Men of Renown*, 65.
18 *Cassell's Union Jack Series*, I (London: Cassell and Co., 1903), 8–9.
19 *Britannia History Readers*, II (London: Cassell and Co., 1882–83), 213.
20 *Cassell's Historical Readers*, II, 146.

21 For further examples, including texts for older scholars, see Heathorn, *For Home, Country and Race: Constructing Gender, Class and Englishness in the Elementary School, 1880–1914* (Toronto: Toronto University Press, 2000), 184–91.
22 David McCrone, 'Scotland and the Union: Changing Identities in the British State', in D. Morley and K. Robins (eds), *British Cultural Studies: Geography, Nationality and Identity* (Oxford: Oxford University Press, 2001), 106; see also Colin Kidd, 'Race, Empire and the Limits of Nineteenth-Century Scottish Nationhood', *The Historical Journal*, 46:4 (2003), 873–7.
23 Robbins, *Nineteenth-Century Britain*, 6.
24 *Britannia History Readers*, II, 138.
25 *Cassell's Historical Readers*, I, 75.
26 Royal School Series, *Stories from English History Simply Told* (London: T. Nelson and Sons, 1884), 151.
27 *Britannia History Readers*, II, 17.
28 This example is extracted from a Civics reader intended for older scholars, and is quoted in Stephen Heathorn, '"Let Us Remember that We, Too, Are English": Constructions of Citizenship and National Identity in English Elementary School Reading Books, 1880–1914', *Victorian Studies*, 38:4 (1995), 399.
29 C.R.L. Fletcher and R. Kipling, *A School History of England* (Oxford: Clarendon, 1911), 21.
30 *Britannia History Readers*, I, 28.
31 *Britannia History Readers*, I, 28.
32 Royal School Series, *Stories from English History Simply Told*, 27.
33 *Britannia History Readers*, I, 46.
34 See Heathorn, *For Home, Country and Race*, 65–6.
35 For further research into residues of 'scientific racism' in late nineteenth-century popular culture, see Douglas Lorimer, 'Nature, Racism and Late Victorian Science', *Canadian Journal of History*, 25:3 (1990), 369–86; and, more generally, Tony Kushner, 'Scientific Racism: History, Heritage, Gender and the (Re) Production of Prejudice', *Patterns of Prejudice*, 33:4 (1999), 67–86.
36 The language pitch of this extract is difficult. I assume it was intended for an older audience than those who would have been reading preliminary literacy primers. It sums up the messages appropriately, however. Anon., *Young Student's English History Reader* (1881), cited in Heathorn, '"Let Us Remember that We, Too, Are English"', 404.
37 *The Newbery Historical Readers*, I, 51.
38 Finnemore, *Black's School Series: Black's Story of the English People* (London: A. & C. Black, 1905), 46.
39 Finnemore, *Black's Story of the English People*, 45. That Finnemore stresses cookery was, I suspect, an attempt to include an attribute fitting for female scholars. One might wonder, more speculatively however, whether it was additionally an attempt to emasculate the Normans by suggesting this as one of their foremost racial characteristics.
40 *Methuen History Readers* (Josiah Turner), II (London: Methuen, 1913), 32.
41 *Britannia History Readers*, I, 57.
42 A. Buckley, *History of England* (London: Methuen and Co., 1892), 18.
43 *Longman's Ship Historical Readers*, I (London: Longmans, Green and Co., 1893), 79.
44 Finnemore, *Black's Story of the English People*, 45.
45 Linda Colley, *Britons: Forging the Nation, 1707–1837*, second edition (London: Pimlico, 2003), 5.
46 Hugh McLeod, 'Protestantism and British National Identity, 1815–1945', in Peter van der Veer and Hartmut Lehmann (eds), *Nation and Religion: Perspectives on Europe and Asia* (Princeton, PA: Princeton University Press, 1999), 44–70.
47 *Tower History Readers*, VII ((London: Pitman, [1907] 1911), 211.
48 See Martin Pugh, *The March of the Women: a Revisionist Analysis of the Campaign for Women's Suffrage, 1866–1914* (Oxford: Oxford University Press, 2000);

Hugh Cunningham, *The Challenge of Democracy: Britain, 1832–1915* (Harlow: Longman, 2001), 180–203.
49 Colley, 'Britishness and Otherness: An Argument', *Journal of British Studies*, 31 (1992), 309–29.
50 Colley admits as much, claiming that 'we can plausibly regard Great Britain as an invented nation superimposed, if only for a while, onto much older alignments and loyalties'. Colley, *Britons*, 5.
51 See also Kathryn Castle, 'India in British History Textbooks for Schools, 1890–1914', in J.A. Mangan (ed.), *The Imperial Curriculum: Racial Images and Education in the British Colonial Experience* (London: Routledge, 1993), 23–39; F. Glendenning, 'Attitudes to Colonialism and Race in British and French History Schoolbooks', *History of Education*, 3:2 (1974), 57–72.
52 Avril Maddrell, 'Empire, Emigration and School Geography: Changing Discourses of Imperial Citizenship, 1880–1925', *Journal of Historical Geography*, 22:4 (1996), 373–87; Teresa Ploszajska, *Geographical Education, Empire and Citizenship* (Historical Geography Research Series, 35, 1999).
53 Heathorn, *For Home, Country and Race*, 119.
54 Cited in W. Marsden, *The School Textbook: Geography, History and Social Studies* (London: Woburn Press, 2001), 151.
55 Maddrell, 'Empire, Emigration and School Geography'. See also Brian Hudson, 'The New Geography and the New Imperialism: 1870–1918', *Antipode*, 2 (1972), 140–53.
56 J. Cowham, *A New School Method: For Pupil-Teachers and Students* (London: Westminster School Book Depot, 1894), 340.
57 Board of Education, 'Outline Schemes of Instruction', in *Handbook of Suggestions for the Consideration of Teachers and Others Concerned with the Work of Public Elementary Schools* (HMSO, 1905), 46.
58 Olive Shropshire, *The Teaching of History in English Schools* (New York: Teachers' College, 1936), 21.
59 Teresa Ploszajska, 'Geographical Education, Empire and Citizenship, 1870–1944' (unpublished PhD thesis, Royal Holloway University of London, 1996). Ploszajska's research demonstrates a veritable wealth of imperial content in geography lessons, and is especially important for its analysis of the visual component of school texts. Despite the weighty evidence for the presence of imperialism in geography texts, she is rightly cautious to agree that sowing seeds of imperial patriotism was the prime objective of lessons.
60 Glendenning, 'Attitudes to Colonialism and Race', 57; F. Glendenning, 'School History Textbooks and Racial Attitudes, 1804–1911', *Journal of Educational Administration and History*, 5:2 (1973), 34.
61 K. Castle, *Britannia's Children: Reading Colonialism through Children's Books and Magazines* (Manchester: Manchester University Press, 1996).
62 Innes' textbook, intended for children aged 14–18, was designed to record the 'development of England with such fullness and lucidity of detail as to afford an effective test of the student's industry, powers of memory, and knowledge of facts'. A.D. Innes, *History of England: For Use in Schools* (Cambridge: Cambridge University Press, 1907), preface.
63 Glendenning, 'School History Textbooks and Racial Attitudes', 39–40.
64 Castle, *Britannia's Children*, 70–3.
65 Castle, *Britannia's Children*, 18–20.
66 *Patriotic Historical Readers*, IV (London: Collins, 1894), 97.
67 Castle, *Britannia's Children*, 70–1.
68 R.S. Pringle, *Local Examination History*, nineteenth edition revised and extended (Manchester: Heywood, 1899), 142.
69 W.F. Collier, *The History of the British Empire* (London: T. Nelson, 1875), 610; H. Ince and J. Gilbert, *Outlines of English History* (London: W.B. Clive, 1906), 128.
70 Cited in Heathorn, *For Home, Country and Race*, 131.
71 *King Edward History Readers*, III, 137, 140.

72 A. Buckley, *History of England for Beginners* (1904), cited in Glendenning, 'The Evolution of History Teaching in British and French Schools in the Nineteenth and Twentieth Centuries, with Special Reference to Attitudes to Race and Colonial History in History Schoolbooks' (unpublished PhD thesis, University of Keele, 1975), 354.
73 Fletcher and Kipling, *A School History of England*, 240.
74 See Glendenning, 'The Evolution of History Teaching', 388–90.
75 G.W. Cox, *England and the English People* (London: Joseph Hughes, 1887), 478.
76 *Patriotic Historical Readers*, II, 112.
77 *King Edward History Readers*, III, 119–20.
78 *Royal Story Book of English History* (For Standard III) (London: T. Nelson and Sons, 1884), 160–4.
79 Heathorn, *For Home, Country and Race*, 184.
80 J.A. Mangan, 'Images for Confident Control: Stereotypes in Imperial Discourse', in J.A. Mangan (ed.), *The Imperial Curriculum: Racial Images and Education in the British Colonial Experience* (London: Routledge, 1993), 15.
81 F.J.C. Hearnshaw, 'The Place of History in Education', *History*, 1 (1913), 39.

CHAPTER FIVE

Enlightened patriots: heroes, heroines and 'pioneers of progress' in the teaching of history

> Patriotism must [...] bring out in bold relief the grand characters which history supplies, and shall make the most of these heroic struggles for right and freedom by which our forefathers gained the privileges we now enjoy. We shall do honour to those pioneers of progress who, by their discoveries, made it possible for England to grow into a mighty Empire.[1]

> Hero-worship ripens a child's intelligence until it becomes quick to recognise noble thought and eager to receive its inspiration. It is this responsiveness which militates against narrowness; the disciple's mind grows until he can understand the conceptions of his master.[2]

Insistence on the pedagogical value of teaching history through moral biographies slotted seamlessly into the English cultural context. Thomas Carlyle's influential lecture series, *On Heroes, Hero-Worship and the Heroic in History*, remained well known a half century after its initial publication in the early 1840s. Carlyle's basic argument was that great men had the power to embody particular cultural values and direct historical change. In Carlyle's formulation, this served to articulate those noble deeds, ideals and aspirations ripe for cultural emulation. 'The History of the World', he averred, is made up by 'the biography of Great Men'. The prevalence of interest in his views is underlined by the frequent re-publication of these lectures throughout the nineteenth century, especially in the 1890s.[3] This is not surprising: late Victorian popular culture was dominated by the cult of the 'hero'; especially the military hero. As Graham Dawson has so convincingly argued, '[s]tories of the colonial adventures of British soldiers, told and retold across many different narrative forms, constituted the very keystone of the hero-industry and constructed a new imperial tradition'. The 'heroic pantheon of historical and contemporary heroes' became part of a project linking all role models to Britain's imperial endeavours.[4] The commodification of heroes through toys, advertising, comics, board games and juvenile literature was widespread,[5] especially when accompanied by increasing participation in youth organisations such as the Scouts and Boy's Brigade which encouraged adulation of military figures.[6] Martial heroes, in particular, became identified sites for the synthesis of imperial propaganda and commerce: together, they served to market imperialism to child consumers.

The 1880s marked a period wherein there began a conscious attempt to inculcate the masses into an imperial world-view that, arguably, had previously been the preserve of the elite few.[7] Even Bernard Porter, sceptical of notions that imperialism exercised a significant influence on national culture, acknowledges that 'what happened after 1880 [. . .] does not simply represent the surfacing of feelings that had been there all along. It *was* something new'.[8] New imperialism required imperial heroes: this is not a shocking assumption. This meant that the empire needed to be flagged as the one point of common pride across class boundaries, locale, gender and occupation. As Dudley Jones and Tony Watkins argue, by the turn of the century 'the moral values of the hero' became 'articulated through the ideological frameworks of gender, imperialism and national identity'.[9] Analysis of those heroes selected to act as bookmarks in the national story enables insight into how contextual fears of domestic and imperial decay were addressed by the transmission of values via historical education. Enlightened patriotic values of fair play, courage, self-sacrifice, obedience, love of liberty and a devotion to Christianity could be presented as civic *and* imperial because they were demonstrated to be characteristics of the English as an imperial race.

A hero, according to Cubitt and Warren, can be defined as '[a]ny man or woman whose existence, whether in his or her own lifetime or later, is endowed with others, not just with a high degree of fame and honour, but with a special allocation of imputed meaning and symbolic significance – that not only raises them above others in public esteem but makes them the object of some kind of collective emotional investment'.[10] As John MacKenzie illustrates, there is 'a difference between the hero and heroic myth' since 'the individual becomes an archetype, representing a set of personal qualities and heroic characteristics that are not only supremely valued by his society but are seen by contemporaries and succeeding generations as having major or instrumental power'. Dead heroes, in particular, proved valuable 'in the hand of others', since their story could be used to form 'not only a moral paradigm' but also serve as an 'exemplar and advocate of policy'.[11] The study of these imputed meanings and symbolic attributes help the researcher to understand more about the perceived definitions of nationhood in turn of the twentieth century Britain. The story of the hero, then, came to represent more than just the values, characteristics and courageous deeds of the individual; the hero's story became invested with contemporary cultural significance.[12] The hero story, or myth, articulated values and characteristics deemed suitable for emulation (or condemnation); heroes were not simply iconic, they embodied national traits and gave human form to representations of the evolution of the national character.

Given pedagogical emphasis on teaching moral biography, and the culture of hero-worship in the 1880s and 1890s, it is not surprising that authors of method manuals were insistent that *values* were best taught through historical stories. Reading books, much more so than textbooks, were part of this process of heroic myth-making. Moreover, pedagogical texts and reading books established a system wherein hero-worship itself became a commendable national trait. Heroes could only be heroic if they were supported by contemporaries and commemorated by posterity. The author of the *Ship Historical Readers* defined what it meant to be a hero: to his audience of young children first learning to read, he declared: 'a hero, you know, is a man who is willing to do all he can for others'.[13] John Gunn, in his influential training manual, wrote that 'there is no sermon [...] so impressive as the life of a good man'.[14] Arthur Garlick insisted that biographies were crucial, since when 'the personality of the hero is ever before them [...] lessons become vivified and successful'.[15] Joseph Landon asserted that 'biography has an important bearing' on how children understand the past. In his view, which was commonly shared, 'the history of the nation is inseparably bound up with the lives of its great men'.[16] He continued:

> There is a human and emotional element in history which can scarcely fail, if the subject is properly presented, to have considerable influence [...] the subject should be so treated that the moral influence is felt, not merely talked about [...] Children are great hero-worshippers; and it is well they should be so, for the contemplation of noble deeds – of what men did and suffered in old times to uphold the right and advance a higher ideal of life – is one of the most potent influences in the formation of character.[17]

How was it anticipated that learning about these 'potent influences' could assist in 'the formation of character' and the child's performance of enlightened patriotic values?

This chapter provides further analysis of four key factors in the teaching of enlightened patriotism. First, it outlines some of those core characteristics of heroism, including those suitable for a working-class audience. Second, this chapter explains the 'pedestal' metaphor: this was the method of connecting stories of heroism to the individual's will to be good. Moreover, this was the system by which children could learn that, by behaving dutifully in their own lives, they could contribute to the continuation of the nation's imperial greatness. Third, this chapter provides some case studies of what might be termed 'specifically' imperial heroes, that is, Nelson, Clive, Wolfe and Wellington. Lastly, given texts were read by girls as well as boys, I offer some thoughts on how enlightened patriotism operated as a carefully gendered construct. Reading books included far more heroines than textbooks. Moreover, texts for young children emphasised the childhood of the hero and often commented on the importance of family relations. Stories of heroes were intended to activate the child's sympathetic interest in order that they become good citizens. Just as recapitulation was used to encourage the child to contrast past stages of English civilisation to their own, stories of individuals showed children about the incremental accumulation of enlightened patriotic values over time: the child's emotional response to stories was to provide the link between learning and doing. These moral biographies aimed not just to promote imperial values but to persuade children to invest in a set of social relations which would bolster collective identity.

Heroic attributes and national-imperial values

To be effective, values and characteristics performed by past actors had to be recognisable to the child. Moreover, in order to engage the child's sympathetic interest, it was essential that the exploits of role models were depicted in accessible language and that their ordinariness as human beings was accentuated. How, for instance, was the crucial characteristic of 'courage' represented to children? From the earliest instance courage was held to be innate: 'The first English were strong and hardy men, brave and fearless, but also cruel and merciless to their foes'.[18] As seen in accounts of the evolution of the national character, cruelty and mercilessness were attitudes eliminated from the national character as the nation evolved. The courage which coursed through the veins of the early English and was carried forth by the first English settlers remained an essential component of the national character centuries later. Note the suitability of the language pitch: stories were highly descriptive and used simple words and phrases to make likelier sympathetic engagement. It is no surprise that a range of individuals, as diverse as Alfred, Harold, Eleanor (wife of Edward I), Drake, Sir Philip Sidney, Nelson and Florence Nightingale, featured as brave

IMPERIAL VALUES AND ENLIGHTENED PATRIOTISM

heroes. The whole social spread of monarchs, military and maritime heroes, nurses and poets, across national chronology, formed a pageant of the onwards march and refinement of English courage. But how were these characters brave? What kind of lessons should children take on board?

Alfred, about whom we have already heard, was lauded especially for his courage. The *Britannia History Readers* narrative style was not atypical: 'Alfred and his little army were much cast down, but the brave king did not lose heart. He was too great a man for that'.[19] Intrinsic to Alfred's valour was his resilience and his inspirational leadership. Likewise, Harold and his men may have lost the Battle of Hastings, but they, nonetheless, were 'brave defenders of their native land'.[20] Their courage, like Alfred's, was lent added prestige because it was the English homeland that they were protecting. As seen in Chapter Three, Alfred was also important because of his link to naval origins. It was the English nation that was being served, and in the process, both saved and advanced. Courage was not just a trait to be performed by English men; women and foreigners could embody enlightened patriotic principles. Eleanor of Castile in a consistently told story was a 'brave princess', not only since she put her own life on the line in order to save another life – she 'sucked the poison from the wound' received by her husband Edward I, and 'so Edward's life was saved' – but because, as a result, Edward was able to continue to become an excellent king.[21] This was true service to the nation, as well as an excellent example of gendered devotion (more on the gendering of civic and national values follows). When the Burghers of Calais, who were prepared to sacrifice themselves in order to save their kin, were helped by the similarly brave Philippa of Hainault,[22] they could return to the 'town which they had saved by their bravery'.[23] Philippa had performed bravery by standing up to her husband's, Edward III's, hot-headedness. Against the Armada, not only was Francis Drake venerated, 'but the hearts of the English were stout and brave', thus demonstrating that courage was not merely an individual trait, but crucially, a national characteristic.[24] Individuals were brave because they stood up to seemingly insurmountable odds; because they led wisely and well, or served their leader dutifully; because they were prepared to sacrifice themselves for the national good – and many did: not only did Harold and Nelson die in their service to the country, but so too did Edmund, Sidney, Grenville, Nelson, General Gordon and many others. In short, these characters were heroic since in their deeds and motivations they legitimated England as the ultimate object of loyalty. The lesson was that this should be the collective ambition for children. Anybody could be brave, even a young child.

Courage enabled the submission of oneself to the greater good which, to recall, constituted the sixth and ultimate objective of the Herbartian method. Other such traits which articulated tenets of enlightened patriotism included: obedience, sacrifice, stoicism, resilience and a passion for learning. Special praise was reserved for those who did their duty but sought neither fame nor financial reward. Thus, a premium was placed on values such as dutifulness, service, loyalty, kindness and humility. Blondel was variously reported as a troubadour, a minstrel and a jester, yet even he became heroic because he was 'true' to his king (by singing to Richard while imprisoned), and was thus loyal to his nation. According to the author of the *Warwick History Readers*, 'Richard I soon returned home to England, but he might have died in prison had Blondel not been so true to him'.[25] Blondel, like Eleanor, performed loyalty to his leader and his king and was rewarded by posterity. Hubert, charged by 'Bad' King John with the unpleasant mission of burning out the eyes of the young heir-apparent Arthur (Richard's son), was venerated in these texts for his common sense and his decision to risk his own safety in order to do the right thing.[26] William Wallace and Joan of Arc were highly thought of and were recorded in reading books focusing on English history as patriotic. This was no paradox: both stood up to oppression in the name of that which they thought to be a good and true cause without (any reported) desire for self-gain: Wallace aimed 'to free his country'; we will hear more on Joan in a later section.[27] Through their patriotism and dedication to their cause they, as did the story of the Burghers of Calais, served as a useful reminder for when the English had lost sight of English values. They were, of course, also very brave.

If children were expected to draw significant lessons by having the lives of these individuals set before them, it was intended they learn that courage, steadfastness and self-sacrifice were only valued if they were performed in defence of the nation and in defiance of those who would seek to undermine English national values. This did, however, pose a significant dilemma. The need, as already stated, was not to promote patriotism *per se*, but 'enlightened patriotism' – that is, the desire to serve one's own country with pride, not pomp, and with full awareness of why the nation was great, rather than with blind and unthinking adulation. The predicament, however, was that the majority of these stories were about *extra*-ordinary characters. It is entirely possible to understand how children might have taken pride in these heroes. Yet, what if children were not content merely to internalise values? Despite clever inclusion of characters shown to be heroic partly because they *did not* seek fame, some feared children might, regardless of these lessons, either expect reward or, worse still, seek to emulate the *actions* rather than the attitudes of role models. George Collar and Charles Crook, co-authors of a manual of method, were aware of this:

> The virtue which is most strongly brought on in the study of historical biographies is that of patriotism. History affords many examples of noble self-sacrifice for one's country, but there is always a danger that the presentation of the grandest examples of patriotism may engender a kind of green-sickness in the pupils which leads to nothing but ineffectual dreams of becoming admirals or generals dying in the defence of the fatherland. The teacher must indicate practical means of giving expression to the patriotic sentiment lest the very boys who dream of emulating Arnold von Winkelreid by gathering a sheaf of the enemy's spears' points into their own bosoms, grow into men who cheat their country by making false income tax returns.[28]

To summarise the story, Arnold was reputed to have led the Swiss victory over the Austrians at Sempach in 1386. When substantially outnumbered, he threw himself into the enemy lines, in full knowledge that this would lead to his death but might cause a breach in the Austrian lines. It was better, educationists posited, for children to want to perform their everyday responsibilities with not only vigour but also the realisation that they need not die in the process (of course, come the Great War and the attrition of trench warfare, Arnold's story took on a different significance). A key lesson intended for children to learn, therefore, was that like Blondel and Hubert they could be heroic in their way and should not seek fame. What mattered, therefore, was that actions undertaken by heroes were represented as expressions of appropriate mental attitudes and national values, not the exclusive pursuit of individual glory. As one text for older scholars confirmed: 'every citizen ought to remember one very important thing about the patriotism which has made our country what it is. Those who love their country best are content to serve it without the hope of immediate reward, or even the encouragement of praise'.[29]

As a result, two techniques were deployed to prevent children from seeking individual fame rather than wanting to devote themselves to work as part of collective unit. First, a number of unexceptional characters were elevated to greatness. Hence, 'ordinary' folk were shown they could contribute to national greatness by the dutiful conduct of their everyday lives. Whereas textbooks tended to privilege martial heroes, diplomats and politicians, reading books incorporated stories of nurses, servants, writers, inventors and unnamed sailors and soldiers. Focus upon ordinary people meant that children could learn that personality traits such as stoical endurance, 'getting on with it', loyalty, common sense and compassion, were just as worthy of national praise as inspirational leadership, military deeds or daring adventures. Stories of Blondel and Hubert made for exciting fare but their pedagogical value resided in their performances of service. Second, famous individuals were represented as great only because they were greatly supported. Everyone could share in national heroism by wisely supporting those individuals who had, and would, receive the plaudits of posterity. Hero-worship was itself cast as an essential ingredient of enlightened patriotism. National progress was depicted as a collective effort, thus strengthening bonds of loyalty and commitment to a common cause. But how was such a supporting role made enticing?

'We can all take our share in forming a firm pedestal in support of a great leader and a great cause'

Terence Raymont recognised that to teach history around the biographies of key military personnel alone might produce exactly the type of crude patriotism which educationists were at pains to prevent. This is why he was keen to emphasise that:

> 'drum and trumpet history' should be put in its right place, and that the personal doings of kings and nobles should be duly subordinated to the story of the nation's social, intellectual and industrial progress. But we must remember that a child's interests – and, for that matter, the average adult's, – are with persons rather than institutions [...] instead of making the biography a mere story, no matter how interesting in itself, we should place the hero amidst his social surroundings, and that the children should realise how his deeds helped or hindered social progress.[30]

More will be said momentarily of industrial and cultural figures, for their contributions to national progress were represented as significant. First, how was the hero positioned in relation to his or her supporters?

John Finnemore (1863–1915) explained the relationship between leaders and led using the analogy of the 'pedestal'. Finnemore, although neither historian nor educationist, was an exceptionally important writer. Not only was he a school book author of some repute, but he had earned himself much contemporary praise for his historical novels and patriotic songs written for schools.[31] He was one of the first to write novels explicitly for the Boy Scouts, and is cited by Marcus Crouch as the most 'prominent of scouting authors'.[32] Within a few months of Baden Powell's *Scouting for Boys* (1908), Finnemore's widely recommended text, *The Wolf Patrol*, had become a bestseller.[33] He was likened to those other great writers of historical fiction, Sir Walter

Scott, Rudyard Kipling and R.M. Ballantyne.[34] Educationists differentiated Finnemore from these: he was widely lauded for his special aptitude for writing for very young children.[35] James Welton, a leading advocate of the power of fiction to convey moral certainties, referenced Finnemore twice in a text of 1906: first as a 'master' storyteller, and second as an example of an author who had the necessary literary skills to entice children to want to become proud and active citizens.[36] Finnemore's texts, according to a report in 1928 by C.H.K. Marten on the teaching of social and economic history, continued to enjoy 'a considerable vogue as books for younger children'.[37] Little wonder that his signature was widely sought after by a range of educational publishers. He was contracted to write historical reading books by A. & C. Black Publishers in 1901, for which he also wrote information books on other countries to be used in geography lessons. He had earlier worked for Chambers.[38] Finnemore, therefore, was a writer of significant import to turn of the twentieth century publishers.

Finnemore's dedication to the Scouts ('its end is good citizenship' he wrote in the preface to *Wolf Patrol*) explains partly why he made it his personal responsibility to ensure that the nameless faces in urban run-down schools were aware of the nameless faces who had sacrificed themselves for the good of their country.[39] Not unsurprisingly, therefore, he devoted much space in one of his most popular historical reading books, *Famous Englishmen* (1901), to explaining why the 'average' boy and girl should feel related to these renowned individuals. This is how he explained the principles of the pedestal. 'A hero needs heroes to follow him', Finnemore informed his elementary-school audience, in the same way that 'a great man must be greatly supported'. He continued: 'In every age we may call the great man the statue, and the people who supported him the pedestal. Few people in our time will become statues, but we can all take our share in forming a firm pedestal in support of a great leader and a great cause'.[40] The pedestal analogy, used as a narrative frame, was intended to enable the vast many to feel pride in, and a putative connection to, the achievements of the select few.

Bernard Porter cites Finnemore's model of the pedestal, yet rather misinterprets its significance. According to Porter, the pedestal encouraged 'working-class imperialists to take the same pride in the empire as, for example, a bricklayer might take in his humble contribution to the building of a great house. It was a serving rather than a participatory kind of imperialism'.[41] Finnemore's objective, however, was neither merely the explicit inculcation of shared imperial ideologies, nor was it an exclusive emphasis on aspects of working-class service. Rather, he advocated lessons about how national progress was best achieved through examples of social harmony rather than discord: the pedestal was about the operation, in tandem, of service and participation. In Finnemore's formulation, it was not just workers who worked hard and were loyal: heroes served their monarchs, monarchs served their people and the people served whoever best represented their collective will. Leaders had a duty towards those they led. Hence, the author of *Cassell's Historical Course for Schools* emphasised the obligations of both: 'our country has grown stronger and better the more its *rulers* and peoples have striven to act rightly', continuing that everyone must 'live worthy and honourable lives'.[42] Hence, the pedestal did not narrowly define 'all' as the working class alone: it emphasised the ideal qualities of leadership but also informed readers of the importance of followership as a civic duty.

The second Boer War, unresolved in 1901 at the time of the publication of *Famous Englishmen*, illustrated this point for Finnemore. The achievements of famous generals, common soldiers and the population at home were synthesised, creating the message that all involved, abroad and at home, were 'great'. 'Getting on with it', for the sake of the greater good, was an essential feature of the national character.[43] Finnemore, however, pointed up the warning that neither those who formed the pedestal, nor those they propped up, should become too lackadaisical in their support of one another:

> Remember, then, that men and women who wisely obey wise laws, who greatly support great men and great aims, are just as necessary as the famous leader himself. We can all become such men and women if we try. Without them it is quite certain that the future will contain very few famous Englishmen.[44]

In terms of ensuring *service*, heroes could only be great because of the pedestal on which ordinary folk placed them. That meant they had a responsibility to their support-base. It was, however, the evolution of human relationships between leaders and led that mattered – and it is this implicit contract, appealing to the tenets of Herbartian educational psychology, to which the pedestal refers. Biographical stories were therefore intended to appeal not only to the child's sympathetic interest, but also to its social and religious interests. After all, these stories urged the child to want to contribute to the ongoing greatness of the whole. 'We can', to recall Finnemore, 'all become such men and women if we try'.

The dominance of the pedestal metaphor also explains why famous people, celebrated neither for their leadership nor their martial achievements, could become part of the story of English progress. Reading books often celebrated English industrial progress: George Stephenson (railways), Caxton (the printing press), Watt (steam power) and Arkwright (king of cotton), featured frequently. Their stories demonstrated characteristics such as thrift and innovation: they provided useful lessons in how one could contribute to the national wellbeing without necessarily having to fight, or die. In an age of railways and industrialisation, children were likely to know about trains and steam power. 'There are few boys and girls who have not seen a railway engine', began the *Britannia History Reader*, continuing, 'whenever we see a railway we should think of George Stephenson'. Stephenson's hard upbringing was noted, in which 'he could neither read nor write'. But once he had worked hard in order to achieve 'a little schooling', he was able to progress and contribute something wonderful to the nation.[45] Lessons in ideal behaviour could hardly have been more explicit! Additionally, cultural icons were celebrated: Chaucer and Milton were occasionally included, Shakespeare and Bunyan frequently. John Bunyan, imprisoned for his beliefs, made shoestrings that were sold by his blind daughter, managed somehow to write *The Pilgrim's Progress* and in the process made his name famous. 'It is still read now', one historical reading book declared, continuing: 'I hope you will see from this lesson that even a poor man can become great by leading an honest and upright life'.[46] A fine lesson indeed. Words lifted directly from Shakespeare, more often than not 'this sceptre'd isle', were used to conclude those texts that ranged up to the Elizabethan period. This is perhaps no surprise, since, as the author of the *King Edward History Readers* (1902) explained, the 'three greatest gifts that England in her long history has given the world are her Empire, her Literature, and her Parliament'.[47] Knowledge of, and pride in, military moments alone would not encourage children to adhere to these lessons in civic duty. In order to effectively transmit enlightened patriotic values, it was essential that these texts contained exciting stories about moments of significant national achievement; these moments, including stories of military glories, could be narrated as the history of the English people writ large, not histories of keynote individuals.

As a result, texts venerated not only famous individuals but also the nameless 'us' who made such powerful contributions to national progress. Stephen Heathorn cites one reader thus: 'the Battle of Crecy [1346] is very important in one respect. It showed that the bravest and boldest knights of France were powerless against the sturdy English yeomen, with their bows and arrows. The men who had left their ploughs and their spades at Edward's call, put to rout the finest nobility of France. The people won the day, and not the nobles'.[48] That the best of the enemy were no match for the combined efforts of the untrained English is significant. The message of 'all in it together' was acutely rendered. On Crecy, Finnemore praised the effort of the ordinary folk too, applying the pedestal in explicit fashion. He wrote: 'We read in our history time and time again of battles such as Crecy and Agincourt, where a small band of English faced overwhelming numbers of a powerful enemy. Their case seemed utterly hopeless, but they won the day, and the name of their leader became great and famous'. The leader became famous because the cumulative effort of the people made it possible. But Finnemore had more to say about the leader. 'Where', he asked, 'would be his glory but for the dauntless English hearts whose names we do not know?'[49] That required mutual trust, as is evident in this passage about the defeat of the Armada: 'But English sailors are very bold and brave. They know no fear, and trust in their generals to lead the way, and where their leaders go they are sure to follow, or die in the attempt'.[50] The message, directly pressed, was therefore that ordinary people had played their part in the shaping of national progress. In supporting the hero, the 'ordinary' citizen at home could also support the common man or woman of the story associated with that hero. In this rendition of collective memory, it was the faceless and nameless heroes who also merited commemoration. This was a sentiment patent in the later erection of the Tomb of the Unknown Soldier: it was the responsibility of those in the present, therefore, not only to pay reverence to celebrated forebears but also revere all who had gone before.

In defining England's onward march to imperial greatness, heroes demonstrated advances of the national character. The pedestal defined a contractual relationship between the people and historical heroes, which had implications for the everyday behaviour of the child reader. The story of Englishness was a story of wise leadership and devoted service since the pedestal not only constituted an accumulation of skills, talents, characteristics and values, but the active demonstration of the Herbartian 'religious interest' in practice. The message was that England had been made great by collective effort. Moreover, the pedestal functioned to reinforce the message that those elevated upon it had their own obligations to the whole. As Sidney lay dying at Zutphen (1586), he gave up a sip of water for the sake of an ordinary footsoldier. His service, therefore, was not only to Queen and country, but to his fellow citizens, represented as equal regardless of rank (see Chapter Three). This model of the leader's service to their countrymen and women held just as true for the monarch (Victoria): 'The Queen has always tried to do her duty. We can all try to do that; and when we grow older we must try to do good for our country by living good lives and helping to make good laws'.[51] This was itself, of course, a nod to late Victorian franchise reform which meant a large number of children would grow up with the responsibility of voting. We will see this aspect of the pedestal in operation in the next section which explores the pedagogical roles of specifically imperial heroes.

Specifically imperial heroes

Although early years reading books concentrated on medieval stories for the youngest children, as children grew older and the concentric system extended to the modern period, texts played up the significance of key stories about individuals more readily identified as imperial heroes. Here, I will focus on the treatment of Clive, Wolfe, Nelson, Wellington and General Gordon since their stories were the most frequently told. However, other characters who merited mention included, among others, Admiral Robert Blake (to maintain the narrative of English maritime dominance), Captain Cook (necessary for the incorporation of the territorial acquisition of Australia into the empire) and Lord Roberts (South Africa). The stories of these heroes constituted the stuff of awe, which was believed could inspire children, and their contributions to national greatness could be told in a relatively straightforward manner. Most significantly, however, stories of their deeds embodied the continuous narrative of the enlargement of the geographical empire as the logical extension of ingrained English attributes. Obviously, the stories of Clive, Wolfe and Gordon were set in India, Canada and Africa, thus introducing stories of colonial control. Likewise, accounts of Nelson served to reinforce stories of English mastery of the seas. All confirm the predisposition of the English towards colonisation. However, these *specifically* imperial heroes also embodied the best of the national character: they served their nation and its people, often dying in the cause; they personified the relationship between responsible and inspirational leadership and communal support; and, crucially, they were living expressions of an accumulation of values which dated back to the early English. All of these individuals were commemorated for their *imperial* achievements: 'we remember Clive as the founder of our Indian Empire', for instance; and, 'Wolfe won a complete victory' which 'made the English masters of Canada'.[52]

It was especially important, from the pedagogical perspective, that these heroes demonstrated continuity. Whereas textbooks often concentrated on the complicated topics of Glorious Revolution, Hanoverian Succession and Walpole's ascendancy, reading books skipped domestic stories from the late seventeenth and eighteenth centuries and concentrated instead on territorial expansion: in particular, texts told stories of Clive in India and Wolfe in Canada. To recap, it must be remembered that it was not until 1892 that 'instruction on British colonies' was incorporated in state recommendations for the teaching of history. Even then, this was only for children staying on beyond the compulsory leaving age. As seen in Chapter Two, reading books were required to teach moral biography rather than detailed dry content. Although texts for primary schoolchildren had always focused on 'the great persons' of English history, it only became statute in the Code of 1904 that moral biographies had to include individuals who had contributed to the 'growth of the British Empire'.[53] Following advice from educationists, stories concentrated on drawing out the human-*ness* of these characters in order to engage the child's sympathetic interest. To achieve this, texts incorporated stories of the hero's childhood and emotive descriptions of his or her personality.

Clive's recalcitrant childhood, for instance, was a topic on which many texts dwelt. 'There was once a boy named Clive, who gave his mother and father a good deal of trouble. He had so many bad friends that his father thought it wise to send him to India, a country which is very far off'. After his numerous achievements, 'everybody now began to talk about the brave young man, who had done such great deeds in India, and Clive found himself quite a hero when he came home to England for a holiday'. So reported the *King Edward History Readers* (1902), concluding that 'the naughty boy had become a great man, and all his friends were very proud of him'.[54] Clearly, in this instance, emphasis was as much on Clive learning to be *good* as it was on the precise details of his deeds and this reflected the pedagogical need to teach civic lessons through these stories. The influence of Herbartian theory is made particularly clear when one examines how textbooks attend to Clive and Wolfe. In Arthur Hassall's text, geared explicitly to teaching imperial history and intended for older children, Wolfe receives one page and Clive two. Neither receives plaudits based on their personality traits.[55] Wolfe did not feature in Ince and Gilbert's *Outlines of English History*; Clive merited one line.[56] In Morris's *Class Book of English History*, Wolfe merely 'expired'.[57]

Another individual – the hero *par excellence* – was Nelson. Although Nelson was held to be the most important hero in the English pantheon, textbooks were similarly dispassionate in their treatment of his death. For Ince and Gilbert, Nelson's story was less important than continental battles against Napoleon and the implications for Pitt's ministry.[58] Hassall, without encomium, did note Nelson's death was the price paid securing the 'supremacy of the sea'.[59] Reading books, on the other hand, enforced the personalities of heroes. For the author of the *King Edward History Readers*, Nelson 'was a small thin child, who did not look like he would ever be a great man. But as he grew up, he showed what a brave boy he was. He never seemed to be afraid'.[60] The *Britannia History Readers* introduced Nelson using a similar approach: 'When he was very young he showed signs of the brave heart that was in him'.[61] Another text summarised the hero's character thus: his 'strength was in his heart and in his will, not in his body' and that should be a lesson to all boys and girls of those 'great deeds [which] may be done by those who are weak in body but strong in mind'.[62] The courage, coolness and commitment to valour that Nelson was later to demonstrate during the Battle of Trafalgar were shown to be childhood traits. In some texts, the story of Nelson confronting a polar bear is told to highlight his innate bravura.[63] Most texts, however, told the story of how, when Nelson and his brother were caught up in a snowstorm on the way to school, Nelson insisted they struggle on since their father had told them it was a matter of personal honour to 'do their best'.[64] Such an association of heroism with youthful commitment and appreciation of schooling resonated with the wider educational context of the time. As a number of studies have shown, absenteeism through truancy or parental influence was a major concern.[65] If a man as great as Nelson considered attendance to be a matter of honour, then clearly children were exhorted to value the importance of their own schooling. Likewise, if such distinction as earned by Clive and Nelson could be achieved by willpower, then the lesson ran that all children had within them the potential to contribute greatly to the national cause.

Nelson, moreover, would not have been able to perform his exceptional talents had he not the full and dutiful support of his crew and, indirectly, the nation back home. When Nelson spoke his famous lines, 'England expects', for instance, his rallying call 'was greeted by loud cheers from every ship'.[66] There was a relationship, therefore, between Nelson, his immediate crew aboard HMS Victory, as well as those on board other ships. But the depiction of a 'collective' experience of this moment did not stop with the moments of the speech and the response it engendered. People 'back home' were said to have echoed the determination of the combatants. Had Napoleon crossed the Channel, 'he would have found a stiff piece of work waiting for him. In England four hundred thousand volunteers sprang to arms, eager to defend their island home'.[67] Further to this, however, manifest in Nelson was the collective aggregate of English history: 'There have always been brave sailors ready to fight for England, and of these the greatest of all was Lord Nelson'.[68] Individually, Nelson had earned his nation a major success. He embodied the relationship between the English and sea: in him was the best of imperial traditions spanning back to Anglo-Saxon antecedents.

Wellington, too, was put to valuable pedagogical use and again provides evidence that it was the demonstration of the hero's personality that mattered as much as accounts of her or his derring-do. 'The British were very proud of him, because he won such a great battle for them', wrote the author of the *King Edward History Readers*, continuing: 'He was a kind man, and always had a good word for those who tried to do what was right'.[69] However, for emphasis, less space was provided for the explanation of continental military campaigns than was to a story in which the retired Duke heaped praise upon a young farm boy. The story runs: Wellington, on a hunt with fellow dignitaries, approached a gate guarded by a young boy. When one of Wellington's company insisted the boy open the gate to allow passage, the boy replied that he had to follow his father's orders and not allow anyone to pass. To this, Wellington's response is telling of the educational context: 'I honour the man or boy who does his duty, and will not be frightened into doing wrong'. Thus, emphasis on duty and obedience were depicted as such important characteristics worthy of emulation that even the Great Duke would celebrate their demonstration by a boy. The boy's response must have generated a smile or two in classrooms: 'Hurrah! I've done what Napoleon could not do; I've kept back the Duke of Wellington'.[70]

Wolfe, Nelson and Gordon died in service of the nation. Like Edmund, Sidney and Grenville, death in the national cause cemented the relationship between the hero figure and the support base at home through collective grief and lessons for communal remembrance: posterity owed heroes, and their contemporaries who held them atop their pedestals, a significant debt of gratitude. On lamenting the death of Wolfe, for instance: 'So Quebec became ours, and because of its fall, the land of Canada was soon won too. But the people at home were very sorry to hear of Wolfe's death, for Britain had lost another great hero'.[71] Gordon was similarly commemorated, with added emphasis on children's duty to feel national pride.[72] That 'every boy and girl should be proud that Gordon was an Englishman, and should say to themselves: "I also will be a hero as Gordon was"' demonstrates just how explicit some of these lessons in civic obligation could be.[73] Texts for older children similarly enjoined the child to honour Gordon. *Chambers' Alternative History Readers*, for children in Standard IV, for instance, explained:

> Thus did a great and good man die, after having endured a siege of over three hundred days. His loss was greatly mourned in England; for, in him, bravery, courage, and sincerity were combined with true goodness, gentleness and charity. Many monuments were erected to his memory,

and probably no other man won the love of his countrymen so entirely as did the great hero, General Gordon.[74]

Stephen Heathorn includes this quotation as an example of how 'the national hero was [...] projected into the classroom in an effort to create social deference'.[75] This was certainly true: heroes, especially martial heroes, embodied those values of valour, courage, leadership, self-sacrifice and commitment to national wellbeing that it was intended children admire. However, Herbartian pedagogy aimed for much more than deference: in particular, these stories were to inspire a will to emulate the everyday values and characteristics of individuals, who – through moral biography – served also as role models exemplifying the best of the national character. Heroes who did not die as martyrs, most notably Wellington, were used to provide lessons in how leaders deserved praise for their treatment of those who formed the pedestal. The *Britannia History Readers*, for instance, informed readers that 'the people welcomed Wellington with the greatest rejoicings'[76] and mourned his death collectively. Grief was expressed, however, not merely because he had won so many battles, but because he had demonstrated so many admirable characteristics. He was compassionate: 'Once when the English had taken a Spanish town it was found that they had lost five thousand men. It is said that when their great leader heard of this he burst into tears; for though he was a stern soldier his heart was full of grief at the loss of life that war ... bring[s]'.[77] He was 'industrious', 'quiet' and 'contemplative' – nice practical lessons in citizenship for child readers – yet he was also 'careful of the health of his men', 'strict', 'respected' and 'trusted'.[78] Wellington epitomised not only the great leader, but the leader who knew how to treat his troops well.

Thus, in reading books, specifically imperial heroes served the pedagogical purpose of activating the sympathetic interest in children and thus encouraging them into dutiful behaviour. Educationists were not concerned that children should know the intricacies of the Wars of Jenkins Ear and Spanish Succession; instead, what mattered most for the creation of enlightened patriots was the telling of stories about the human characteristics of role models. Indeed, whereas textbooks and readers for older children were packed with dense material, moral biographies emphasised those human traits which were recognisable to, and could be reproduced by, all children. This method also enabled the incorporation of unexceptional people into the national pageant, including those whom posterity did not remember by name and those in the present who, together, held historical heroes in the highest regard. This was especially the case with the creation of *heroines*. The higher frequencies of female role models in reading books, as compared to subject-specific textbooks, also provide evidence to suggest that context-sensitive civic values became intertwined with imperial attributes.

Gendering national and imperial values

Females performing exceptional deeds, be it Philippa, Eleanor, Joan of Arc or Grace Darling, invariably were lauded for their femininity; yet femininity itself was conjoined to notions of service and characteristics of courage in order to demonstrate that young girls could equally share in collective memory and contribute to ongoing national prestige. This corresponded with the dominant separate spheres ideology of the times, in which the public world of politics and foreign policy was defined as the masculine realm and girls were fitted for the domestic sphere of house and home.[79] Girls, of course, were an especial target for education policies aimed at socialisation: their elementary education prioritised lessons in needlework and other aspects of domestic life.[80] Historical stories justified precisely why they should grow up determined to be good mothers and to serve their men. Trepidation about motherhood as midwife to the future necessitated that reading books were replete with stories which reproduced dominant gender ideologies. These female role models articulated how girls should fulfil a role for their community and their nation.[81]

The story of Grace Darling demonstrated that those of humble birth who performed extraordinary deeds could be rewarded by posterity. The daughter of a lighthouse keeper, Grace had risked her own life in 1838 in order to rescue the stranded passengers of the S.S. Forfarshire. Her story was introduced thus by the *Ship Historical Reader* (note the pedestal in action as well as the appropriately maritime intonation of the text's title):

> We have read of brave soldiers and sailors who did noble deeds. We have read of heroes who stood up against kings, and gave up their lives for what they thought was right. There are also many heroes whose brave deeds are never heard of. But there was a brave deed done by a girl named Grace Darling that we all ought to hear of and copy, if we ever have the chance.[82]

Hugh Cunningham has found much so far that is of relevance to this work. At times when Britain's maritime authority was under threat, he argues, the legend of Grace Darling was invoked. It is not surprising that Grace featured more significantly in the 1890s and 1900s given the increase and subsequent fear of German sea power;

nor is it surprising that she became popular in the Second World War (the Battle of the Atlantic). After all, she personified grit, sacrifice and, in the words of a popular song, 'Grace had an English heart'.[83] Despite this, however, she was soon returned to the female role: she nursed the men back to health and her gendered service was depicted as just as important as the act on the rowboat itself.[84] She was a nineteenth-century working-class female Northumbrian child. Heroic individuals with these properties were not two-a-penny. She showed that even ordinary children could perform heroic deeds, yet also demonstrated that girls could serve their nation by caring for men.[85] Specifically, Grace showed the endurance of the English characteristics of courage and self-sacrifice into the nineteenth century. She also showed how the English maintained their relationship to the sea.

Florence Nightingale also featured in reading books, demonstrating the domestic qualities of nurture. She was brave for travelling overseas and helping nurse the army but, likewise, she was 'proud of our brave men, who were not afraid of anything'.[86] In being proud of England's fighting fellows, Florence exuded collective pride. Readers, likewise, were encouraged to be proud of her. In Florence's story, both she and the war-wounded she tended are linked by their dedication to commemorate the great and the good. In this telling of the story, she is not too far removed from the story of Eleanor of Castile. Both served men dutifully, a useful lesson contemporaries wanted working-class girls to learn; both were prompted into action by enlightened patriotic principles; both put their own lives on the line for the national wellbeing; and both were rewarded with enduring fame by posterity. Eleanor was heroic since she not only stared death in the face in sucking poison from her husband's wounds (Edward I), but also reverted to role as the loyal devoted wife. Eleanor was commemorated thus: 'When Queen Eleanor died the king was in great grief. "I loved her in her lifetime", said the weeping king, "I do not cease to love her now she is dead". The queen's body was brought to London to be buried'.[87] Accompanying the text was a picture of Charing Cross, her burial place. Eleanor was loved not only by her husband and her contemporaries, but – if texts were successful in cultivating the sympathetic interest and generating an emotional response – by those reading about her. It must have helped that she gave birth to the first Prince of Wales.[88] Joan of Arc and Boudicca showed that women might be brave in primarily masculine ways, but their stories were told in the language of females tenaciously defending their territory. Philippa of Hainault, wife of Edward III, demonstrated that the calmness of women was as essential to national progress as the spontaneity of men: hence her composure allowed the Burghers of Calais to demonstrate their courage.

In addition to hailing the contributions of individual women to the national story, stories often invoked the language of the nation as *family*, which has additional implications for how reading books contributed to the construction of gendered ideals of nationhood and citizenship. In particular, this enabled depictions of the national past which invoked human relationships, especially that of mother and child. The pedestal was given flesh by encouraging adulation of wives and mothers; the unbroken narrative of the national story made for a representation of the nation as united through blood and inheritance. Two examples suffice to demonstrate this role of women in the formative development of the nation. It cannot be a coincidence that the childhoods of Alfred and Nelson, two of the most revered heroes in the pantheon, were the most frequently retold. Cowham, in his manual, suggested to teachers that in order to render stories more meaningful, the 'social upbringing' of the individual should be related in order to aid the understanding of the contrast between 'life now and then'.[89] Nelson's transformation from naughty boy – he was often scolded by his mother – to national hero was attributed to his education:

> So Horatio went back to school and tried to learn all he could. He was very much liked by his school fellows, because he was good-natured and fond of a good game, and he was in high favour with his teachers, because he was obedient, frank and truthful. Like all really brave boys, he scorned to tell a lie; nor would he ever take praise to himself if he thought others were more deserving of it.[90]

We have seen the invocation of *normal* aspects of the hero's childhood in relation to Clive too, but the motherly role was most explicitly told in the case of Alfred. 'The king's mother had taught him to read and write when he was a boy. He knew what a good thing it was to be able to read books and put his thoughts into writing. Many schools were built during his time'.[91] The lesson to be learnt from this consistently told story was both explicit and implicit. The author of *Longman's Ship Historical Readers* placed Alfred firmly atop the pedestal: 'he spent his life in teaching his people' and 'helping them'; 'he set up schools'; and, 'although it is a thousand years since he lived, we still love him, as a King who did nobly, and always loved that which is good'.[92] Texts lauded the merits of reading: 'I hope you all become like Alfred', Oscar Browning wrote in his reading book, 'and grow up wise and good. Learn when you are young, and do not forget, that you can never learn too much'.[93] This reminded children of their good fortune to have schools.[94] However, in depicting the pivotal role of women in raising the hero and ensuring the hero's education, stories celebrated domestic virtues.

Additionally, mobilisation of the family metaphor not only enlivened the deeds of past actors, but contributed to the teaching of chronology. This was deemed essential to Herbartian principles, to recall, because in order for children to identify the values upon which to act, they needed to be able to evaluate progress over time. Accordingly, the story of the English people was told as the story of a national family, united, importantly, through blood. This is explicit in the following extract from *Cassell's Historical Course for Schools*:

> The reason why we like to read English history is because it tells the story of our own ancestors. You all know of your fathers and grandfathers, and you must remember that each of these had grandfathers and grandfathers before them, and so on backwards as far as we can go; so that forefathers of every English child who reads this book must have been living at every time in the history of the English People. English History, therefore, is the history of our families as well as that of our nation.[95]

The family was mobilised by more precise methods too. The monarchy was used as a chronological template: Victoria, for instance, embodied the story of the English people as the inheritor of the Anglo-Saxon tradition. She was labelled by the *Raleigh History Readers* as the 'the descendant of the Saxon chiefs who settled in Wessex more than fourteen centuries ago'. The text continued:

> She represents the growth of our people from very small beginnings to its present worldwide power: and all who know the history of our country feel a thrill of pride and joy when they think of its wonderful past and its prosperous present, with all of which our royal family has been so closely associated. When we sing 'God Save the Queen', we think not only of the Queen, but of the people whose past and present life she represents. For [...] we remember that, after all, we are one nation, closely related in blood and community of interest.[96]

The national story was depicted, therefore, as the history of a chronologically expanding family, writ-large, with its genealogical roots positioned as far back in time as the history of the 'English' in these isles.

In his analysis of the cultural reception of soldier heroes, Graham Dawson has convincingly argued that '[w]ithin nationalist discourse, narratives about soldier heroes are both underpinned by, and powerfully reproduce, conceptions of gender and nation as unchanging essences'.[97] These examples were intended to teach stories about past female deeds in order to provide putative lessons for female students; yet, they also served to remind boys of *their* gendered obligations. It is no surprise, therefore, to read in one manual that lessons drawn from history should teach how 'the love of country united brave men, not for themselves, but for the defence of hearth and home'.[98] Boys were reminded that part of the collective effort required of them was the defence of both the homeland and the womenfolk back home. According to Norman Vance, 'manliness' can be reduced to four types: the chivalric, the benevolent, the sturdy English and the moral.[99] Kelly Boyd informs us that adventure story fiction focused predominantly on the upper middle-class boy hero.[100] In that regard, it was important that stories in reading books demonstrated that the working-class lad could be 'manly'. While those attending the public school might have had reason to identify predominantly with aspects of 'sturdy' Englishness, *all* of Vance's masculine 'types', but especially the 'moral', were set before the working-class boy in reading texts.

Although it can readily be argued that this presentation of gendered values neatly fitted turn of the century gender boundaries, one must be more cautious in assuming that there was necessarily an impact on how the child understood its place and responsibilities within civic, national and imperial life. One can, however, engage in some speculation about what these intentions represent about the construction of identity. Nationhood was depicted as 'timeless', insofar as the national story told the onward march of English national progress from the fixed origin-point of Anglo-Saxon settlement. The extent to which individuals were represented as rooted within this narrative was reinforced further by the gendering of the national story. Representation of the nation-as-family, in Anne McClintock's words, 'offered an invaluable trope for figuring historical time',[101] since it discursively constructed the nation as endowed with female properties. Family is the most natural unit for human relationships: the conflation of that *natural* condition to the *national* reinforced hierarchies of power. Men were heads of household; so too were they leaders of the nation. Women played the subservient role of dutiful wife and dedicated mother (or nurse in the case of Florence and Grace); so too should they serve their national leaders in a similar manner. Feminine image emphasised domestic stability and this was mapped on to national chronology. The female nation was inert and authentic. 'She' embodied national progress and reproduced those national values through the nurture of the young. Masculine image, however, was shown as powerful and dynamic. Whereas women articulated stability and symbolically represented essentially timeless and eternal characteristics of the nation, men were agents of historical change – immediately noticeable in the use of active verbs to describe them.[102] Men fought, struggled, sailed, rode, bargained, wrote great literature, invented, defended female honour, and so on. The empire, on this interpretation, was a masculine accomplishment.[103]

The gendering of national chronology, therefore, served to position boys and girls within a collective framework of narrative time. Via the approach of the pedestal, emphasis was placed upon the child undertaking action in order to meet the criteria for national belonging. Genealogical bonds of belonging conferred gender-specific expectations for how children would perform their enlightened patriotism at home, in school, or in their duty to fellow countrymen and women. Historical stories contributed to the codification of these civic values, collectively depicted as the cumulative aggregate of English history from barbaric beginnings to beneficent imperial modernity. Children might not have known enough specifically imperial content for the liking of some, but the evidence from the content of reading books demonstrates that the historical stories they would have read fused imperial and civic values.

Summary

Finnemore, respected as an exceptional writer, created neither a new approach to telling historical stories, nor a methodological rationale to ensure their effectiveness. He merely coined the pithy phrase – the pedestal – which described so aptly the approach. Other reading books, incorporating pedagogical methodologies evident in reading books, implied the pedestal contract. The reason why this was so popular was that it captured perfectly the requirement, in keeping with Herbartian principles, to use historical stories to teach children that they were part of a collective national whole and were, consequently, expected to want to 'do their bit' towards the greater good. That was how the requirements and obligations of citizenship could be coupled onto representations of national – and by extension – imperial identities.

A number of national traits were therefore presented in these reading books which explained the ongoing evolution of the national character. Five conclusions can be drawn about this recognised need to render the national past through biographical stories. First, heroes were selected because children could identify with them: that is, stories emphasised the human*ness* of these characters, concentrated on bringing their stories alive through deployment of emotive prose, and thus nourished the child's sympathetic engagement. Second, heroes need not have been *great men* alone: the cast of heroes included servants, court entertainers and poets, for instance. Moreover, texts lauded the significant contributions of women, from a variety of backgrounds, to the forging of the national story. Third, the deeds of the meek were lauded as fervently as the achievements of the mighty. That was the crucial component of the pedestal since it aimed to impress upon children that the ways in which they conducted their lives contributed to the national effort. Fourth, children were reminded that the hero could only be great if he or she was greatly supported: not only by his or her contemporaries, but in the reverence shown by subsequent generations. The onus in these stories was therefore on what the child could do to maintain and contribute to the unfinished national story. It is no surprise that when reading book authors did ask the children to think about questions, the questions usually required them to assess character, consider moral actions and evaluate the advantages enjoyed by modern-day children by contrasting past and present. After telling how Canute turned back the waves, children were asked: 'What do you think of Canute? In what ways was he well fitted to be king?'[104] Similarly, questions such as, 'How would you describe Blondel?'; or, on Joan of Arc, 'Do you think the English did right in putting her death',[105] were not uncommon. Following the story of Alfred learning to read, children were asked to consider: 'What difficulties would a person who could not read or write get into today?'[106] Thus, children were enjoined to form moral judgements about past characters and answers were intended to exercise a direct effect on how they thought about their conduct and their world-view. Lastly, heroes represented how these values were innate to the English story: these values were depicted as historically embedded and, thus, they demonstrated not only the progress of individuals towards civilisation, but the onward chronological march of the English race.

Tom Nairn observed of the late nineteenth century that, '[T]he new middle-class intelligentsia of nationalism had to invite the masses into history; and the invitation card had to be written in a language they understood'.[107] These reading books, written in language appropriate for young working-class scholars, constituted precisely this. Not only did texts set the questions, they also provided children with examples in both the wrong and right ways in which to answer that invitation into shared history and thus nationhood. The gendered dimension of this call to nationalism demonstrates, moreover, that values presupposed as fitting for working-class children reinforced dominant gender and class ideologies of the period. This is important since children were expected to act upon these lessons. Not all boys, for instance, would serve their country in battle (though a fair few of them did so in the not too far removed future), but all of them could conduct their lives according to a masculine code comprising common sense, courage, loyalty, hard work and commitment to family. Likewise, it would be possible for all girls to serve their country well by being good daughters, wives and mothers. Thus, these historical stories lent credibility to, and justified, the *status quo* both between the sexes and between the social classes. We cannot be certain about whether or not these intentions met with success. We can, however, emphasise that much more thought was put into history teaching than has been allowed for in previous studies. If we take the yardstick to measure success to be the *representation* within school books of intentions articulated by educational theorists, then it is possible to argue for a significant accomplishment.

Thus, it was the prevalence of educational psychology which accounts for the esteemed role of history in the curriculum; not discrete lessons in history based on textbooks, but historical stories which encouraged emotive and empathic responses in children. These texts may not always have preached the glory of empire, and they certainly did not teach children detailed knowledge of imperial history. They did, however, aim to mobilise cutting-edge pedagogical developments to influence the world-view of the child. As a result, the nation to which children were to feel allegiance was an imperial nation, and those everyday values deemed suitable for emulation were depicted as imperial values.

To what extent, however, did this relationship between pedagogy and practice persist through times of war in the face of international pressure to promote peace education in the 1920s? To what extent did the First World War prompt a revaluation of the teaching of history, especially the teaching of imperial history?

Notes

1 Joseph Cowham, *A New School Method: For Pupil-Teachers and Students* (London: Westminster School Book Depot, 1894), 342.
2 L.H. Montagu, 'Hero-Worship as a Factor in Education', *Parents' Review*, 12 (1901), 561–73.
3 Thomas Carlyle, *On Heroes, Hero-Worship and the Heroic in History* (London: Chapman and Hall, 1840 [1903]), 12. Some of the best-selling editions include: Chapman and Hall (1872, 1895, 1898 and 1903), Routledge (1888), Ward, Lock and Bowden (1896 and 1910).
4 G. Dawson, 'Heroes of History, Heroes of Phantasy: Idealisation, Masculinity and the Soldiers of Empire', *Soundings*, 3 (1996), 149.
5 On advertising, see: Thomas Richards, *The Commodity Culture of Victorian England: Advertising and Spectacle* (London: Verso, 1991), especially Chapter Three: 'Selling Darkest Africa'; Lori Anne Loeb, *Consuming Angels: Advertising and Victorian Women* (Oxford: Oxford University Press, 1994), especially Chapter Four: 'The Hero for Sale'; Richard Fulton, 'The Sudan Sensation', *Victorian Periodicals Review*, 42:1 (2009), 37–63; Anne Cronin, 'Rags and Refuse: The Newspaper, Empire and Nineteenth-Century Commodity Culture', *Cultural Studies*, 20:6 (2006), 574–98. For juvenile literature, magazines and comics, see: Kelly Boyd, *Manliness and the Boys' Story Paper: A Cultural History, 1855–1940* (Basingstoke: Palgrave, 2003); the various essays in J. Richards (ed.), *Imperialism and Juvenile Literature* (Manchester: Manchester University Press, 1989); Ymitri Mathison, 'Maps, Pirates and Treasure: The Commodification of Imperialism in Nineteenth-

Century Boy's Adventure Fiction', in Dennis Denisoff (ed.), *The Nineteenth-Century Child and Consumer Culture* (Aldershot: Ashgate, 2008), 173–85; Michelle Smith, *Empire in British Girls' Literature and Culture: Imperial Girls, 1880–1915* (Basingstoke: Palgrave, 2011). For toys, see Kenneth D. Brown, 'Modelling for War? Toy Soldiers in Late Victorian and Edwardian Britain', *Journal of Social History*, 24:2 (1990), 237–54; Ashley Jackson and David Tomkins, *Illustrating Empire: A Visual History of British Imperialism* (Oxford: Bodleian Library, 2011), especially Chapter Six: 'Empire, Leisure and Popular Culture'.

6 John Springhall, *Youth, Empire and Society: British Youth Movements, 1883–1940* (London: Croom Helm, 1977); S. Pryke, 'The Popularity of Nationalism in the Early British Boy Scout Movement, *Social History*, 23 (1998), 309–24; R.H. MacDonald, *Sons of Empire: The Frontier Movement and the Boy Scout Movement, 1890–1918* (London: University of Toronto Press, 1993).

7 On this, see Steve Attridge, *Nationalism, Imperialism and Identity in Late Victorian Culture: Civil and Military Worlds* (Basingstoke: Palgrave, 2003), 2–8; Andrew Thompson, *The Empire Strikes Back: The Impact of Imperialism on Britain from the Mid-Nineteenth Century* (Harlow: Longman, 2005), 97–8.

8 Bernard Porter, *The Absent-Minded Imperialists: What the British Really Thought about Empire* (Oxford: Oxford University Press, 2004), 194 (emphasis in original).

9 Dudley Jones and Tony Watkins (eds), 'Introduction', in their *A Necessary Fantasy? The Heroic Figure in Children's Popular Culture* (New York: Garland, 2000), 4.

10 Geoff Cubitt and Allen Warren, 'Introduction', in their *Heroic Reputations and Exemplary Lives* (Manchester: Manchester University Press, 2000), 2.

11 John MacKenzie, 'Heroic Myths of Empire', in J. MacKenzie (ed.), *Popular Imperialism and the Military* (Manchester: Manchester University Press, 1992), 112; Max Jones, 'What Should Historians Do With Heroes? Reflections on Nineteenth- and Twentieth-Century Britain', *History Compass*, 5:2 (2007), 439–54.

12 For analysis of case studies, see Fulton, 'Sudan Sensation'; R.H. MacDonald, *The Language of Empire: Myths and Metaphors of Popular Imperialism* (Manchester: Manchester University Press, 1994), especially Chapter Three: 'Deeds of Glory'; K.T. Surridge, 'More Than a Great Poster: Lord Kitchener and the Image of the Military Hero', *Historical Research*, 74:185 (2001), 298–313.

13 *Longman's Ship Historical Readers*, I (London: Longmans, Green and Co., 1893), 26.

14 John Gunn, *Class Teaching and Management* (London: T. Nelson and Sons, 1895), 136.

15 Arthur Garlick, *A New Manual of Method*, sixth edition (London: Green and Co., 1904), 267.

16 Joseph Landon, *The Principles and Practice of Class Teaching and School Management* (London: Alfred M. Holden, 1894), 404.

17 Landon, *Principles and Practice*, 404.

18 *Britannia History Readers, Introductory Book* (London: Edward Arnold, 1901), 12.

19 *Britannia History Readers, Introductory Book*, 14.

20 *Britannia History Readers, Introductory Book*, 28.

21 *Britannia History Readers, Introductory Book*, 47.

22 Philippa was the wife of the Edward III, and featured frequently in readers. Her main activity is the restraint she urged her war-tired and frustrated husband to show at the conclusion of the Siege of Calais (1346–47).

23 *Britannia History Readers, Introductory Book*, 61.

24 *Britannia History Readers, Introductory Book*, 77.

25 *Warwick History Readers*, I (London: Blackie and Son, 1895–96), 29.

26 See *Warwick History Readers*, I, 35.

27 The examples of Wallace and Joan as non-English heroes appear consistently in texts. See, for instance, *Britannia History Readers*, I, 50–2 (for Wallace), 64–7 (Joan).

28 G. Collar and C.W. Crook, *School Management and Methods of Instruction with Special Reference to Elementary Schools* (London: Macmillan and Co., 1900), 183–4.
29 Cited in S.J. Heathorn, '"Let Us Remember that We, Too, Are English": Constructions of Citizenship and National Identity in English Elementary School Reading Books, 1880–1914', *Victorian Studies*, 38:4 (1995), 416.
30 T. Raymont, *The Principles of Education* (London: Longmans, Green and Co., 1904), 141.
31 See, for instance, *Kindergarten Action Songs* (1891) and *The Red Men of the Dusk* (1899).
32 M. Crouch, *Treasure Seekers and Borrowers: Children's Books in Britain, c. 1900–1960* (London: Library Association, 1962), 40. Finnemore's wide contribution to A. & C. Black's 'Peeps at Other Lands Series' is indicative. He contributed (among others): *France* (1907); *Italy* (1908); *Switzerland* (1909); *Japan* (1910); *Morocco* (1910); *Holland* (1912); *America* (1912); *Germany* (1913); *India* (1913); and *The Holy Land* (1925).
33 Eric Quayle, *The Collector's Book of Boys Stories* (London: Studio Vista, 1973), 124.
34 Martin Green, *Dreams of Adventure, Deeds of Empire* (London: Routledge, 1980).
35 J.D. Newth, *Adam and Charles Black, 1807–1957: Some Chapters in the History of a Publishing House* (London: A. & C. Black, 1957), 82.
36 J. Welton, *Principles and Methods of Teaching*, second edition (London: University Tutorial Press, 1909), 272, 236.
37 C.H.K. Marten, 'The Teaching of Economic History in Schools', *Economic History Review*, 1:2 (1928), 204.
38 For the youngest, *Social Life in England* (1902) and *Black's Story of the English People* (1905). For the slightly older, *Famous Englishmen* (1901) and for higher grades *Men of Renown: King Alfred to Lord Roberts* (1902). Finnemore also wrote for other publishers. His text, *Children of Empire* (1905) was a supplement for older scholars to Chambers' School Series. See also his two-volume *Boys and Girls of Other Days Told in the Form of Romance, etc.* (London: White Horse, 1898). *The Story of Robin Hood and His Merry Men* (London: A. & C. Black, 1909) is but one example of his continued forays into historical fiction.
39 Quayle, *The Collector's Book of Boys Stories*, 124.
40 J. Finnemore, *Famous Englishmen*, I (London: A. & C. Black, 1901), 3.
41 Porter, *Absent-Minded Imperialists*, 174.
42 *Cassell's Historical Course for Schools*, I (London: Cassell and Co., 1884), *Simple Outline*, 75 (my emphasis).
43 This, obviously, had slightly different connotations to the public school language of 'mucking in'. This was one of the few public school traits to be expected of the elementary schoolchild. On public schools, see J.A. Mangan, 'Social Darwinism and Upper Class Education in Late Victorian and Edwardian England', in J.A. Mangan and J. Walvin (eds), *Manliness and Masculinity: Middle-Class Masculinity in Britain and America, 1800–1940* (Manchester: Manchester University Press, 1987), 135–59.
44 Finnemore, *Famous Englishmen*, I, 5.
45 *Britannia History Readers, Introductory Book*, 121–4.
46 *The Newbery Historical Readers* (Oscar Browning), II (London: Griffith, Farran and Co., 1893), 57.
47 *King Edward History Readers*, IV, *The Evolutionary History of England* (London: Isaac Pitman and Sons, 1902), 119.
48 *Raleigh History Readers*, IV (London: Blackie and Son, 1896–98), 96. Cited in Heathorn, '"Let Us Remember that We, Too, Are English"', 407.
49 Finnemore, *Men of Renown*, I, 2–3.
50 *The Newbery Historical Readers*, II, 78.
51 *Longman's Ship Historical Readers*, II, 116.
52 Finnemore, *Black's Story of the English People*, II, 122, 124.

53 John MacKenzie, *Propaganda and Empire: The Manipulation of British Public Opinion* (Manchester: Manchester University Press, 1984), 175; Olive Shropshire, *The Teaching of History in English Schools* (New York: Teachers' College, 1936), 21.
54 *King Edward History Readers*, II, 89–90.
55 A. Hassall, *The Making of the British Empire* (London: Blackie and Son, 1896), 49–50; 50–1.
56 H. Ince and J. Gilbert, *Outlines of English History* (London: W.B. Clive, 1906), 111.
57 D. Morris, *Class Book of English History* (London: Longmans, Green and Co., 1902), 429.
58 Ince and Gilbert, *Outlines of English History*, 118.
59 Hassall, *Making of the British Empire*, 118.
60 *King Edward History Readers*, II, 97.
61 *Britannia History Readers*, I, 126.
62 *King Alfred Readers*, III (London: Edward Arnold, 1900), 43.
63 See, for example, *Britannia History Readers*, I, 128.
64 *King Edward History Readers*, II, 99.
65 J. Rose, 'Willingly to School: The Working-Class Response to Elementary Education in Britain, 1875–1918', *Journal of British Studies*, 32 (1993), 114–38.
66 *Britannia History Readers*, I, 129.
67 Finnemore, *Story of the English People*, I, 130.
68 *Longman's Ship Historical Readers*, II, 83.
69 *King Edward History Readers*, II, 107.
70 *King Edward History Readers*, II, 108–10.
71 *King Edward History Readers*, II, 88.
72 On the treatment of Gordon's death, more specifically, see: Douglas Johnson, 'The Death of Gordon: A Victorian Myth', *Journal of Imperial and Commonwealth History*, 10 (1982), 185–310; Brook Miller, 'Our Abdiel: The British Press and the Lionisation of "Chinese" Gordon', *Nineteenth Century Prose*, 32:2 (2005), 127–53; John Wolffe, *Great Deaths: Grieving, Religion, and Nationhood in Victorian and Edwardian Britain* (Oxford: Oxford University Press, 2000), especially Chapter Five, 'Martyrs of Empire'.
73 *Longman's Ship Historical Readers*, II, 111.
74 *Chambers' Alternative History Readers*, IV (London: Chambers, 1898), 160; Stephen Heathorn, *For Home, Country and Race: Constructing Gender, Class and Englishness in the Elementary School, 1880–1914* (Toronto: University of Toronto Press, 2000), 50.
75 Heathorn, *For Home, Country and Race*, 54.
76 *Britannia History Readers*, II, 232.
77 *Britannia History Readers, Introductory Book*, 136.
78 *Britannia History Readers*, II, 225.
79 This notion has been applied to education of working-class girls in a short article by Anna Davin, '"Mind That You Do as You Are Told": Reading Books for Board School Girls, 1870–1902', *Feminist Review*, 3 (1979), 89–98. For middle-class girls, see Carol Dyhouse, 'Social Darwinistic Ideas and the Development of Women's Education, 1880–1920', *History of Education*, 5:1 (1976), 41–58.
80 To name but a few of the studies on female education: Jane Lewis, 'The Working Class Wife and Mother', in Lewis (ed.), *Labour of Love: Women's Experience of Home and Family, 1850–1940* (Oxford: Blackwell, 1986), 99–120; Annmarie Turnball, 'Learning Her Womanly Work: The Elementary School Curriculum, 1870–1914', in Felicity Hunt (ed.), *Lessons for Life: The Schooling of Girls and Women, 1850–1959* (Oxford: Blackwell, 1987), 83–100; and Felicity Hunt, *Gender and Policy in English Education, 1902–44* (Hemel Hempstead: Harvester Wheatsheaf, 1991).
81 This section owes a significant debt to Heathorn's analysis. See Heathorn, *For Home, Country and Race*, 141–76, for a more detailed reading of gender and the

domestication of imperial ideology. My emphasis is on explaining the incorporation of female role models as pedagogical technique.
82 *Longman's Ship Historical Readers*, II, 101–2.
83 Hugh Cunningham, *Grace Darling: Victorian Heroine* (London: Hambledon Press, 2007) and personal communication.
84 *Longman's Ship Historical Readers*, II, 101–2.
85 This observation echoes that made by Jacky Bratton in her analysis of juvenile adventure fiction that featured female protagonists. Jacky Bratton, 'Imperialism and the Reproduction of Femininity', in J. Richards (ed.), *Imperialism and Juvenile Literature* (Manchester: Manchester University Press, 1989), 195–215.
86 *Britannia History Readers, Introductory Book*, 144.
87 *Britannia History Readers, Introductory Book*, 49. Of the 'cross' at Charing Cross, 'It is not there now, but a model of it has been set up on the place where it stood', 49.
88 See Chapter Three.
89 Cowham, *A New School Method*, 343.
90 *Holborn Historical Readers*, I (London: Educational Supply Association, 1900), 105–7.
91 *Britannia History Readers, Introductory Book*, 18.
92 *Longman's Ship Historical Readers*, I, 47–8.
93 *The Newbery Historical Readers*, I, 39.
94 It is interesting to note the ways in which Alfred was politicised in Victorian debates about working-class education. See Joanne Parker, *England's Darling: The Victorian Cult of Alfred the Great* (Manchester: Manchester University Press, 2007), 137–42.
95 *Cassell's Historical Course for Schools*, I, 9.
96 *Raleigh History Readers*, IV, 24.
97 Graham Dawson, *Soldier Heroes: British Adventure, Empire and the Imagining of Masculinities* (London: Routledge, 1994), 11.
98 Quoted in Heathorn, *For Home, Country and Race*, 157.
99 Norman Vance, 'The Ideal of Manliness', in Brian Simon and Ian Bradley (eds), *The Victorian Public School* (London: Gill and Macmillan, 1975), 115–28; Kelly Boyd, *Manliness and the Boys' Story Paper*, 46.
100 Kelly Boyd, *Manliness and the Boys' Story Paper*, 45–69.
101 Anne McClintock, *Imperial Leather: Race, Gender and Sexuality in the Colonial Contest* (London: Routledge, 1995), 45.
102 Jan Jindy Pettman, 'Boundary Politics: Women, Nationalism and Danger', in Mary Maynard and June Purvis (eds), *New Frontiers in Women's Studies: Knowledge, Identity and Nationalism* (London: Taylor and Francis, 1996), 187.
103 McClintock, *Imperial Leather*, 28–30.
104 *King Edward History Readers*, I, 64.
105 *King Edward History Readers*, I, 89, 108.
106 *King Edward History Readers*, I, 48.
107 T. Nairn, *Faces of Nationalism: Janus Revisited* (London: Verso, 1997), 340.

CHAPTER SIX

History in war and peace

> I distinguish very sharply in my mind patriotism from nationalism. Patriotism is an essential constituent of the gift of historical thinking. It is a principle, not only reasonable and elevating in itself, but also possessing a power of sympathy and understanding which makes it an influence, not of international strife, but of mutual understanding between peoples.[1]

When the First World War began, few would have foreseen a four-year conflict which would claim the lives of millions; nor could many have anticipated the complete sundering of society to the war effort. On some interpretations, many thousands of volunteers, convinced by the 'over by Christmas' slogan, went to combat in the expectation of adventure and the pursuit of personal heroism and self-sacrifice, their enthusiasm fuelled by a blaze of nationalist emotion stoked by imperial propaganda. For many 'the Empire was not only something to die for', argues W.J. Reader, 'it was an ideal to live for'.[2] The Hackney shoemaker Arthur Newton recalled that the 'population of the country had been schooled in the glories of the British Empire and the deeds of her victorious armies'.[3] If the evidence of Newton's autobiography is universal, such an explanation might carry weight. Other scholars, with good reason, have been more circumspect. The evidence for why so many enlisted does not adequately support the supposition that imperial propaganda in general, let alone nationalism in the teaching of history in particular, played such a crucial role.[4] The average child had left compulsory education by the age of twelve and influences of the world beyond school, be that work, leisure or family life, would likelier have made a more direct impact on the decision to enlist.

Contemporary observers, writing in the 1920s, however, seemed in little doubt. The fostering of nationalism, especially in schools, was to be held directly accountable for the outpouring of patriotic emotion witnessed in the war years.[5] The Earl of Meath (about whom we heard in Chapter One), founder of Empire Day, claimed his movement was to be thanked for British military success:

> evidently, then, a large proportion of those young men from all parts of the Empire, who Rushed to the Colours during the bloody years from 1914, must have learnt at school the watch-words of the Movement. Would they have answered their country's call so readily if they had not acquired in their early years a knowledge of the obligations of free citizenship? We may claim that the movement was not without effect on the successful prosecution of the world war in defence of liberty and justice.[6]

Others, as will be seen, concurred with his general conclusion about the pervasive nature of pre-war nationalism. However, instead of feeling pride, they recoiled in horror. Noble sentiments of patriotism had been usurped by the worst excesses of animalist jingoism. The need for many in the 1920s was to rid society of its xenophobia and to promote international understanding so that such an event could never recur.

Before the war, educationists had fought to choke off imperialists' demand to use school history to foster overt nationalism through promotion of extreme pride in empire. Enlightened patriotism was preferred. Following the war, however, pressure was exerted to teach European and world history rather than focus on English history alone. This reopened debates about the relationship between the teaching of history, especially imperial history, and citizenship education. If enlightened patriotism had been the key phrase for educationists before the war, since it combined healthy pride in the national past and promoted the willingness to serve the collective as dutiful subject, then the war necessitated renewed discussion in order to clarify this relationship. This was the key point made by Charles Grant Robertson, Vice Chancellor of Birmingham, in his Creighton Lecture at the London School of Economics in 1928: 'we all, I presume, know what history is; but what is citizenship? If this is an absurd question to ask, the answer ought to be obvious and easy. Yet is it?' Despite this lack of clarity, as Robertson continued, teachers and educationists were 'instructed with monotonous regularity, by laymen even more than professional experts, that the chief function of and end of education from the nursery school and the home to the University is to produce good citizens'.[7] Educationists were not confused about the desired relationship between the teaching of history and citizenship. Citizenship, for them, was to remain the dutiful role played by the individual in the promotion of national wellbeing. The teaching of historical stories remained the best means to achieve that end.

HISTORY IN WAR AND PEACE

This chapter serves three purposes. First, it demonstrates the continuation of pre-war methods and rationales for state primary schools. Although imperialists continued to demand a more explicit teaching of content which would boost pride in empire, there was no immediately discernible shift to syllabi – especially for younger children. Second, it considers the challenge of internationalism which meant, if anything, that by the mid-1920s, the demand to teach imperial *values* as well as content became even more explicit. Third, however, it examines arguments for the teaching of empire that were different from those proposed in the 1880s and 1890s. Public anxieties about militarism, with memories of war freshly to mind, had to be taken into account. The terrain of imperial studies was widened in the 1920s, yet the teaching of history through sympathetic engagement with past characters persisted and became the vital ingredient in inculcating citizenship beyond the elementary school. Much greater emphasis, then, was placed on the teaching of a context-sensitive enlightened patriotism.

Continuity of practice

Much has been written on the effect of the First World War on the public school system (and vice versa),[8] but less analysis has been given to how the war helped to identify both the value of elementary schools and the need for their improvement: to their buildings, educational provision and the quality of teacher training.[9] The Board of Education announced in 1917 that the war had 'brought a clearer and wider recognition of the value of education, and, while showing the defects and short-comings of our system, has produced the resolution to improve it'.[10] Pressures of war, however, obviated reform of education. Absenteeism soared, as was to be expected, and local authorities refused to prosecute parents – often mothers – for their children's non-attendance: after all, child labour in agriculture had by 1916 been deemed an essential component of the domestic war effort.[11] One estimate suggests 600,000 children were taken out of schooling. Male teachers were expected to volunteer, to the extent that by 1918 the number of men in training colleges was less than 10 per cent of what it had been in 1914.[12] Buildings themselves were requisitioned for military use, and it was not uncommon for children to share playgrounds and toilets with billeted soldiers. Ordinary syllabi were cancelled as schools put children to work as urban gardeners, fruit pickers and textiles manufacturers: needlework became a national priority and boys were trained in elementary metal- and woodwork.[13] Spending on education was slashed by a third during the war, which meant an effective 'ban on the introduction of new schemes'.[14] Under such circumstances, it is entirely understandable that the 1918 Education Act did not institute any fundamental reforms to syllabi. Nor is it surprising that the Board recommended the continuation of pre-war methods.[15]

As a result, Herbartian influences continued to shape both the content of primary school texts and the educational objects underpinning historical education. The teaching of tub-thumping imperial history remained a hazy subject, not in the least because of the war; yet imperial values derived from storytelling remained of central importance for the curricular delivery of civic values. Children who studied in state primary schools continued to read from historical stories. The compulsory leaving age was set at fourteen as a result of the Education Act of 1918. At age eleven, some children transferred to the secondary system. Both these, and those who stayed in elementary school, would continue to read in their two hours per week of compulsory history teaching, from primers specially designed for children their age. From fourteen years of age, children would be introduced to textbooks and from sixteen, specialist texts set for preparation for examinations. Moreover, the Board decided that there would be no examinations in history *until* the age of sixteen. Teachers were encouraged to continue to use history to draw out civic lessons in order to ensure history remained 'pre-eminently an instrument of moral training'.[16]

Up to the age of fourteen, the syllabus should be 'built around the stories of the great men and women of the past', which could range from prehistory to the present day: so confirmed several reports commissioned by the Board of Education in 1928 on the condition of history teaching in London's schools.[17] Emphasis on the teaching of moral biography was not controversial. Whether or not to include more imperial history, however, was a hotly contested topic. The content of late Victorian and Edwardian imperial history, specifically, remained in suggestions for older scholars. Specific examinations in imperial history were set for the first time for the small minority who remained in school post-sixteen.[18] For children between eleven and fourteen, the Board had reasoned in its 1924 report that stories from English history should lead up to nineteenth-century empire, which it justified as important since 'the study of Empire is not merely a school of patriotism but even an inspiring and ennobling theme'.[19] C.H.K. Marten was unsure, given the paucity of time and resources available, how all the Board's prescriptions could be included (he wondered, mischievously, if the Board might like to make some suggestions).[20] The Board, in fact, had only repeated its advice of 1908. Despite pressure from propagandists, it was especially keen *not* to advise on the teaching of colonial history. As B.J. Elliot neatly explains, the debate about the purpose of historical education had, by the early 1920s, 'resolved itself into a tug of war between the "horrors of war" school and those with a patriotic pride in the navy, the army and the unity of Empire'.[21] Had the Board heeded calls for the teaching of world history (effectively, international relations), it would have been held to account for its lack of national pride; certainly not an accusation any agency of government was willing to face in the aftermath of war. Had the Board ratified the compulsory teaching of imperial triumphalism,[22] then that too would have led to criticism.[23] Hence the Board compromised and the only prescriptive element for younger scholars, beyond vague pre-war suggestions, was its proposal to incorporate more naval history and to teach the navy's 'connection with the building up of the Empire'.[24]

John MacKenzie informs us that many pre-war textbooks which incorporated imperial history remained in use until after the Second World War.[25] Frank Glendenning's thesis confirms that many of those textbooks noticeable for their inclusion of prejudicial representations of colonial subjects remained commonplace into the 1950s.[26] Kathryn Castle's study of school books and other reading material for children reveals that if there was any discernible post-war change in their emphasis on representations of other races, it was towards the promotion of favourable relations with India.[27] Texts written in the 1920s certainly reflect this: R.B. Mowat's *A New History of Great Britain* (1926) was more sympathetic to the Indian plight than pre-war textbooks and was even prepared to condemn English atrocities.[28] Moreover, texts for older scholars increasingly mimicked the prose style and methodological approach of reading books. C.S. Lucas, that propagandist historian who was furious about insufficient teaching of colonial history before and – as discussed momentarily – during the war, was specially commissioned to write the *Story of the Empire* in 1924. The text was intended first as an accompaniment for children attending the 1924 Empire Exhibition at Wembley but was later to be a general purpose resource for schools.[29] Lucas's text aped the approach of reading books. This is how he explained the growth of the English race:

> What was there in the invaders who came to tame the island and whom the island tamed? They were all, in less or more remote degree, brothers in blood, all of northern stock, Teuton, Scandinavia, Northmen moulded in France. There was the Saxon, with his sense of freedom, his instinct for self-government, rooted in freedom and the countryside. For a while he had lost his prowess on the sea, but King Alfred brought it back to life when he created a fleet to match the Danes; and when, many centuries

later, in the days of Queen Elizabeth, English Rovers harried the Spanish Main and sailed into all corners of the world, they hailed for the most part from the borderland of Saxon England, from parts of Devon. Meanwhile, what may have been wanting in the Saxon in this regard, the Danes more than made good. Baddest of seafarers, most ruthless of seafighters, they wedded the island more than ever to the sea. Close of kin with them were the Northmen who had gone raiding up the Seine, but who for a century and a half before the Conquest had in France grown from wayward infancy to man's estate, and having learnt to rule, brought that great quality and much more to swell the island's store.[30]

This extract clearly emulates both the prose style and content of reading books. It is also valuable to examine Mowat's popular text in more detail, especially so given it was a textbook for older scholars written after the war. Again, the influence of reading books is immediately apparent. Mowat eulogised heroes by concentrating on their public service and personality traits and, in doing so, drew connections between historical moments by incorporating increased coverage of Anglo-Saxon settlement. Mowat, for instance, had this to say on Wolfe: 'In his life, as in his death, he seems to anticipate the career of Nelson; like Nelson he was delicate, studious, daring, and had a rare genius'.[31] On the Anglo-Saxons, Mowat waxed:

> The Angles and Saxons were rough, strong men [who] took readily to the sea, and battled with the waves and the winds, with all the potent forces of nature, as bravely as they battled with the British tribes that stood in their way [...] We find a people faithful to their word, fond of their country, fond of their wives and children, looking upon treason and impurity as the greatest of crimes.[32]

Mowat paid similar tribute to Gordon, positioning him atop the pedestal, adopting the storytelling mode and reminding the child reader of character values ripe for emulation:

> Gordon was a man of noble, unselfish character. He was a first-class soldier, a capable practical administrator, and thoroughly honourable [...] Every boy in the land [...] knew the cool soldier who went into the thick of a fight with only a light cane in his hand, and yet brought victory everywhere to his men. And all England passionately admired the man, who fought all of his life against cruelty, corruption and spiritual ignorance, and counted his own life as nothing in the balance.[33]

David Cannadine identifies Mowat's textbook at one of the most popular, by sales statistics, of the 1920s. The most frequently used textbook for older children in secondary schools in the 1920s remained *The Groundwork of History*, first published in 1911 by G.T. Warner and C.H.K. Marten.[34] Their text was retained because schools lacked finances for new purchases. Yet, whereas Mowat's text was written after the war, and thus embodied pedagogical recommendations, Warner and Marten's textbook was lambasted for its 'traditional' preoccupation with the 'conception that history is mainly concerned with the actions of politicians and with the details of wars'.[35] Other texts written in the 1920s, as will be shown, were closer to Mowat's in both prose style and content.

The most popular set of historical reading books in use in London was Nelson's *Highroads of History*, which corresponded to pre-war models in that it incorporated pedagogical advice and emphasised moral biography.[36] Cannadine's research team have found that the *Piers Plowman* series, first published to little acclaim in 1912, became popular with the youngest children in the interwar years:[37] this is no surprise; its concentration upon everyday life made it both accessible and interesting. John Finnemore's *Social Life in England* was re-issued frequently and for the last time in 1955.[38] The format of reading books remained consistent with pre-war practice. Educationists *and* historians emphasised the fundamental importance of reading lessons, the essential value of moral biography and storytelling, and the need to evoke emotional investment in national history by focusing on 'primitive' stories. A.H. Dodd commented, in 1928, that 'historical stories' remained 'desirable', since:

> by wide reading the pupils may store up a hoard of information. These stories, historically true in substance, may sometimes be fiction [...] it is not accurate and detailed knowledge that is wanted, but an extensive acquaintance with the leading personages.

Secondary school teachers, Dodd continued, expected nothing more.[39] The view that reading books were valuable since they merged history and fantasy in a series of meaningful tales which would provoke an emotional response is clearly Herbartian. Yet, what needs noting here is the extent to which such techniques were used in the new generation of 1920s textbooks for older children.

Although explicit reference to Herbartianism had slipped out of pedagogical language, to be replaced primarily by Dewey and then Piaget in the 1940s,[40] the endurance of methods formalised under the Herbartian system in the 1890s and 1900s is striking. D.P. Dobson informed the Historical Association in 1928 of developments in educational psychology, explaining that 'psychologists tell us that each child develops, mentally as well as physically, by some type of recapitulation ... To put it baldly, a child is a primitive being, and primitive occupations appeal more to him'.[41] As A. Rogers summarised in

1962, 'educational theory and practice have altered greatly' since the state introduced compulsory history in 1902:

> Four main developments have influenced the general attitude to history. First, a better psychology of learning has resulted in vastly improved methods of instruction. Learning is based on interest and activity. Secondly (in order to base training on interest), there came that movement which might be labelled 'paedocentricity'. The child, his interests and his limitations, became central in educational theory. The effect upon the *content* of historical education was marked. Thirdly, the emphasis on the imparting of attitudes rather than facts has had a great influence upon both the content and the methods of history teaching in schools.

His fourth point was that exams in secondary schools stifled progress.[42] J.J. Findlay, advocate of Herbartianism, had made clear in a text aimed at promoting internationalism that historical stories remained 'essential to the cultivation of the civic spirit, patriotism, citizenship, devotion to public service; these terms and phrases make a great appeal, both to teachers and to the public. The state, through its offices of public instruction, has a direct interest in stimulating young people to a lively sense of national obligation and of social service'.[43] In both cases, history was best taught to children younger than fourteen through the appeal to emotions rather than to intellect.

Very few would have disagreed with this statement. Manual authors continued to be active in the field: James Welton was still writing on method well into the 1920s, John Gunn's manual was reissued in 1932 and Terence Raymont's in 1941. New manuals urged teachers to use reading books with older scholars. Charles Jarvis, teacher educator at Leeds, argued in 1917 that one reason why older scholars often found history drab owed to teachers' reluctance to use stories: children have a 'permanent interest in historical tales. When teachers in the upper part of the school fail to arouse interest in history, it is due to the fact that they have not continued the storytelling methods of the lower classes, but have troubled children with vague incomprehensible ideas'.[44] Helen Madeley (in 1920) reminded her contemporaries that the tradition of introducing children to the study of the past through fairy stories, moral biography and hero worship was commendable: 'the romance of certain human qualities [...] contains much heroic material' which provides children with a value system of how to behave and how to measure good attitude.[45] Sir Fred Clarke (in 1929) argued that 'interest in a fanciful world of fairies, of wild stories, of distant adventures in strange lands' were all very important since social concerns were the 'real and essential scheme of behaviour with which History teaching is properly concerned'.[46] The Historical Association, in a discussion in 1929 of school book content, repeated that schools 'should include those romantic tales of action which are the child's heritage from early times'.[47] This was endorsed by a London County Council memorandum on curriculum planning of 1933.[48] Such views were enshrined in texts by educationists concerned specifically with the teaching of citizenship. Eric Walker argued in 1935, 'under the plea of meeting the fustian of the public examination requirements', the teaching of history 'is frequently unimaginative and pedestrian', thus 'making little or no appeal' and failing to confer civic values.[49] M.V.C. Jeffreys's popular text promoted the 'lines of development' methodology, confirming the persistence of the race recapitulation approach which was made a core of Herbartian influence.[50]

The Handbook of Suggestions for the Consideration of Teachers and Others Concerned in the Work of Public Elementary Schools (1927) rendered explicit such methods and their desired outcome. The *Handbook* advised on lessons which make clear in 'how many ways the patriot has helped his country and by what sort of actions nations and individuals have earned the gratitude of posterity'. 'Lessons', the *Handbook* continued, 'should bring out the splendour of heroism, the worth of unselfishness and loyalty and the meanness of cruelty and cowardice'.[51] The content of reading books, unsurprisingly, remained consistent and reflected such ambition. Some were brought up to date to include the First World War itself, yet maintained the message of individual service and communal endurance. In the 1931 reissue of the *Highroads of History*, the war was introduced thus:

> In this book you have read of many wars. You are now to learn how the most terrible war of history began. Very likely your fathers or uncles fought in this war, and if so, they will show you the medals which they then won. Everywhere in this country you can see something to remind you of this Great War. You can see monuments to the brave men who fell, or guns that were captured from the enemy. Almost every grown up person can tell you stories of long, sad years when nearly all the strong young men of our race were fighting as soldiers of the King.

The text then explained German aggression and how 'we were obliged to stand by our friends'. The book concluded: 'Then began a terrible struggle in which sixteen great nations took part. It lasted fifty-two months and before it ended nine millions of men had been killed, and millions more had been crippled for life. In November 1918 Germany begged for peace, and the wretched emperor, who had ruined his country, was forced to give up his throne and flee'.[52] Such honest reflection was not uncommon: it would be impossible to teach the most recent of history without acknowledging the ravages of war. Yet what the author of this text was careful to include was comment on sacrifice, heroism and the confirmation that, when called upon, the pedestal had worked. The message was that England endured because of communal effort and collective sacrifice. The depiction of the collective war effort as part of Britain's imperial trajectory was made explicit in the conclusion of a *Headway Histories* series volume for older children:

> Our story of Britain and its Empire has now reached the days in which we are living [...] The boys and girls who read this book can find out a great deal about the events of the earlier years by asking their parents to tell them the history of those wonderful days. For their parents played an important part in the story of our race when they shared in the Great War against Germany and her allies.[53]

For, as Hensley Henson argued (quoted at the onset of this chapter), it was imperative that all history education should be geared towards an 'enlightened' and 'sympathetic' study of the past.[54]

Thus, the teaching of history remained consistent after the war. The central message of enlightened patriotism was retained as the core objective underpinning the teaching of history. Given the 'tug of war' between those who wanted to rid history education of nationalistic impulses, and those who believed not enough patriotic material was taught, it is little wonder that the Board recommended the status quo.

The challenges of internationalism

During the war, David Parker argues, the shock of wartime conditions served to reinforce tradition and 'ensure[d] that Victorian perceptions of class, place and role withstood the war unscathed [...] the war engendered a high national regard for old values'.[55] As a source of collective pride, the British empire was often the topic of patriotic rallying calls and fundraisers. The response of the colonies and dominions to the collective war effort encouraged all-embracing warmth towards the empire and gave imperialists further ammunition for the promotion of imperial enthusiasm. According to the *Times Educational Supplement*, 'before the war' the empire had sometimes 'seemed remote, unreal, too high for ordinary men and women'. Little wonder, then, that the periodical recommended schools forge an appreciation of 'the common heritage' of the empire, bestowing on them the task of establishing a 'tradition of kinship'.[56] Sarah Winfield and Marjory Harper have shown how exchange programmes for teachers and school tours became popular.[57] Parker's close study of the Hertfordshire Local

Education Authority reveals that county councillors, education committee members, local dignitaries, churches and charities urged schools to undertake greater exertions to promote patriotism through imperial pride. This bore fruit in wartime, Parker finds, in the form of a 'plethora of sermons, hymns, prayers, plays, poems, tableaux', which revealed that 'emphasis was firmly on the watchwords of the League of Empire movement: responsibility, duty, sympathy and self-sacrifice, and the rallying cry, "For God, duty and Empire"'.[58] Prior to the war (as seen in Chapter One), the Earl of Meath had failed to make compulsory Empire Day celebrations. However, under duress of war, Meath's vision was finally sanctioned by the state in 1916.[59] The London County Council reminded teachers that the day should awaken 'in the minds of the children attending the schools a true sense of the responsibilities attaching to their inheritance as children of the Empire, and the close family tie which exists among all British subjects'.[60] Its success was uneven, admittedly, but that it endured into the interwar years in the face of failures to acknowledge formal observations of an Armistice Day is indicative.[61]

The war, moreover, focused the attention of historians onto the teaching of nineteenth-century history in general and colonial history in particular. In 1916, A.F. Pollard informed the Historical Association that in some schools the teaching of English history, under the guise of the teacher-led oral lesson, had become 'inseparable' from the history of the British empire.[62] This, he explained, owed to wartime context. By December 1919, A.C. Dewar urged more teaching of naval history since, if 'history may be regarded as the memory of community', then the 'in the nineteenth century, a century of peace, large portions of society forgot the innate meaning of war and the methods essential for success in war'. If eighteenth-century naval success had been better taught before the war, the fighting mentality necessary for eventual victory would have been evident from the outset.[63] In Chapter One, Lucas was given as an example of a historian wanting more emphasis on the teaching of imperial pride. In 1916, he welcomed that war had proved to be a 'wholesome corrective' to the idea that to teach empire was to indulge 'bombast and vainglory'. The Historical Association agreed, remaining by general consensus and a show of hands at the Annual General Meeting, 'exhilarated with the imperial ideal', especially naval history.[64] Lucas anticipated an altered curriculum in which wartime trends would be inscribed in statute, especially for older boys.[65] However, he was to be disappointed in the short term. The Board of Education refused to sanction the use of history to 'encourage national animosities'. This refusal sparked serious debate – Elliot's 'tug of war'. The debate was to continue into the 1920s as the very nature of history teaching was put on trial: was the teaching of history to be held accountable for the bloodshed of war?

Mark Starr complained in 1929 that within schools 'the cult of King and Empire now noticeable appears therein as objects of conscious inculcation'.[66] He claimed that textbook writers had been infected with 'poisoned blood and feverish vision', and that the results of their endeavours were 'written in the tens of millions of casualties of 1914–18'.[67] In H.G. Wells' well-known phrase, history education was not only itself 'poisoned'; it had demonstrated its potential to poison international relations.[68] A number of comparative studies had emerged which sought to measure such assertions.[69] The emergence of these surveys came as no shock: in the atmosphere of the 1920s, many interpreted the outbreak of the First World War to be the end-result of a half-century of embittered diplomacy that had been broken down further by the rise of European nationalisms.[70] School history, it was claimed, had been the fuel for the conflagration of harmless patriotism to xenophobic jingoism and thus had paved the way for hatred and enmity to characterise relations between combatant nations.[71] The American researcher Jonathan French Scott praised the British for not having a 'State cult of patriotism' in their school system generally, and history teaching specifically (unlike Germany). He did warn, however, of 'one important force militating against the success of internationalism in British education: the Briton's belief in the essential rightness of the British Empire', and subsequently, 'his tendency to identify the welfare of the Empire with the welfare of humanity'. Scott concluded that 'John Bull cannot do his best for enduring peace as long as so many of his sons and daughters cling to this dogma'.[72] Whereas Scott worried about such an arrangement, by the late 1920s many historians and educationists were satisfied that the teaching of empire had been stripped of its militaristic bite and was aligned to the principles of enlightened patriotism.

Historians and educationists had also reflected on the teaching of nationalism, and urged reappraisal. E.L. Hasluck, in addressing the outbreak of war, argued in 1920 that teachers now realised that they should have done more to educate children in the history of other nations.[73] C.H.K. Marten confessed: 'probably most teachers will agree that the teaching of history has been in the past too narrowly national, and that it is possible, while making the history of our own island the main road, to have a good understanding and a good many interesting excursions en route'.[74] Findlay claimed in 1923 that overt patriotism needed rooting out of classrooms: 'we do not ask [the student] to cease to be a nationalist, for unless a man continue to be a good Englishman he is scarcely likely to be a good European. But *internationalist* he must be; to leave our children as ignorant as their fathers were of the state of Europe and Asia, lulled in the pride of the past and the conceited security of our exalted power, is to invite disaster'. Such a task, Findlay maintained, 'is the one contribution which the teacher through his syllabus can make towards the healing of nations'.[75] Emphasis on international history and cooperation among nations was recommended. This need not be to the detriment of teaching of colonial or naval history. Indeed, this demand was to prompt renewed attention to how the empire was explained to children. Rejection of attempts to formalise the teaching of international relations signified both continued enthusiasm for the British 'tradition' but also its revaluation.

Under the aegis of the League of Nations, the 1920s was a noteworthy decade for its degree of international textbook collaboration, the aim of which was to promote international understanding by harmonising the principles of history education.[76] This was the case among League members from both the newly formed (or re-formed) Baltic and Balkan states. It was also central to Franco-German efforts to work together to represent in their school books a balanced and equally acceptable account of the outbreak of the First World War (needless to say, this cooperation collapsed by the mid-1930s).[77] By the end of the 1920s, the League of Nations Union seemed to be enjoying considerable success not just in Europe but in Britain too. Indeed, schools were encouraged to teach about the League by the Hadow Report (1926), which recommended that 'the growing sense of interdependence of communities, as shown for example in the League of Nations, should receive due prominence'.[78] Miss H.A. Drummond argued every school should have its own branch of the League of Nations Union. By 1930 the Chief Inspector of the London County Council offered his opinion that 'reference to the inauguration of the League, to its constitution, machinery and the scope of its activities' should be taught in the final year of compulsory history education.[79] The *Handbook* of 1929 even contained a detailed history of the League for the sake of helping teachers swot up on the subject, should schools wish to teach it.[80]

The Historical Association wavered between caution and hostility. The Association, which had exercised only limited influence prior to the war, had grown in membership and influence and, by the 1920s, packed quite considerable punch.[81] Its concerns were pedagogical (even benevolent bias was worrisome) and practical (where, members worried, would League prescriptions fit into the curriculum?).[82] As one correspondent wrote to *The Times* in 1927, in response to proposals to 'internationalise' history, 'it is an old vice in idealists [...] to pervert the past in order to gain new sanctions for visions of the future. But our business as historians, or as teachers of history, is not to deal with things as they ought to have been but with what actually happened [...] a more international appreciation of history is as foolish as it is incorrect'.[83] T.F. Tout found the idea of rewriting textbooks 'from the standpoint of the League of Nations' ludicrous.[84] American observer, Olive Shropshire, lamented that the League was 'quietly ignored' in many British schools, and 'openly attacked' in many others.[85] Certainly by the 1930s any enthusiasm had waned, to the extent that the Historical Association in 1934 dismissed the teaching of the League as 'sheer propaganda'.[86] By this time of course, the League was more or less a spent force: Hitler had withdrawn Germany from the League in the 1930s, nullifying notions of European textbook cooperation. The most significant cause for why the Association took immediate umbrage, however, was that the suggested tinkering with the teaching of continuous national history would threaten to dislocate the English imperial present from its deep roots in Anglo-Saxon history.

Thus, the teaching of history up to the age of fourteen was not to vary from pre-war approaches. Before the war, the challenge was to face down those who demanded the teaching of overtly jingoistic history. Now, the challenge was twofold: to counterbalance those who demanded explicit imperial propaganda *and* those who sought the promotion of international harmony at the expense of national history. The latter challenge was considered a hazard to English traditions: it would mean radically rethinking the teaching of naval history and would raise questions about encouraging adulation of martial heroes. In doing so, it threatened to undermine the pedagogical vitality of moral biography.

Justifying empire

Bernard Porter speculates that a raft of new textbooks, which focused on modern European history and British imperial history, signalled a desire to teach in accordance with League recommendations.[87] A. Browning's *Britain as a European Power* (1922), E. Hasluck's *Short History of Modern Europe* (1923) and Arthur Innes' *Classbook of European History for Public and Secondary Schools* (1930) were specially prepared for use by older scholars. Similarly, E.A. Hughes' *Britain and Great Britain* (1919), Arthur Innes' *Classbook of the British Commonwealth* (1921) and C.S. Higham's *History of the British Empire* (1921) exemplified a trend towards the publication of textbooks for older scholars focusing specifically on Britain's colonial expansion and the contemporary empire.[88] Naturally, the inclusion of examination courses on European history, 1815–1902, and the expansion of the British empire necessitated specific texts. In addition, textbooks were less bombastic in articulating imperial zeal. This is explained by two factors: first, authors realised explicit enthusiasm was unsuited to a period which remained wary of nationalism; second, they had absorbed pedagogical lessons. In his address to the Royal Colonial Institute's textbook conference, for instance, J.C. Stobart argued that the 'temper of the times is wholly unfavourable to work of a propagandist nature'.[89] He continued that the need was 'to teach Empire, not imperialism' since overconcentration on content, and rote learning, would fail to make children 'like, even love, the idea of Empire'. Instead, Stobart advised that 'you can implant loyalties, prejudices, tendencies, in the young by appealing to their sentiments of affection and their habit of imitation'.[90] The gentler approach to teaching imperial patriotism was not atypical of pro-imperial lobby groups and organisations. As Matthew Hendley makes clear in his recent book, such groups had learnt by the 1920s that their future success depended upon sensitivity to context, especially public distaste for militarism and patriotic excess. That required both recognition of 'public mood' and adaptability to established institutions – including the education system.[91]

What these texts demonstrate is *not* that the British had forsaken its understanding of itself as the pre-eminent contemporary and historical power: on the contrary, the empire became *the* model for teaching world history and authors sought to adopt pedagogical principles which had proven popular, and effective, before the war. The Board of Education confidently asserted that the British model of imperialism was 'the only safe road to internationalism', as well as 'the only safe basis of humanitarianism'. According to Bill Marsden, a study by the British Association movement concluded that the British empire was 'the greatest secular organisation on earth', and defined the 'British type of patriotism as the surest route to promoting international citizenship'.[92] As was made clear in the Norwood report (1943), 'the history of Britain must remain the core of the history syllabus, and to that core the history of other peoples must be organically related'.[93] Pre-war pedagogical ideals thus became manifest in post-war texts geared explicitly to the teaching of empire.

Although designed for older children, this new genre of textbook merits attention, not only because they were written for older children but also because they were increasingly used as resources to assist the cramming of subject knowledge by teachers of younger children. Sentiments explaining the importance of empire were redolent within these books. T. Bevan's *The British Empire Overseas* (1930) informed that the British empire was 'nearer to perfection than any state that went before'.[94] Innes explained to children that 'British history is not the history of the British Isles but of the British Empire'.[95] Texts specifically designed to teach citizenship followed suit. H. Newland's *The Model Citizen* (1924) reiterated the central message of reading books: the empire was 'one of the marvels of the world', and 'we' owed our presently exalted position to 'the pluck, enterprise, and tact of our forefathers'.[96] Another author deliberately drew from reading books, and in his text for children entering secondary schools, wrote that the British empire was 'greater than any that have existed in the world before'.[97] Demands to teach world history prepared the way for the teaching of the specifically British experience of global history.

Clearly, educationists and historians had changed tack: when they were pressured to teach world history they did so through the lens of settlement, territorial expansion and stories of Britain's civilising mission. That required a different emphasis in how the merits of the imperial past and present were taught. Grand celebratory statements endured, but emphasis was instead placed on the British colonial history as a history of benevolent expansion. Lucas, previously so keen to celebrate the armed forces, came instead to argue that 'the Empire is very commonly held to be a misnomer, as indicating military power, domination and dependence'.[98] Stripping imperial history of its militarism did not mean failure to honour martial heroes, but rather required teaching 'the development of the Commonwealth ideal and the gift of imperial trusteeship'.[99] On the League of Nations itself, H.F.B. Wheeler mocked those that 'dream of an unpractical world-notion' and who would 'surrender the Empire in pursuance of their will-o'-the-wisp'.[100] Reading books and textbooks became aligned. F.W. Tickner's *Building the British Empire* (Volume 4 of the *Headway Histories* series, so nominally for children aged twelve to thirteen) explained: 'just as the League of Nations stands for peace in the world, so also this smaller League of British Nations stands for peace and good fellowship within the Empire, and for peace and goodwill towards all the nations of the world'.[101] The empire continued to demonstrate British power but became recast with a beneficent face. This tallied with the historiographical remodelling of imperial history as a 'moral progress'. Rather than concentrate on teaching systems of colonial administration or economic expansion, by the late 1920s imperial history taught that the British were already adept at international partnership. The contribution of colonial subjects to the war effort was sufficient evidence of the global uptake of English imperial values and commitment to righteous causes.[102]

The war had thus sharpened historians' desire for the teaching of imperial history as a means to explain contemporary context to children. Pressures exerted by those who baulked at the celebration of militarism and demanded the use of history for peace education added further incentives for historians to try their best to influence the Board of Education. They clearly had their way when it came to the official teaching of history: whereas reading books retained their emphases on moral biography, texts for older children included coverage of the expansion of the empire. Patrick Brindle's oral historical research into teachers of history who were educated in the interwar elementary schools not only suggests the continued focus on moral biography, but the retention of values even though there was no recollection of specific history lessons. Leaving the complexities of oral historical research methodology to one side,[103] a brief summary of some of the testimonies Brindle recounts is illustrative: 'We were never ever taught anything that wasn't patriotic', recalled one interviewee; 'We were taught to be proud and patriotic', remembered another. 'I left school proud of being a member of a great nation'; 'our teachers instilled in us a great love of our country', claimed others.[104] As Brindle summarises: 'For the most part, imperial history was taught and it was made up, moreover, of a common canon of character-dominated stories based around the semi-mythic adventures of heroes'.[105] It is not a surprise, therefore, that his interviewees located Alfred, Drake and Raleigh as part of the same historical trajectory as Clive, Wolfe, Nelson and Wellington. It did not matter that children did not know the intricate details of complex colonial law, the specifics of battles in Africa, or power struggles with the French in Southern India: what mattered is that younger students were taught a history, through stories, which evoked patriotic sentiments. Had these interviewees stayed in school beyond sixteen, and opted to study history as an examination subject, then the explicit content taught might well have given factual form to these abstract notions of national sentiment.

Summary

This chapter has demonstrated the persistence of pre-war teaching methods and approaches in the interwar period. If anything, the empire became much more important to those debating the aims of history teaching than it had been in the years of intense imperial propaganda before the First World War. Reading lessons, for the vast majority of the nation's children, retained their structure and their content: an approach endorsed by a Department of Science and Education Report of 1952. The authors of the report, *Teaching History*, encouraged the primary school teacher to continue 'to feed his pupils' imaginations with good stories' for the reason that, in moral biographies, 'the virtues which they esteem – skill, audacity, courage and loyalty' might be realised in the child's conduct of its life.[106] A teaching manual of 1962 was similar: 'History is traditionally first presented as story and experience endorses the soundness of this approach'.[107]

If one contrasts the teaching of empire in 1900 and 1930, the obvious conclusion is that there had been a dramatic change of attitude. In effect, however, this change of attitude was part of the continuity of teaching enlightened patriotism. As Findlay explained in 1923, 'up until 1914 the school system in Britain appeared by comparison [to the early 1920s] far less anxious to stir the hearts of children, but this apparent lack of zeal admits of a simple explanation'. The 'national sentiment' did not require explicit exegesis, or jingoistic expression, since respect for the institutions of monarchy and empire were part of the nation's 'unconscious mind'.[108] In the context of war and its aftermath, tangible form had been given to what Lord Roberts in 1911 labelled an 'immense wave of helpless incoherent patriotism striving for an outlet'.[109] That was the intention of historical reading books: to sow national sentiments, to inculcate enlightened ideals and to create a communal sense of national responsibility. This lack of explicit patriotic emotion in the years leading up to war perhaps explains J.A. Mangan's opinion that 'it was not until well after the First World War that the empire became part of the educational consciousness of the state-educated [...] imperial propaganda in British education in its earlier years [was] concerned essentially with the growing awareness of empire among public schoolboys'.[110] A search for *explicit* imperial propaganda in the conduct and content of the pre-war teaching of history, as experienced by the vast majority the nation's children, reveals much less obvious evidence of jingoistic propaganda than one might expect. That might be why Porter confidently claims that English educational culture, despite the demands of mandarins, was noticeable for its lack of immediately apparent imperial enthusiasm. Yet, if one digs a little deeper and examines pedagogical culture and the teaching of values and attitudes, then a different story emerges. The teaching of history, for the many rather than the narrow few, emphasised values, not knowledge; enlightened patriotism, not crude nationalism. These values were both civic and imperial and informed new approaches to the teaching of empire at all levels into the interwar period.

Once the post-war suggestions of the pacifist school had been rejected, foundations were therefore set for the introduction of an era of history teaching that cemented the pro-imperial island story narrative at the heart of twentieth-century history education. This was the golden age in practice, later to be cemented by grammar school teaching and systematised through the two-tier English educational system. The shift towards reliance on exam-oriented teaching of content-led curricula meant that the input of educational psychologists was gradually rendered less important in schools for older children. Yet, they retained their influence in the teaching of stories for the young. When educational theorists re-entered national debate in the 1960s, it was not to introduce something new to the teaching of history, but to once again attempt to fit historical education to contextual demands. 'New' approaches to history teaching in the 1960s and 1970s, promoted by the Schools Council, paid significant attention to methodologies of teaching.[111] The rationale of historical education was reorganised in order to make history an inquiry-led system, building on skills of sympathetic engagement and recapitulation.[112] This was the type of historical education attacked by the New Right – somewhat ironically – for its newness, novelty and its alleged disrespect for tradition.

A further incentive for radical change, however, related to the notion of relevancy to the modern child. Mary Price, in an infamous polemic, argued that the existence of history 'was in danger': unless it taught global history through a study of sources, instead of giving children a compendium of dry dusty facts about British political and diplomatic history, it faced the very real threat of being relegated from classrooms in much the same way as had been the study of Classics.[113] Martin Ballard was not alone in his endorsement of 'new' history. For him, classroom history needed to 'break out of the narrow nationalistic straitjacket in which it had lived for so long'. Change was needed, he argued, since the consensus approach to history teaching for older students in the 1950s did not, and could not, explain to the majority of children the development of the modern world.[114] In the period of its creation, therefore, the *majority* teaching of history was attuned to the contemporary requirements of citizenship and identity exactly because it embraced pedagogy. By the 1960s, however, the external context had changed. History lessons for older children focused on the same content as texts of old, but had lost the flexibility afforded by a pedagogical system which was able to match educational ambitions to the social requirements of the time.

Notes

1. H. Hensley Henson, 'The Gift of Historical Thinking', *History*, 10 (1925), 6–7.
2. W.J. Reader, *'At Duty's Call': A Study in Obsolete Patriotism* (Manchester: Manchester University Press, 1988), 56. See also Pamela Horn, 'English Elementary Education and the Growth of the Imperial Ideal', in J.A. Mangan (ed.), *Benefits Bestowed: Education and British Imperialism* (Manchester: Manchester University Press, 1988), 39–55.
3. David Cannadine, Jenny Keating and Nicola Sheldon, *The Right Kind of History: Teaching the Past in Twentieth-Century England* (Basingstoke: Palgrave, 2011), 55–6.

4 G. De Groot, *Blighty: British Society in the Era of the Great War* (London: Longman, 1996), 36–53; B. Porter, *The Absent-Minded Imperialists: What the British Really Thought about Empire* (Oxford: Oxford University Press, 2004), 260. F.M.L. Thompson, *The Rise of Respectable Society* (London: Fontana, 1988), 147–50. See also David Silbey, *The British Working Classes and Enthusiasm for War, 1914–16* (London: Frank Cass, 2005); Adrian Gregory, 'British "War Enthusiasm" in 1914: A Reassessment', in Gail Braybon (ed.), *Evidence, History and the Great War* (Oxford: Berghahn, 2003), 67–85.
5 See, for instance, H.E. Barnes, *The Genesis of the World War* (New York: Alfred A. Knopf, 1926). For discussion, see J.W. Langdon, *July, 1914: The Long Debate, 1918–1990* (Oxford: Berg, 1991), 26–30.
6 Cited in J. Springhall, 'Lord Meath, Youth and Empire', *Journal of Contemporary History*, 5:4 (1970), 107.
7 C.G. Robertson, *History and Citizenship: Being the Creighton Lecture* (Oxford: Clarendon Press, 1928), 3.
8 See, for instance, C.B. Otley, 'Militarism and Militarisation in the Public Schools, 1900–72', *British Journal of Sociology*, 29:3 (1978), 321–39; J.A. Mangan, '"The Grit of Our Forefathers": Invented Traditions, Propaganda and Imperialism', in J.M. MacKenzie (ed.), *Imperialism and Popular Culture* (Manchester: Manchester University Press, 1986).
9 Keith Vernon, 'Science and Technology', in S. Constantine, M. Kirby and M. Rose (eds), *The First World War in British History* (London: Edward Arnold, 1995).
10 John Stevenson, *British Society, 1914–45* (London: Allen Lane, 1984), 89–90.
11 David Parker, '"Something a Little Sterner and Stronger": World War One and the Enhancement of Bias in English Elementary Education', *Journal of Vocational Education and Training*, 52:3 (2000), 438.
12 Cannadine, Keating and Sheldon, *The Right Kind of History*, 59.
13 Parker, '"Something a Little Sterner and Stronger"', 452–3.
14 J. Greenlee, *Education and Imperial Unity, 1901–1926* (New York and London: Garland, 1987), 180.
15 De Groot, *Blighty*, 303.
16 Cannadine, Keating and Sheldon, *The Right Kind of History*, 71.
17 A.H. Dodd, 'The Selection and Provision of History Books for Elementary Schools', and J.A. White, 'The Board of Education Report on the Teaching of History in London', both in *History*, 12 (1928), 230–1.
18 B.J. Elliot, 'History Examinations at 16 and 18 Years in England and Wales between 1918 and 1939', *History of Education*, 20:2 (1991), 121.
19 Board of Education, *The Weekly Bulletin of Empire Study* (1924), 346, cited in Atsuko Mizobe, 'Nationalism and School Textbooks: A Comparative Study of Britain and Japan, 1919–1955' (unpublished PhD Dissertation, University of Lancaster, 1997), 219.
20 C.H.K. Marten, 'The Board of Education Report on the Teaching of History', *History*, 9 (1924), 33.
21 B.J. Elliot, 'An Early Failure of Curricular Reform: History Teaching in England, 1918–1940', *Journal of Educational Administration and History*, 12:2 (1980), 40.
22 For more detailed analysis of the role of imperial pressure groups during the war, see Matthew Hendley, *Organised Patriotism and the Crucible of War: Popular Imperialism in Britain, 1914–32* (Montreal: McGill Queens University Press), 67–114.
23 Elliot, 'An Early Failure of Curricular Reform', 40.
24 Board of Education, *Report on the Teaching of History* (London: Educational pamphlet, no. 37, 1923), 28, 33.
25 John MacKenzie, *Propaganda and Empire: The Manipulation of British Public Opinion* (Manchester: Manchester University Press, 1984), 193.
26 Frank Glendenning, 'The Evolution of History Teaching in British and French Schools in the Nineteenth and Twentieth Centuries, with Special Reference to

Attitudes to Race and Colonial History in History Schoolbooks' (unpublished PhD thesis, University of Keele, 1975), 58–62.
27 This would make sense in the context of India's contribution to the war effort. Children need not be told of Amritsar, however. Kathryn Castle, *Britannia's Children: Reading Colonialism through Children's Books and Magazines* (Manchester: Manchester University Press, 1996), 162–181. See also Derek Sayer, 'British Reaction to the Amritsar Massacre, 1919–1920', *Past and Present*, 131 (1991), 130–64.
28 R.B. Mowat, *A New History of Great Britain* (Oxford: Oxford University Press, 1926), 255.
29 On the Wembley Exhibition, see MacKenzie, *Propaganda and Empire*, 107–13; Trevor May, *Great Exhibitions* (Oxford: Shire, 2010), 36–41.
30 C.P. Lucas, *The Story of the Empire* (London: W. Collins Sons and Co., 1924), 10–11.
31 Mowat, *New History of Great Britain*, 503.
32 Mowat, *New History of Great Britain*, 15–16.
33 Mowat, *New History of Great Britain*, 897–8.
34 Warner and Marten, *The Groundwork of History* (London: Blackie and Son, 1911); Cannadine, Keating and Sheldon, *The Right Kind of History*, 81–3.
35 Cannadine, Keating and Sheldon, *The Right Kind of History*, 81.
36 *Highroads of History* (London: T. Nelson and Sons, 1907), including reprints in 1910, 1920, 1931.
37 Cannadine, Keating and Sheldon, *The Right Kind of History*, 81.
38 J. Finnemore, *Social Life in England*, new and revised edition (London: A. & C. Black, [1902] 1955).
39 Dodd, 'The Selection and Provision of History Books for Elementary Schools', 229.
40 D. Hamilton, 'The Pedagogic Paradox (Or, Why No Didactics in England)?' *Pedagogy, Culture and Society*, 7:1 (1999), 135–52; H. Dunkel, *Herbart and Herbartianism: An Educational Ghost Story* (Chicago: Chicago University Press, 1970), 1–10.
41 D.P. Dobson, *The Teaching of Prehistory in Schools* (London: Historical Association, leaflet no. 74, 1928), 2.
42 A. Rogers, 'Why Teach History? The Answer of Fifty Years, Part I', *Educational Review*, 14:1 (1962), 10–11.
43 J.J. Findlay, *History and its Place in Education* (London: University of London Press, 1923), 178.
44 C.H. Jarvis, *The Teaching of History* (Oxford: Clarendon, 1917), 56.
45 H. Madeley, *History as a School of Citizenship* (London: Oxford University Press, 1920), 19.
46 F. Clarke, *The Foundations of History Teaching: A Critique for Teachers* (London: Oxford University Press, 1929), 11.
47 'Courses for Study in History for Children under Eleven in Elementary Schools', *History*, 14 (June, 1929), 112.
48 T.D. Cook, 'Changing Attitudes to the Teaching of History in Schools, c. 1900–1970' (unpublished MPhil dissertation, University of Lancaster, 1970), 48.
49 Eric Walker, 'History and the Unemployed Adolescent', *History*, 20 (1935), 142–3.
50 M.V.C. Jeffreys, *History in Schools: The Study of Development* (London: Pitman, 1939).
51 Board of Education, *Handbook of Suggestions for the Consideration of Teachers and Others Concerned in the Work of Public Elementary Schools* (HMSO, 1927), 115, 39. Peter Gordon, 'The Handbook of Suggestions for Teachers: Its Origins and Evolution', *Journal of Educational Administration and History*, 17:1 (1985), 41–8.
52 *Highroads of History*, II (London: T. Nelson and Sons, 1931 edition), 139–42.
53 *Headway Histories*, IV (London: University of London Press, 1928), 141.
54 Hensley Henson, 'The Gift of Historical Thinking', 8.
55 Parker, '"Something a Little Sterner and Stronger"', 437–8.
56 Cited in Parker, '"Something a Little Sterner and Stronger"', 446–8.

57 Marjory Harper, '"Personal Contact Is Worth a Ton of Textbooks": Educational Tours of the Empire', *Journal of Imperial and Commonwealth History*, 32:3 (2004), 48–76. See also S. Winfield, 'Travelling the Empire: The "School Empire Tours" and Their Significance for Conceptual Understandings, 1927–39', *History of Education Review*, 40:1 (2011), 81–95.
58 Parker, '"Something a Little Sterner and Stronger"', 445.
59 Robin Betts, 'A Campaign for Patriotism in the Elementary School Curriculum: Lord Meath, 1892–1916', *History of Education Society Bulletin*, 46 (1990), 38–45; Porter, *Absent-Minded Imperialists*, 186–7.
60 Derek Heater, 'The History of Citizenship Education in England', *Curriculum Journal*, 12:1 (2001), 118.
61 W. Marsden, '"Poisoned History": A Comparative Study of Nationalism, Propaganda and the Treatment of War and Peace in the Late Nineteenth and Early Twentieth-Century School Curriculum', *History of Education*, 29:1 (2000), 43; Springhall, 'Lord Meath, Youth and Empire', 105–6. The definitive recent study of Empire Day is Jim English, 'Empire Day in Britain, 1904–58', *The Historical Journal*, 49:1 (2006), 247–76.
62 A.F. Pollard, 'The Teaching of Imperial History', in *Report of the Proceedings of the Tenth Annual Meeting of the Historical Association* (London: Historical Association, leaflet no. 41, 1916), 11.
63 A.C. Dewar, 'The Need of Naval History', *History*, 4 (1919), 198.
64 Elliot, 'An Early Failure of Curricular Reform', 40. See also the various contributions to E.C. Martin (ed.), *Imperial Studies in Education: Papers Read at the Imperial Studies Conference Held at Wembley, 26th, 28th, 29th May, 1924, and Published under the Auspices of the Royal Colonial Institute* (London: Sir Isaac Pitman and Sons Ltd, 1924).
65 C.P. Lucas, 'On the Teaching of Imperial History', *History*, 1 (1916), 5.
66 Mark Starr, *Lies and Hate in Education* (London: Leonard and Virginia Woolf, 1929), 5.
67 Starr, *Lies and Hate in Education*, 61.
68 Discussed at length by William Marsden, '"Poisoned History"', 29–47.
69 See S.H. Bailey, *International Studies in Modern Education* (Oxford: Oxford University Press, 1938) and especially Jonathan French Scott, *The Menace of Nationalism in Education* (London: Allen and Unwin, 1926).
70 David Lloyd George's famous dictum that 'nations had slithered over the brink and into the boiling cauldron of war', although not necessarily a consensus opinion, appeared to resonate with many by the mid-1920s. Hartmut Pogge von Strandmann, 'Germany and the Coming of War', in R.J.W. Evans and H. Pogge von Strandmann (eds), *The Coming of the First World War* (Oxford: Clarendon, 1988), 95; Annike Mombauer, *The Origins of the First World War: Controversy and Consensus* (London: Longman, 2002).
71 See, V.R. Berghahn and H. Schissler (eds), *Perceptions of History: An Analysis of School Textbooks* (Oxford: Berg, 1987), especially their introductory chapter 'Introduction: History Textbooks and Perceptions of the Past', 1–16.
72 French Scott, *The Menace of Nationalism*, 145, 159, 160.
73 E.L. Hasluck, *The Teaching of History* (Cambridge: Cambridge University Press, 1920), 87.
74 Marten, 'Board of Education Report', 35.
75 Findlay, *History and its Place in Education*, 178.
76 B.J. Elliot, 'The League of Nations Union and History Teaching in England: A Study in Benevolent Bias?' *History of Education*, 6 (1977), 137–46.
77 Bernadotte E. Schmitt, '"War Guilt" in France and Germany: Resolutions Adopted by a Committee of French and German Historians for the Improvement of Textbooks in Both Countries', *American Historical Review* (January, 1938), 321–41.
78 Elliot, 'The League of Nations Union and History Teaching in England', 134.
79 Elliot, 'The League of Nations Union and History Teaching in England', 134–5. On the League of Nations Union more generally, see Helen McCarthy, 'The League

of Nations, Public Ritual and National Identity in Britain, c. 1919–56', *History Workshop Journal*, 70 (2010), 109–33.
80 Cook, 'Changing Attitudes', 32.
81 Keith Robbins, '*History*, the Historical Association and the National Past', *History*, 66 (1981), 412–25.
82 Elliot, 'The League of Nations Union and History Teaching in England', 137
83 Elliot, 'The League of Nations Union and History Teaching in England', 137
84 T.F. Tout, 'The Middle Ages in the Teaching of History', *History*, 8 (1923), 4.
85 Olive Shropshire, *The Teaching of History in English Schools* (New York: Teachers' College, 1936), 85.
86 C.H.K. Marten, *On the Teaching of History and Other Addresses* (Oxford: Basil Blackwell, 1938), 54–5.
87 Porter, *Absent-Minded Imperialists*, 260–3.
88 Cited in Porter, *Absent-Minded Imperialists*, 260.
89 J.C. Stobart, 'The Child: The Empire', *The Royal Colonial Institute Journal*, 16:3 (1925), 175–6. For more, see Greenlee, *Education and Imperial Unity*, 196–7.
90 Stobart, 'The Child: The Empire', 175–6.
91 Hendley, *Organised Patriotism and the Crucible of War*, 214, 114.
92 Marsden, '"Poisoned History"', 34.
93 For discussion, see Cook, 'Changing Attitudes', 71.
94 T. Bevan, *The British Empire Overseas: Historical and Geographical* (London: Sampson, Low, Marston and Company, 1930), 1.
95 Cited in Porter, *Absent-Minded Imperialists*, 260.
96 H.O. Newland, *The Model Citizen* (London: Sir Isaac Pitman and Sons, 1924), 2, 277.
97 R. Wilson, *The Complete Citizen: An Introduction to the Study of Civics* (London: J.M. Dent and Sons, 1920), 215. On these, and others, see W. Marsden, *The School Textbook: Geography, History and Social Studies* (London: Woburn Press, 2001), 155–7.
98 Cited in Porter, *Absent-Minded Imperialists*, 275.
99 G.W. Morris and L.S. Wood, *The English-Speaking Nations* (Oxford: Clarendon, 1924). For discussion of this, and other texts which embraced 'commonwealth' over militaristic empire, see Porter, *Absent-Minded Imperialists*, 275.
100 H.F.B. Wheeler, *Makers of the British Empire* (London: George Harrap and Co., 1927), 7–8.
101 F.W. Tickner, *Building the British Empire*, cited in Porter, *Absent-Minded Imperialists*, 277.
102 J.H. Grainger, *Patriotisms: Britain 1900–1939* (London: Routledge and Kegan Paul, 1986), 323–8.
103 On this, *apropos* the history of education specifically, see the excellent synthesis of theory in Phil Gardner, 'Oral History in Education: Teacher's Memory and Teachers' History', *History of Education*, 32:2 (2003), 175–88.
104 Quoted from Patrick Brindle, 'Past Histories: History and the Elementary School Classroom in Early 20th-Century England' (unpublished PhD thesis, University of Cambridge, 1999), 210–11.
105 Brindle, 'Past Histories', 209.
106 Cook, 'Changing Attitudes', 113.
107 A.K. Davies, 'Syllabus Construction in the Junior School', in W.H. Burston and C.W. Green (eds), *Handbook for History Teachers* (London: Methuen, 1962), 17.
108 Findlay, *History and its Place in Education*, 31.
109 Lord Frederick Roberts, *Fallacies and Facts* (London: John Murray, 1911), 169.
110 Mangan, '"The Grit of Our Forefathers"', 116.
111 R. Aldrich, 'New History: An Historical Perspective', in A.K. Dickinson, P.J. Lee and P.J. Rogers (eds), *Learning History* (London: Heinemann Educational, 1984), 210–24.
112 Findings of a government survey were reported in the publication of the Schools Council's *Young School Leavers* (1976): these showed that the subject was losing

relevance and was considered by the majority of children to be depressing, boring and dull. The survey found that out of 9,677 girls and boys aged fifteen that had just left secondary schools, history was considered the school subject least 'useful and interesting' and the second most 'useless and dull'. See also Martin Booth's influential survey of history teaching in grammar schools and his conclusion that a radical re-evaluation of the pedagogical principles underpinning the teaching of history was required to safeguard its place in the curriculum. Schools Council, *Young School Leavers* (London: HMSO, 1968), 45; M. Booth, *History Betrayed* (London: Longman, 1973), especially 120; Schools Council 13–16 Project, *A New Look at History* (Edinburgh: Holmes MacDougal, 1976).

113 M. Price, 'History in Danger', *History*, 53 (1968), 342–7.
114 M. Ballard (ed.), *New Movements in the Study and Teaching of History* (London: Temple Smith, 1970), 5.

Conclusion

Some years ago the people of this country determined to alter the state of things. So a law was passed in Parliament by Mr Forster, one of our rulers. It provided for the education of every child, and for the making of new and good school-houses [. . .] Schoolchildren are now taught, not only reading and writing, but the history of their own land, much about other lands, and many other useful things. As our country has done so much for its little citizens, they ought to pay great attention to their teachers, to attend school regularly, and to learn their lessons carefully. Thus, they will grow up to be wise and happy men and women. They will be able to do good to their fellow-countrymen, and they will be honoured by them.[1]

Stories of collective national progress placed children, in their schools, as the direct inheritors of the national past. Contemporary provision of elementary education, children were told, was but one example of how the nation had improved over time. In keeping with Herbartian recommendations to encourage children to understand national progress by comparing the present to the past, authors informed children that they could be good citizens by doing their best at school. Finnemore, for instance, urged his child readers to be grateful since in the past 'people had not learnt that education is the most important thing in the world, and the greatest attention must be paid to it, if a nation is not to lose its place among other nations'.[2] Such explicit lessons were intended to attach the child's dedication to its schooling to the national wellbeing. Even more explicitly, the author of the *Warwick History Readers* reminded children that unlike in the past when 'boys and girls did not learn to read and write [. . .] we can learn now far more things than boys and girls could learn then'. That was 'because many wise men have lived since then, and have found out how to do things. But we must not forget that there are some lessons now, which are just the same as they were then. These lessons are the best of all, for they teach us how to be good, brave and true'.³ Statements such as these remind us that the primary objective underpinning history teaching in elementary schools was to encourage dutiful conduct. The reward for their devotion, as expressed through collective pride in a shared history, was communal happiness in the present. As one reading book of 1884 concluded:

> thus we now live in peace and prosperity under the rule of our gracious Queen. But we should never forget that it has been through the labours and suffering of many good and brave men that a country which began as ours did, is now one of the happiest in the world.⁴

As has been demonstrated, children were encouraged to recognise that as the English nation advanced over time English people inherited more rights, responsibilities and privileges (including schooling). Children were told, in no uncertain terms, that they were expected to be good citizens. Part of this included their self-conduct in the school, but the demands of citizenship reached further. Lessons in civic values, taught in historical stories, were intended to help them understand the attitudes and characteristics they should emulate for the sake of the enduring national good. As A. Rogers was later to summarise in his assessment of the teaching of history in the first half of the twentieth century, 'good citizenship' was sought through the combination of two approaches. First, history could convey to older children the 'information necessary for the execution of the rights and duties of citizenship'. This would include the teaching of constitutional history and the machinations of national and local government for older scholars. On the other hand, Rogers emphasised that history teaching first needed to inculcate in children appropriate 'attitudes of mind, strength and character'.⁵

Educationists believed that these enlightened patriotic values would include both moral and imperial dimensions. The most commonplace teaching of history did not seek, as historiographical orthodoxy suggests, to bombard children with imperial propaganda. Instead, the aim was to present children with a series of moral lessons to be taught via biographical stories. Absence of attention to educational theory in established historiography has, I have argued, been to the detriment of a deeper understanding of the intended outcomes of historical education. The majority of past studies into the history of history teaching have concentrated on research into the subject-specific textbook; this study – in contrast – has indicated that historical reading books constitute the better sources out of which to further understand the type of history the majority of children read. These texts were written with the dual aim of providing interesting stories which prompted senti-

CONCLUSION

ments of national pride, and also, primarily, of imparting lessons in citizenship. Significantly, historical reading books – especially those written in the 1890s and after – encapsulated developments in educational psychology.

Moreover, educationists believed that historical stories were of far greater pedagogical value than textbooks and a number of reasons for this have been demonstrated. First, storytelling was thought likelier to invoke the child's emotional identification with past characters. Second, stories would better appeal to the imagination and thus provide an enhanced probability that children would internalise values. Third, these stories could activate the imagination because they especially concentrated upon the human-ness of past actors. This not only encouraged children to revere such actors, but also to want to emulate their values. Fourth, these stories adopted a narrative framework which presented the national story as one of unproblematic development: as such, children could form judgements about values and actions by comparing past and present and witnessing for themselves the extent of progress over time. This indicated, fifth, that improvements to the *national* character could be demonstrated in these texts: stories about individuals reflected the collective advancement towards the present-day standard of civilisation. Thus, such an approach was able to instruct children not only in values, but in the incremental enlargement of Englishness itself. Sixth, onto this structure could be added descriptions which explained the origins of the imperial present day as resident in the aspirations, blood and destiny of the earliest English. Finally, this approach developed out of Herbartian theories of teaching and learning. That Herbartian educational theorists emphasised an education for the transmission of moral values must not be underestimated. The dominant contemporary belief was that lessons in the national past, such as these, could exercise an effect on how children chose to conduct their lives.

Moreover, representations of the nation in which children were to be enlightened patriots emphasised the centrality of specifically English values to the acquisition and the existence of the British empire. The civic values children were exhorted to use as the framework within which to conduct their daily lives were depicted as consonant with the story of Englishness evolving and progressing over time. That mattered, first, since it tied the demands of citizenship to the requirements of national allegiance. Second, it was of crucial contemporaneous significance, because in placing a premium on the ethnic origins of the English, stories portrayed a history of the English people which was racially flexible and thus had the capacity to adapt to the needs of colonisation, and the demands of maintaining an empire. The late Victorian and Edwardian English understood themselves to be an imperial race. As a result, national identity was represented in school books as developed from the combination of a successful maritime tradition, propensity towards settling new territory, Christianity and a predisposition towards the love of liberty. In short, the primary aim of historical education was to teach citizenship or – to adopt the contemporary terminology – enlightened patriotism. These civic values, if successfully internalised and understood by children, would serve to reinforce the paradigmatic national self-understanding of the empire as part of England's manifest historical destiny. It was anticipated, thus, that the ideal student – as constructed in the educational theory of the time – should learn from the ideal historical reading lesson how to become an enlightened patriotic citizen. Moreover, this ideal student should come to view his or her own behaviour and mental attitude as an important component in the perpetuation of national greatness. The rejection of calls to teach more international content in the interwar period indicates the extent to which history's contribution towards citizenship education was perceived to be unique. After all, history's unique appeal was its potential to conjoin civic and imperial values.

The conditional clause, inserted in the above paragraph, reminds us, however, that one needs to exercise caution when considering the success of these lessons. In her critique of Stephen Heathorn's research, for instance, Gillian Sutherland suggested we need to know much more about the social history of the classroom in order to be in a better position to theorise how children negotiated their identities. Regrettably, there has not been space to undertake that project in this book. However, Heathorn, Bernard Porter and Jonathan Rose make use of autobiographical sources to search for evidence of popular uptake of imperial ideals. Their findings are inconclusive: their samples – as they recognise – are too small to be anything other than illustrative, at best.[6] That does not preclude the testimonies they cite from being of potential indicative value, however. In terms of how the empire and history teaching were recalled, a brief glimpse can be used to both confirm *and* refute the notion that children were influenced by their schooling. Rose argues that despite the extent to which everyday life was 'supersaturated with imperialist propaganda', and the myriad efforts towards 'unrelenting indoctrination', 'most working people knew little of empire and cared less'.[7] Porter provides a number of examples in the aim of reinforcing Rose's statement. He suggests that, even *if* explicit patriotism was taught, those who were educated in this period actively resisted it. 'With reference to History or Geography', Porter quotes from one of his autobiographical sources, 'I only had the haziest idea'.[8]

CONCLUSION

Another described how a socialist teacher had deliberately undermined the recommended curriculum and taught a history sympathetic to the cause of the Indians in the mid-nineteenth century, allowing him to realise 'what a load of rubbish we've been taught in the past'.[9] 'Patriotism never struck me as very clever', wrote another (who had read Tom Paine).[10] It seems, therefore, that the teaching of explicit patriotism could be seen to have exercised a negligible impact on its working-class target. Paradoxically, however, that the author rejected imperial patriotism indicates precisely that patriotism – or something like it – had been taught. In order to reject something, one must first have some awareness of what is being rejected.

Porter and Rose both comment that when schooling was reflected upon at all, literacy lessons were remembered over and above any subject-specific lessons.[11] One autobiographer noted his education 'was concentrated on reading and writing'.[12] Another reminisces, with a well-observed commentary on the intended social functions of his education (this is a London hatter named Frederick Willis): 'We were great readers of school stories', 'we thought British people were the salt of the earth' and 'the object of our education was to train us to become honest, God-fearing, useful workmen'. He continued by demonstrating his acceptance: 'I have no complaints', he writes, 'against this very sensible arrangement'.[13] Evidence such as this confirms the argument that appropriate focus should be placed on reading lessons, rather than the content of textbooks, in order better to understand the mass experience of historical education. Moreover, this lack of explicit 'knowledge', or – arguably – the active resistance to *imperial* propaganda, need not indicate that messages from reading lessons were not partially absorbed. Heathorn is therefore surely correct to emphasise that 'before symbols and narratives can be reconfigured for another purpose [...], some understanding of the original purpose is necessary'.[14] The object of reading lessons, we must remember, was not to create a blindly patriotic populace, but to recast the status quo of social life and its attendant class relationships within a civic language of belonging. Frederick had quite clearly hit the nail on the head.

He was not a lone example of someone who seems to have learnt his lessons. 'Patriotism in those days was an ideal of love and service to one's country', according to Dorothy Burnham's memoir, '[i]t did not conjure up pictures of an intolerably supercilious British Raj arrogantly wielding the big whip on cowering, depressed natives. Rather, it inspired courage, promoted unselfishness and a concern for others which overrode purely private considerations'.[15] Dorothy certainly seems to have learnt her lessons well! Another noted that she could not remember much about the content of her lessons, but was 'aware that we were exceptional because we were English'.[16] 'Schooling made no lasting impression on me', recalled another, except 'to establish that I was a freeborn Englishman and the world was my oyster'.[17] Selective as these extracts may be, they demonstrate the success of elementary schooling in moulding the world-view of some children: in these examples, they all rejected the idea that they had been indoctrinated by imperial propaganda, but they all bear witness to the internalisation of a sensation of nationhood. Thus, one could speculatively conclude from these examples that reading lessons implanted ideas of civic and national identity in children.

We must, however, remain vigilant about assuming impact. Brindle warns, tellingly, that 'if we really want to understand the nature of history teaching we need to move from the textbooks and into the classroom'.[18] That historical stories were taught as a statutory part of the compulsory reading lesson we can be certain. That the majority of the nation's children learnt to read through the use of the historical reading book is, additionally, a reasonably secure supposition. However, teachers might not have taught from historical stories according to the recommendations in teaching manuals. Even if they did, we cannot be sure that children internalised these lessons in civic values. There are many contingent factors additional to their schooling, analysis of which is beyond the scope of this study, which would be likely to have exercised an influence on how children perceived their identities. To cite but a few: their parents and family; their confidantes and playground chums; their teachers; in some cases their employers; other materials they went on to read and so on.[19] All of these would have had the potential to offer up explanations of home, community and nation that were potentially antagonistic to the messages central to reading books. This is why the focus of this study has remained closely concentrated on the question of *intent* and on representations of civic, national and imperial identities. Quite simply, we cannot be certain; we can only hypothesise that *some* identified that their schooling influenced their national identity. We can, however, make more of this question of intent.

The language of belonging

Given that texts were intended to engage the child's emotions by use of conversational prose style, it might be valuable to concentrate on the language of stories. As I read and re-read historical reading books and method manuals, it became obvious not only that the same stories recurred but that the prose style was essentially similar. Historical reading books combined to produce collective acts of reading in the classroom; however, the uniformity of their prose suggests that the classroom could represent the nation in microcosm. *All* children were subject to literacy lessons; *all* children, therefore, must have been subject to these historical stories at some time. Walker Connor argues that identity 'does not draw its sustenance from facts but from perceptions; not from chronological/factual history, but from sentient/felt history'.[20] If Connor is correct, and I find his argument compelling, then one could tentatively suggest that stories might well have influenced the child. Stories prioritised the engagement of the child's sympathetic interest. That emphasis was placed on children's emotive and imaginative relationship with the nation would *imply* a greater likelihood that these stories exercised some emotional impact on children. The representation of the nation as family, and efforts to connect the present-day child in the classroom to his or her ancestors, signifies a biological ethnicity. In this formula, otherness mattered less than 'sameness'. Indeed, to follow the work of Ruth Wodak and the Vienna School, knowing that 'we' are the same as one another is as crucial to identity formation as understanding that we are not the same as others (be those other races, other nations, or other religions.)

This sense of belonging linguistically relates to what Ruth Wodak and her colleagues describe as the 'historically expanding we'. When deployed within the framework of the 'national', 'we' relates not only to those in our immediate shared environment, but also to those with whom 'we' share national territory ('our' homeland) and national time ('our' shared history). 'We' have in common with 'our forefathers' a place in the evolving national story. One simple pronoun – 'we' – is a complex and powerful word in the English language. It encapsulates all other personal pronouns: it can, in short, be used to refer both to immediately localised settings and vague, abstract, and all-encompassing historical moments. For ease of explanation, the flexibility of 'we' is demonstrated below in list form. 'We' can be all of the following:

(a) I + you.
(b) I + he/ I + she.
(c) I + you (plural) = (I + any number of people, hereafter n).
(d) I + they (I + n multiplied by any number of she/he).
(e) I + you + he/she (I + them + they).[21]

When texts use words such as 'us', 'them', and 'they', in reference to people, the reader is discursively positioned as part of a collective. There is a welter of examples within reading books, which when applying this linguistic-analytical approach, demonstrate a discursive construction of Englishness which positioned the child reader as a part of communal unit, united in the experience of national time. It is especially evident in the following extract:

> *We* have now read the story of the English people during their life in England. *We* have seen *them* land on our shores, a race of rude, savage warriors. *We* have seen *them* grow in strength and in knowledge until *they* have become a leading nation of the world. And let *us* remember that *we*, too, are English. In our hands lies the future of our great race. Let *us* resolve to do all *we* can to uphold the fame of our country, so that fresh honours may yet be added to the story of the English People.[22]

Italicisation draws attention to the range of ways in which 'we', 'us' and 'them' feature, whereas underlined words denote both 'our' collective possessions and the historically embedded essences of Englishness. This extract highlights just how chronologically pervasive was both the national 'we' and an inclusive ownership of the national story in which 'we' have evolved, and in which 'we' will surely continue. Evident within this extract is a sense of both a language of belonging, but precisely a language rooting that belonging within a sense of national time. The 'we' in the extract 'Let us remember that we, too, are English' denotes the modern 'we': the children together; the children with their teacher in their classroom; their school; their contemporaries in and out of school; all those that they know, including family, friends and foes, heroes and others in the public spotlight; and all those they might never know, but are aware of as English. The suggestion that 'we' need to remember denotes an expansion of that 'we' back in time, so that 'we' are the same as the 'them' who made England the 'leading nation', and that it is 'our' responsibility that 'we' continue their efforts to ensure the future of 'our' race.

Brief analysis of the discursive construction of nationhood, as evidenced here, signifies that history might be understood as a series of lessons onto which projected outcomes could be mapped: it was intended that children would consider themselves the inheritors of the national past. It thus placed the child within both the instantaneous now but also the historically expanding story of the English people. Furthermore, it could be speculated that such an invocation of a time-transcending national 'we' placed responsibility onto readers to act according to their vested responsibilities. Thus, on one reading, the language of the pedestal discursively united readers within a common linguistic framework of who 'we' are and enjoined those who formed the pedestal to be prepared to act in order to maintain national progress.[23]

CONCLUSION

Discourse analysis presents itself as a precise science, yet to apply it to the past without all due consideration of past contexts of classroom-based learning requires caution. *If* the language of belonging did engender emotional identification to the nation, then the discursive intertwining of Englishness and imperialism is highly significant.

Empire and citizenship in teaching of history today

Tentative as these speculations are, we can make firm conclusions about the intent underpinning the teaching of history in its 'golden age'. Knowing that educationists did not intend historical lessons to teach knowledge, but rather values, has a significant bearing on contemporary debates. At the turn of the twentieth century, educationists were convinced that continuous national history was the essential foundation for the teaching of citizenship and national identity. Clearly, the current demand for a return to a narrative teaching of history aims also to promote an emotional identification to the nation. In order to evoke collective identity, it is presumed that an uncomplicated history needs to be known by all. This explains why there was such a positive response to Civitas's centenary reissue of Henrietta Marshall's *Our Island Story* (1905 [2005]). Amanda Craig, of *The Times*, lauded *Our Island Story* on the grounds that 'it is precisely the kind of old-fashioned, sequential, kings and queens, history-as-story approach which the National Curriculum has jettisoned so disastrously'.[24] Another reviewer wrote that 'the delight of *Our Island Story* lies in its emphasis on personality, in the unalloyed certainty that Britain has produced some remarkable people, and some extraordinary tales'.[25] What is noticeable here, therefore, is the identification of a golden age of history teaching which privileged exciting biographies and blended storytelling with historical certainty. Thus far, critics of modern approaches have interpreted the 'golden age' correctly. In this sense, it is possible to understand despair at the 'patch' approach used in some primary schools in which content is not taught chronologically. Where critics have misinterpreted past practice, however, is in their distrust of educational theory in general and the teaching of historical skills in particular. To them, the teaching of skills is threatening because encouraging students to evaluate sources and understand historical writing as interpretative renders received knowledge relative. Neo-conservative attempts to gain control of school history are best seen as a need to reconcile these uncertainties with a need for factual accounts out of which fixed meanings can be derived.[26] Thus, Jenkins's and Brickley's explanation of Thatcherite attacks on historical skills is equally valid today:

What Thatcherism would have liked for history was an interpretation we might call *certaintist*. Such a reading would confidently construct for Britain (especially England) a unique and pioneering historical journey from which traditional (natural) values, liberties and freedoms have evolved [...] together with invocations of overriding solidarities: the people, the nation, patriotism, in order to curb any excesses such notions as liberty and freedom may suggest. Cautious, empirical in its mode of enquiry; factual and knowledge led; anti-intellectual in its distrust of theories so British history would act as the privileged centre and yardstick around which all other histories would revolve and be judged. Champion of free trade, Thatcher would close down the market-place of competing historical commodities (interpretations) erecting just one stall from which everyone would purchase authorised historical products all stamped with the legend 'Made in Britain' or, better still, 'Made in England'.[27]

Consumer histories needed to be tempered by an *official* history for the nation: this was to be the standard by which other histories could be judged.

The advance of social history in the 1960s, which found form in School's History Project syllabi, contributed to the fracturing of grand narratives. New British history, in recognising past dominance of the English pitch in the British voice, similarly played a part in the dismantling of historical certainties out of which comforting assurances of belonging had been drawn.[28] There is now no longer one unified History with a capital H; rather, there is a multiplicity of histories. The variety of theoretical approaches to the study of British history in universities, including British imperial relations, has further complicated the teaching of history in schools. At the turn of the twentieth century, focus was on how the shared past could be mobilised for the promotion of collective national identity. It was not paradoxical to warn against the teaching of jingoism, but still hail the empire a cause for collective celebration. Relative academic agreement, *then*, on the Englishness of imperial origins contributed to a majority of history teaching which untied Englishness and imperialism. The intent, *then*, was to use historical stories to produce loyal and obedient citizens, proud of their nation and its history, keen to contribute to its continued wellbeing and actively aware of the requirements and rewards of citizenship.

In her Millennium Lecture, Linda Colley differentiated between citizenship ('which is political and functional') and identity ('which is more ancestral and visceral') in her definition of twenty-first-century Britishness.[29] In doing so, she recognised that history could no longer provide the emotional glue that tied a nation together through collec-

CONCLUSION

tive memory. History had the potential to rupture as well as unify. The introduction of discrete lessons in 'Education for Citizenship' in September 2002, with emphasis on moral behaviour as well as political literacy, was an attempt to convey civic pride because history teaching could no longer provide a consensual narrative of shared memory. For that reason, Colley argued that 'modern' allegiance should be to the political state rather than to collective history. Little wonder that the current government, and their forbears in the 1980s, sought to create a state-sanctioned curriculum for history: the crisis of national identity requires the creation of historical certainty as the first ingredient in the renewal of nostalgic patriotism. However, Britain is no longer an empire; and England no longer dominates the United Kingdom union in the way it once did. Rather than take collective comfort in the imperial possession, as was possible before, the English now face a set of moral dilemmas about engaging with that past. Should the shadier aspects of English history be taught? How can a continuous history of the English be taught which pays due attention and respect to other nations, races and religions? Can history still be used to convey lessons in civic and national pride? Should history be used to such an end?

These questions barely scratch at the surface of what is a vivid and ongoing debate. However, there is one aspect of this 'golden age' of historical education which needs to be emphasised since it is absent in assumptions about the traditional teaching of history. Educational theorists played a pivotal role in shaping a curriculum oriented to teach values rather than knowledge. *If* children did learn their lessons, they would be aware that one of the central parts of their nation's story was its ability to absorb, intermix and interact with other races. Although our twenty-first-century context is significantly different from a century ago, such a model might be made appropriate for today. There is no reason why such a model, in which the history to be taught is chronologically arranged and exciting, should not be considered. Children could learn stories of how the English (or British) met and engaged with others. Children could be taught about the positives and negatives of England's past relationships not only with other Britons but with Europeans and the peoples of the world writ-large. Such a proposal would require serious thought about syllabus design. Such a proposal would, moreover, be politically contentious – of that there can be no doubt. It would almost certainly need to draw on the expertise of professionals: academic historians, educationists and teachers. Nonetheless, what premium *now*, I wonder, on the teaching of a context-sensitive, and values-oriented, enlightened patriotism?

Notes

1 *Chambers' Historical Readers*, I (London and Edinburgh: Chambers, 1882), 149–50.
2 John Finnemore, *Black's School Series: Black's Story of the English People* (London: A. & C. Black, 1905), 146.
3 *Warwick History Readers*, I (London: Blackie and Son, 1895–96), 8–9.
4 *Chambers' Historical Readers*, I, 112.
5 A. Rogers, 'Why Teach History? The Answer of Fifty Years, Part I', *Educational Review*, 14:1 (1962), 14.
6 Bernard Porter, *The Absent-Minded Imperialists: What the British Really Thought about Empire* (Oxford: Oxford University Press, 2004), 199–203; Stephen Heathorn, *For Home, Country and Race: Constructing Gender, Class and Englishness in the Elementary School, 1880–1914* (Toronto: Toronto University Press, 2000), 212–18; Jonathan Rose, *The Intellectual Life of the British Working Classes* (New Haven and London: Yale University Press, 2001).
7 Rose, *Intellectual Life*, 322.
8 Porter, *Absent-Minded Imperialists*, 201.
9 Porter, *Absent-Minded Imperialists*, 201.
10 Porter, *Absent-Minded Imperialists*, 201.
11 Rose, *Intellectual Life*, 322–3; Porter, *Absent-Minded Imperialists*, 200–1.
12 Porter, *Absent-Minded Imperialists*, 201.
13 Rose, *Intellectual Life*, 323.
14 Heathorn, *For Home, Country and Race*, 217.
15 Cited in Rose, *Intellectual Life*, 240.
16 Cited in Rose, *Intellectual Life*, 240.
17 Cited in Rose, *Intellectual Life*, 240.
18 Patrick Brindle, 'Mr Chips with Everything', *History Today*, 46:6 (1996), 14.
19 J. Springhall, 'Building Character in the British Boy: The Attempt to Extend Christian Manliness to Working-Class Adolescents, 1880 to 1914', in J.A. Mangan and J. Walvin (eds), *Manliness and Morality. Middle-Class Masculinity in Britain and America, 1800–1940* (Manchester: Manchester University Press, 1987), 52–74.
20 Walker Connor, 'The Timelessness of Nations', *Nations and Nationalism*, 10:1–2 (2004), 45.
21 Adapted from R. Wodak, R. de Cillia, M. Reisigl and K. Liebhardt, 'The Discursive Construction of National Identities', *Discourse and Society* 10:2 (1999), 164–5.
22 Finnemore, *Black's Story of the English People*, II, 154.
23 If the scope of this book allowed, one could apply more techniques of discourse analysis to the language in these school books. James Martin, 'Making History: Grammar for Metaphor', in James Martin and Ruth Wodak (eds), *Re/reading the Past: Critical Functional Perspectives on Time and Value* (Amsterdam: John Benjamins, 2003), 19–57; James Martin, S. Eggins and P. Wignell, 'The Discourse of History: Distancing the Recoverable Past', in M. Ghadessy (ed.), *Register Analysis* (London: Pinter Publishers, 1993), 75–109; M. Billig, *Banal Nationalism* (London: Sage, 1995).
24 Amanda Craig, *The Times* (December 2005). Cited at: www.civitas.org.uk/islandstory/reviews.htm (accessed 26 March 2014).
25 *The Times* (September 2005). Cited at: www.civitas.org.uk/islandstory/reviews.htm (accessed 26 March 2014).
26 Gary McCulloch, 'Privatising the Past: History and Education Policy in the 1990s', *British Journal of Education Studies*, 45:1 (1997), 69–82; Dave McKiernan, 'History in a National Curriculum: Imagining the Nation at the End of the Twentieth Century', *Journal of Curriculum Studies*, 25:1 (1993), 33–53; Keith Crawford, 'A History of the Right: The Battle for Control of National Curriculum History, 1989–1994', *British Journal of Educational Research*, 43:4 (1995), 433–56; and V. Little, 'A National Curriculum for History: A Very Contentious Issue', *British Journal of Education Studies*, 38:4 (1990), 319–34.

CONCLUSION

27 K. Jenkins and P. Brickley, '"Always Historicise": Unintended Opportunities in National Curriculum History', *Teaching History* (January 1991), 8–14.
28 Raphael Samuel, 'Grand Narratives', *History Workshop Journal*, 29 (1990), 120–33; David Cannadine, 'British History: Past, Present and Future?' *Past and Present*, 116 (1987), 169–91.
29 L. Colley, 'Britishness in the 21st Century', Millennium Lecture, Downing Street, 2001. Full text available at: www.number-10.gov.uk/output/Page3049.asp (accessed 12 June 2009).

SELECT BIBLIOGRAPHY

Reading books, textbooks and other classroom resources

Berry, A.J., *England and the English* (Glasgow: Blackie and Son, 1910).
Bevan, T., *The British Empire Overseas: Historical and Geographical* (London: Sampson, Low, Marston and Company, 1930).
Britannia History Readers, 6 volumes (London: Edward Arnold, 1901).
British History in Periods: A New Series of Historical Readers, 6 volumes (London: Blackie and Son, 1904).
Browning, O., *The Citizen: His Rights and Responsibilities* (London: Blackie and Sons, 1893).
Buckley, A., *History of England* (London: Methuen and Co., 1892)
Cassell's Historical Readers, 3 volumes (London: Cassell and Co., 1882–83).
Cassell's Historical Course for Schools, 3 volumes (London: Cassell and Co., 1884).
Cassell's Union Jack Series, 5 volumes (London: Cassell and Co., 1903).
Chambers' Historical Readers, 4 volumes (London and Edinburgh: Chambers, 1882).
Collier, W.F., *The History of the British Empire* (London: T. Nelson, 1875).
Collins' School Series, *Patriotic Historical Readers*, 6 volumes (London: Collins, 1894).
Cox, G.W., *England and the English People* (London: Joseph Hughes, 1887).
Dick, A.H., *First Historical Reader for Standard II: English History, Roman and Saxon Period* (London: Gall and Inglis, 1881).
Finnemore, J., *Boys and Girls of Other Days: History Told in the Form of Romance, etc.* (London: White Horse, 1898).
Finnemore, J., *Famous Englishmen*, 2 volumes (London: A. & C. Black, 1901).
Finnemore, J., *Men of Renown: King Alfred to Lord Roberts* (London: A. & C. Black, 1902).
Finnemore, J., *Social Life in England*, 2 volumes (London: A. & C. Black, 1902 and 1955).
Finnemore, J., *Black's School Series: Black's Story of the English People*, Volumes I and II (London: A. & C. Black, 1905).
Finnemore, J., *Chambers' Supplementary Readers: Children of Empire*, 2 volumes (London: Chambers, 1905).

SELECT BIBLIOGRAPHY

Fletcher, C.R.L. and R. Kipling, *A School History of England* (Oxford: Clarendon, 1911).
Green, J.R., *A Short History of the English People*, illustrated edition, 4 volumes (London: Macmillan and Co., [1874] 1902).
Hassall, A., *The Making of the British Empire* (London: Blackie and Son, 1896).
Headway Histories, 9 volumes (London: University of London Press, 1928).
Highroads of History, 8 volumes (London: T. Nelson and Sons, 1930).
Holborn Historical Readers, I (London: Educational Supply Association, 1900).
Ince, H. and J. Gilbert, *Outlines of English History* (London: W.B. Clive, 1906).
Innes, A.D., *History of England: For Use in Schools* (Cambridge: Cambridge University Press, 1907).
Jack's Concentric Histories, 5 volumes (London: T.C and E.C. Jack, 1905).
King Alfred Readers, 8 volumes (London: Edward Arnold, 1900).
King Edward History Readers, 8 volumes (London: Isaac Pitman and Sons, 1901–4).
Longman's Ship Historical Readers, 7 volumes (London: Longmans, Green and Co., 1893).
Lucas, C.P., *The Story of the Empire* (London: W. Collins' Sons and Co., 1924).
Mee, A., *Little Treasure Island: Her Story and Her Glory* (London: Smith and Elders, 1920).
Morris, D., *Historical Readers: History of England*, 4 volumes (London: William Ibister, 1883).
Morris, D., *Class Book of English History* (London: Longmans, Green and Co., 1902),
Mowat, R.B., *A New History of Great Britain* (Oxford: Oxford University Press, 1926).
The Newbery Historical Readers (Oscar Browning) (London: Griffith, Farran and Co., 1893).
Newton, A.P., *An Introduction to Colonial History* (London: SPCK, 1919).
Oman, C., *The History of England* (London: Methuen, 1895)
Pringle, R.S., *Local Examination History*, nineteenth edition revised and extended (Manchester: Heywood, 1899).
Raleigh History Readers, 4 volumes (London: Blackie and Son, 1896–98).
Royal School Series, *Royal English History Readers*, 4 volumes (London: T. Nelson and Sons, 1880).
Royal School Series, *Stories from English History Simply Told* (London: T. Nelson and Sons, 1884).
Salmon, E., *The Story of the Empire* (London: Newnes, 1902).
Spence, C.H., *History and Geography Examination Papers* (London: George Bell and Sons, 1888).
Tower History Readers, 5 volumes (London: Pitman, 1907).
Turner, J., *Methuen History Readers*, 8 volumes (London: Methuen, 1913).
Warner, G.T., *A Brief Survey of British History* (London: Blackie and Son, 1899).

Warner, G.T. and C.H.K. Marten, *The Groundwork of History* (London: Blackie and Son, 1911).
Warwick History Readers, 7 volumes (London: Blackie and Son, 1895–96).
Wheeler, H.F.B., *Makers of the British Empire* (London: George Harrap and Co., 1927).

Texts on Herbartian method and educational theory

Adams, J., *The Herbartian Psychology Applied to Education* (London: Isbister and Company, 1897).
Allemandy, V.H., 'The Herbartian Principles of Education', *Parent's Review*, 12:9 (1901), 888–9.
Darrock, A., *Herbart and the Herbartian Theory of Education* (London: Longmans, Green and Co., 1903).
de Garmo, C., *Herbart and the Herbartians* (London: Sonnenschein, 1895).
Dodd, C., *Introduction to Herbartian Principles of Teaching* (London: Sonnenschein, 1901).
Felkin, H.M. and E. Felkin, *An Introduction to Herbart's Science and Practice of Education* (London: Sonnenschein, 1895).
Fennell, M., *Notes of Lessons on the Herbartian Method* (London: Longmans, Green and Co., 1902).
Hayward, F.H., *The Reform of Moral and Biblical Education in the Lines of Herbartianism, Critical Thought and the Ethical Needs of the Present Day* (London: Sonnenschein, 1902).
Hayward, F.H., *The Critics of Herbartianism* (London: Sonnenschein, 1903).
Hayward, F.H., *Three Historical Educators: Pestalozzi, Froebel, Herbart* (London: Ralph, Holland and Co., 1905).
Herbart, J.F., *The Science of Education*, trans. H.M. and E. Felkin (London: Sonnenschein, 1892).
Lange, K., *Apperception: A Monograph on the Psychology and Pedagogy of Education*, trans. Elmer E. Brown (Boston: D.C. Heath and Co., [1879] 1894).
Rooper, T.G., 'A Pot of Green Feathers', *Parent's Review*, 4 (1893–94), 8–16.
Üfer, C., *Introduction to Herbart*, trans. J.C. Zinser (London: Isbister and Co., 1895).

Manuals of method

Adamson, J.W., *The Practice of Instruction: A Manual of Method General and Special*, second edition (London: National Society's Depository, 1912).
Browning, O., *An Introduction to the History of Educational Theories* (London: Kegan Paul, Trench and Co., 1881).
Clarke, F., *Foundations of History Teaching: A Critique for Teachers* (London: Oxford University Press, 1929).
Collar G. and C.W. Crook, *School Management and Methods of Instruction with Special Reference to Elementary Schools* (London: Macmillan and Co., 1900).

SELECT BIBLIOGRAPHY

Cowham, J., *A New School Method: For Pupil-Teachers and Students* (London: Westminster School Book Depot, 1894).
Cox, T.A. and R.F. Macdonald, *The Suggestive Handbook of Practical School Method* (London: Blackie and Son, 1896).
Dexter, T.F.G. and A.H. Garlick, *Psychology in the Schoolroom* (London: Longmans, Green and Co., 1901).
Findlay, J.J., *Principles of Class Teaching* (London: Macmillan, 1904 and 1911 editions).
Fitch, J., *Lectures on Teaching* (Cambridge: Cambridge University Press, 1881).
Garlick, A.H., *A New Manual of Method*, sixth edition (London: Longmans, Green and Co., 1904).
Green, J.A. and C. Birchenough, *A Primer of Teaching Practice* (London: Longmans, Green and Co., 1911).
Gunn, J., *Class Teaching and Management* (London: T. Nelson and Sons, 1895).
Howard, M.A., 'History', in J.W. Adamson, *The Practice of Instruction: A Manual of Method General and Special* (London: National Society Repository, 1907).
Jarvis, C., *The Teaching of History* (Oxford: Clarendon, 1917).
Landon, J., *The Principles and Practice of Class Teaching and School Management* (London: Alfred M. Holden, 1894).
Raymont, T., *The Principles of Education* (London: Longmans, Green and Co., 1904).
Salmon, D., *The Art of Teaching* (London: Longmans, Green and Co., 1898).
Welton, J., *Principles and Methods of Teaching*, second edition (London: University Tutorial Press, [1906] 1909).

Contemporary books, essays and articles concerned with education policy in general and the teaching of history in particular

Archer, R.L., L.V.D. Owen and A.E. Chapman, *The Teaching of History in Elementary Schools* (London: A. & C. Black Ltd., 1916).
Bailey, S.H., *International Studies in Modern Education* (Oxford: Oxford University Press, 1938).
Beale, D., 'The Teaching of Chronology', *Parent's Review*, 2 (1891–92), 81–91.
Board of Education, *Report on the Teaching of History* (London: Educational pamphlet, no. 37, 1923).
Bray R., 'Patriotism and Education', in Lucian Oldershaw (ed.), *England: A Nation* (London: Brimley and Johnson, 1904).
Davies, A.K., 'Syllabus Construction in the Junior School', in W.H. Burston and C.W. Green (eds), *Handbook for History Teachers* (London: Methuen, 1962).
Dewar, A.C., 'The Need of Naval History', *History*, 4 (1919), 198–202.
Dobson, D.P., *The Teaching of Prehistory in Schools* (London: Historical Association, leaflet no. 74, 1928).

SELECT BIBLIOGRAPHY

Dodd, A.H. 'The Selection and Provision of History Books for Elementary Schools', *History*, 12 (1928), 230–1.

Findlay, J.J., *History and its Place in Education* (London: University of London Press, 1923).

Firth, C.H., *A Plea for the Historical Teaching of History*, Inaugural lecture delivered at Oxford University (Oxford: Clarendon Press, 1904).

Haldane, R.B., *Education and Empire: Addresses on Certain Topics of the Day* (London: John Murray, 1902).

Hasluck, E.L., *The Teaching of History* (Cambridge: Cambridge University Press, 1920).

Hayward, F.H., *An Educational Failure: A School Inspector's Story* (London: Duckworth, 1938).

Headlam, J., 'The Effect of the War on the Teaching of History', *History*, 3 (1918), 10–13.

Hearnshaw, F.J.C., 'The Place of History in Education', *History*, 1 (1913), 34–41.

Hensley Henson, H., 'The Gift of Historical Thinking', *History*, 10 (1925).

Holmes, E.A.G., *In Defence of What Might Be* (London: Constable, 1914).

Hughes, R.E., *Schools at Home and Abroad* (London: Sonnenschein, 1902).

Jeffreys, M., *History in Schools: The Study of Development* (London: Pitman, 1939).

London County Council, Education Committee, 'Report of a Conference on the Teaching of History in London Elementary Schools' (London: P.S. King and Son, [1911] 1923).

Lucas, C.P., 'On the Teaching of Imperial History', *History*, 1 (1916), 5–11.

Madeley, H., *History as a School of Citizenship* (London: Oxford University Press, 1920).

Mantoux, P., 'The Effect of the War on the Teaching of History', *History*, 3 (1918), 13–24.

Marten, C.H.K., 'Some General Reflections on the Teaching of History', *History*, 2 (1913), 85–98.

Marten, C.H.K., 'The Board of Education Report on the Teaching of History', *History*, 9 (1924), 33.

Marten, C.H.K., 'The First School Examinations and the Teaching of History', *History*, 13 (1928), 24.

Marten, C.H.K., 'The Teaching of Economic History in Schools', *Economic History Review*, 1:2 (1928), 204.

Marten, C.H.K., *On the Teaching of History and Other Addresses* (Oxford: Basil Blackwell, 1938).

Martin, E.C. (ed.), *Imperial Studies in Education: Papers Read at the Imperial Studies Conference Held at Wembley, 26th, 28th, 29th May, 1924, and Published under the Auspices of the Royal Colonial Institute* (London: Sir Isaac Pitman and Sons Ltd, 1924).

Montagu, L.H., 'Hero-Worship as a Factor in Education', *Parents' Review*, 12 (1901), 561–73.

Newland, H.O., *The Model Citizen* (London: Sir Isaac Pitman and Sons, 1924).

SELECT BIBLIOGRAPHY

Pollard, A.F., *On the Educational Value of the Study of History* (London: Historical Association, leaflet no. 26, 1911).

Pollard, A.F., 'The Teaching of Imperial History', in *Report of the Proceedings of the Tenth Annual Meeting of the Historical Association* (London: Historical Association, leaflet no. 41, 1916).

Roberts, Lord F., *Fallacies and Facts* (London: John Murray, 1911).

Robertson, C.G., *History and Citizenship: Being the Creighton Lecture* (Oxford: Clarendon Press, 1928).

Rogers, A. 'Why Teach History? The Answer of Fifty Years, Part I', *Educational Review*, 14:1 (1962).

Schmitt, B.E., '"War Guilt" in France and Germany: Resolutions Adopted by a Committee of French and German Historians for the Improvement of Textbooks in Both Countries', *American Historical Review* (January, 1938), 321–41.

Scott, J. French, *The Menace of Nationalism in Education* (London: Allen and Unwin, 1926).

Seeley, J.R., *The Expansion of England* (London: Macmillan and Co., [1883] 1914).

Shropshire, O., *The Teaching of History in English Schools* (New York: Teachers' College, 1936).

Smith, F., *History of English Elementary Education, 1760–1902* (London: University of London Press, 1931).

Starr, M., *Lies and Hate in Education* (London: Leonard and Virginia Woolf, 1929).

Stobart, J.C., 'The Child: The Empire', *The Royal Colonial Institute Journal*, 16:3 (1925), 175–6.

Strong, C.F., *History in the Secondary School* (London: University of London Press, 1958),

Tout, T.F., 'The Middle Ages in the Teaching of History', *History*, 8 (1923), 1–18.

Waldegrave, A.J., *Lessons in Citizenship* (London: Thomas Nelson and Sons, 1912).

Walker. E., 'History and the Unemployed Adolescent', *History*, 20 (1935), 138–46.

Webb, W.H., 'History, Patriotism and the Child', *History*, 2:1 (1913), 53–4.

White, J.A. 'The Board of Education Report on the Teaching of History in London', *History*, 12 (1928), 230–1.

Williams, T., 'The Place of Economic History in the Teaching of History: A Discussion', *History*, 31 (1936).

Williamson, G.C., *On Learning and Teaching History in Schools and on the Results Obtained by Such Teaching* (London: Longmans, Green & Co., 1891).

Wilson, R., *The Complete Citizen: An Introduction to the Study of Civics* (London: J.M. Dent and Sons, 1920).

Withers, H.L., *The Teaching of History and Other Papers* (Manchester: Sherrat and Hughes, 1904).

SELECT BIBLIOGRAPHY

Journals, newspapers and periodicals

Economic History Review
Educational Review
Educational Times
History
Parents Review
Royal Colonial Institute Journal
Times
Times Educational Supplement

Sources relating to national curriculum debates

Aldrich, R., 'New History: An Historical Perspective', in A.K. Dickinson, P.J. Lee and P.J. Rogers (eds), *Learning History* (London: Heinemann Educational, 1984), 210–24.

Aldrich, R., 'Imperialism in the Study and Teaching of School History', in J.A. Mangan (ed.), *Benefits Bestowed? Education and British Imperialism* (Manchester: Manchester University Press, 1988), 23–38.

Aldrich, R., 'The National Curriculum: An Historical Perspective', in D. Lawton, and C. Chitty (eds), *The National Curriculum* (London: Institute of Education, Bedford Way Papers, number 33, 1988).

Aldrich, R. (ed.), *History in the National Curriculum* (London: Institute of Education, 1991).

Arthur, J., I. Davies, A. Wrenn, T. Haydn and D. Kerr, *Citizenship through Secondary History* (London: Routledge, 2001).

Bage, G., *Narrative Matters: Teaching and Learning History through Story* (London: Falmer, 1999).

Ball, S.J., 'Education, Majorism and the Curriculum of the Dead', *Curriculum Studies*, 1:2 (1993), 195–214.

Ballard, M. (ed.) *New Movements in the Study and Teaching of History* (London: Temple Smith, 1970).

Batho, G., 'The History of the Teaching of Civics and Citizenship in English Schools', *Curriculum Journal*, 1:1 (1990), 91–100.

Berghahn, V.R. and H. Schissler (eds), *Perceptions of History: An Analysis of School Textbooks* (Oxford: Berg, 1987).

Bourdillon, H. (ed.), *Teaching History* (London and New York: Routledge, 1994).

Brocklehurst, H. and R. Phillips, '"You're History!" Media Representation, Nationhood and the National Past', in H. Brocklehurst, and R. Phillips (eds), *History, Nationhood and the Question of Britain* (Basingstoke: Palgrave, 2004).

Clark, J.C.D., 'National Identity, State Formation and Patriotism: the Role of History in the Public Mind', *History Workshop Journal*, 29 (1990), 95–102.

Coltham, J. and J. Fines, *Educational Objectives for the Study of History: A Suggested Framework* (London: Historical Association, Teaching of History Series 35, 1971).

SELECT BIBLIOGRAPHY

Crawford, K., 'A History of the Right: The Battle for Control of National Curriculum History, 1989–1994', in *British Journal of Educational Research*, 43:3 (1995), 433–56.

Deuchar, S., *History and GCSE History* (London: Centre for Policy Studies, 1987).

Elwyn Jones, G., 'The Debate over the National Curriculum for History in England and Wales, 1989–90: The Role of the Press', *The Curriculum Journal*, 11:3 (2000), 299–322.

Evans, R., '"The Wonderfulness of Us" (the Tory Interpretation of History)', *London Review of Books*, 33:6 (March, 2011), 9–12.

Gardiner, J. (ed.), *The History Debate* (London: HarperCollins, 1990).

Goalen, P., 'The History Curriculum and National Identity: Exploring Children's Perceptions of National Identity', *Curriculum* 19:1 (1998), 23–32.

Guyver, R. and T. Taylor (eds), *History Wars and the Classroom: Global Perspectives* (London and Charlotte, NC: Information Age Publishing, 2011).

Haydn, H., '"Longing for the Past": Politicians and the History Curriculum in English Schools, 1988–2010', *Journal of Educational Media, Memory and Society*, 4:1 (2012), 7–25.

Jenkins, K. and P. Brickley, '"Always Historicise": Unintended Opportunities in National Curriculum History', *Teaching History* (January 1991), 8–14.

Johnson, R., 'Thatcherism and English Education: Breaking the Mould or Confirming the Pattern?' *History of Education* 18:2 (1989), 91–121.

Jones, K., *Right Turn: The Conservative Revolution in Education* (London: Hutchinson Radius, 1989).

Lawton, D., *The Tory Mind on Education, 1979–94* (London: Falmer, 1994).

Little, V., 'A National Curriculum for History: A Very Contentious Issue', *British Journal of Education Studies*, 38:4 (1990), 319–34.

McCulloch, G., 'Privatising the Past: History and Education Policy in the 1990s', *British Journal of Education Studies*, 45:1 (1997), 69–82.

McKiernan, D., 'History in a National Curriculum: Imagining the Nation at the End of the Twentieth Century', *Journal of Curriculum Studies*, 25:1 (1993), 33–53.

Phillips, R., 'History Teaching, Cultural Restorationism and National Identity in England and Wales', *Curriculum Studies*, 4:3 (1996), 385–99.

Phillips, R., 'Thesis and Antithesis in Tate's Views on History, Culture and Nationhood', *Teaching History*, 86 (1997), 30–3.

Phillips, R., *History Teaching, Nationhood and the State: An Exploration of Policy Sociology* (London: Cassel, 1998).

Phillips, R., 'History Teaching, Nationhood and Politics in England and Wales in the late Twentieth Century: a historical comparison', *History of Education*, 28:3 (1999), 351–63.

Phillips, R., P. Goalen, A. McCully and S. Wood, 'Four Histories, One Nation: History Teaching, Nationhood and a British Identity', *Compare*, 29:2 (1999), 153–70.

Price, M., 'History in Danger', *History*, 53 (1968), 342–7.

Quicke, J., 'The "New Right" and Education', in *British Journal of Educational Studies*, 26 (1988), 5–20.

SELECT BIBLIOGRAPHY

Samuel, R., 'Grand Narratives', *History Workshop Journal* 29 (1990), 120–33.
Samuel, R., 'Empire Stories: The Imperial and the Domestic', in his *Island Stories: Unravelling Britain (Theatres of Memory, Vol. II)* (London: Verso, 1998), 74–97.
Sylvester, D., 'A Historical Overview: Change and Continuity in History Teaching, 1900–1993', in H. Bourdillon (ed.), *Teaching History* (London and New York: Routledge, 1994), 9–23.
Visram, R., 'British History: Whose History? Black Perspectives on British History', in H. Bourdillon (ed.), *Teaching History* (London and New York: Routledge, 1994).

Other secondary sources

Attridge, S., *Nationalism, Imperialism and Identity in Late Victorian Culture: Civil and Military Worlds* (Basingstoke: Palgrave, 2003).
August, T.G., *The Selling of the Empire: British and French Propaganda, 1890–1940* (London: Greenwood Press, 1985).
Barczewski, S., *Myth and National Identity in Nineteenth Century Britain: The Legends of King Arthur and Robin Hood* (Oxford: Oxford University Press, 2000).
Barker, E., *National Character and the Factors in its Formation* (London: Methuen, 1927).
Batho, G.R., 'Sources for the History of History Teaching in Elementary Schools, 1833–1914', in T.G. Cook (ed.), *Local Studies and the History of Education* (London: Methuen, 1972), 139–43.
Beaven, B., *Visions of Empire: Patriotism, Popular Culture and the City, 1870–1939* (Manchester: Manchester University Press, 2012).
Beaven, B. and J. Griffiths, 'Creating the Exemplary Citizen: The Changing Notion of Citizenship in Britain, 1870–1939', *Contemporary British History*, 22:2 (2008), 203–25.
Bell, C.M., *The Royal Navy, Seapower and Strategy Between the Wars* (Basingstoke: Macmillan, 2000).
Bentley, M., *Modernizing England's Past: English Historiography in the Age of Modernism, 1870–1970* (New York: Cambridge University Press, 2006).
Berghahn, V. and H. Schissler (eds), *Perceptions of History: An Analysis of School Textbooks* (Oxford: Berg, 1987).
Betts, R., 'A Campaign for Patriotism in the Elementary School Curriculum: Lord Meath, 1892–1916', *History of Education Society Bulletin*, 46 (1990), 38–45.
Biddiss, M., 'Racial Ideas and the Politics of Prejudice, 1850–1914', *Historical Journal*, 15:3 (1972), 570–82.
Bolt, C., *Victorian Attitudes to Race* (London: Routledge and Kegan Paul, 1971).
Booth, M., *History Betrayed* (London: Longman, 1973).
Boyd, K., *Manliness and the Boys' Story Paper in Britain: A Cultural History, 1855–1940* (Basingstoke: Palgrave, 2003).

SELECT BIBLIOGRAPHY

Bramwell, R.D., 'Curricular Determinants: An Historical Perspective', *History of Education Society Bulletin*, 12 (Autumn, 1973), 40–9.

Bratton, J.S., '"Of England, Home and Duty": The Image of England in Victorian and Edwardian Juvenile Fiction', in J.M. MacKenzie (ed.), *Imperialism and Popular Culture* (Manchester: Manchester University Press, 1986), 73–93.

Bratton, J., 'Imperialism and the Reproduction of Femininity', in J. Richards (ed.), *Imperialism and Juvenile Literature* (Manchester: Manchester University Press, 1989), 195–215.

Briggs, A., *Collected Essays of Asa Briggs*, II (London: Harvester, 1985).

Brindle, P., 'Mr Chips with Everything', *History Today*, 46:6 (1996), 11–14.

Brocklehurst, H. and R. Phillips (eds), *History, Nationhood and the Question of Britain* (Basingstoke: Palgrave, 2004).

Brockliss, L. and D. Eastwood (eds), *A Union of Multiple Identities: The British Isles, c. 1750–1850* (Manchester: Manchester University Press, 1997).

Brown, K.D., 'Modelling for War? Toy Soldiers in Late Victorian and Edwardian Britain', *Journal of Social History*, 24:2 (1990), 237–54.

Brundage, A., *The People's Historian: John Richard Green and the Writing of History in Victorian England* (London: Greenwood, 1994).

Burroughs, P., 'John Robert Seeley and British Imperial History', *Journal of Imperial and Commonwealth History*, 1:2 (1973), 191–212.

Calhoun, C., *Nationalism* (Buckingham: Open University Press, 1997).

Cannadine, D. (ed.), *Admiral Lord Nelson: Context and Legacy* (Basingstoke: Palgrave, 2005).

Cannadine, D., J. Keating, and N. Sheldon, *The Right Kind of History: Teaching the Past in Twentieth-Century England* (Basingstoke: Palgrave, 2011).

Carlyle, T., *On Heroes, Hero-Worship and the Heroic in History* (London: Chapman and Hall, [1840] 1903).

Castle, K., 'India in British History Textbooks for Schools, 1890–1914', in J.A. Mangan (ed.), *The Imperial Curriculum: Racial Images and Education in the British Colonial Experience* (London: Routledge, 1993), 23–39.

Castle, K., *Britannia's Children: Reading Colonialism through Children's Books and Magazines* (Manchester: Manchester University Press, 1996).

Caunce, S., E. Mazierska, S. Sydney-Smith and J.K. Walton (eds), *Relocating Britishness* (Manchester: Manchester University Press, 2004).

Chancellor, V., *History for their Masters: Opinion in the English History Textbook, 1800–1914* (London: Adams and Dart, 1970).

Cole, E.A. (ed.), *Teaching the Violent Past: History Education and Reconciliation* (Plymouth: Powman and Littlefield, 2007).

Colledge, S., 'The Study of History in the Teacher Training College', *History of Education Society Bulletin*, 36 (1985), 45–51.

Colley, L., 'Britishness and Otherness: An Argument', *Journal of British Studies*, 31 (1992), 309–29.

Colley, L., 'Britishness in the 21st Century', Millennium Lecture, Downing Street, 2001. Full text available online: www.number-10.gov.uk/output/Page3049.asp (accessed 12 June 2009).

SELECT BIBLIOGRAPHY

Colley, L., *Britons: Forging the Nation, 1707–1837*, second edition (London: Pimlico, 2003).

Colls, R., 'Englishness and the Political Culture', in R. Colls and P. Dodd (eds), *Englishness: Politics and Culture, 1880–1920* (London: Croom Helm, 1986), 29–61.

Colls, R., *The Identity of England* (Oxford: Oxford University Press, 2002).

Colls, R. and P. Dodd (eds), *Englishness: Politics and Culture, 1880–1920* (London: Croom Helm, 1987).

Colquhoun, A., P. Lyon and E. Alexander, 'Feeding Minds and Bodies: The Edwardian Context of School Meals', *Nutrition and Food Science*, 31:3 (2001), 117–25.

Conlon, M., *From Jack Tar to Union Jack: Representing Naval Manhood in the British Empire, 1870–1918* (Manchester: Manchester University Press, 2009).

Connor, W., 'The Timelessness of Nations', *Nations and Nationalism*, 10:1–2 (2004), 35–47.

Copelman, D., *Class Acts: London's Women Teachers* (London and New York: Routledge, 1996).Cronin, A., 'Rags and Refuse: The Newspaper, Empire and Nineteenth-century Commodity Culture', *Cultural Studies*, 20:6 (2006), 574–98.

Crouch, M., *Treasure Seekers and Borrowers: Children's Books in Britain, c. 1900–1960* (London: Library Association, 1962).

Cubitt, G. and A. Warren (eds), *Heroic Reputations and Exemplary Lives* (Manchester: Manchester University Press, 2000).

Cunningham, H., *The Challenge of Democracy: Britain, 1832–1915* (Harlow: Longman, 2001).

Cunningham, P., 'Progressivism, Decentralisation and Recentralisation: Local Education Authorities and the Primary Curriculum, 1902–2002', *Oxford Review of Education*, 28:2–3 (2002), 218–20.

Cunningham, H., *Grace Darling: Victorian Heroine* (London: Hambledon Press, 2007).

Czisnik, M., 'Admiral Nelson's Tactics at the Battle of Trafalgar', *History*, 89:296 (2004), 549–59.

Davin, A., '"Mind That You Do as You Are Told": Reading Books for Board School Girls, 1870–1902', *Feminist Review*, 3 (1979), 89–98.

Davin, A., 'Imperialism and Motherhood', in Raphael Samuel (ed.), *Patriotism: The Making and Unmaking of British National Identity* (London: Routledge, 1989).

Davin, A., *Growing Up Poor: Home, School and Street in London, 1870–1914* (London: Rivers Oram Press, 1996).

Dawson, G., *Soldier Heroes: British Adventure, Empire and the Imagining of Masculinities* (London: Routledge, 1994).

Dawson, G., 'Heroes of History, Heroes of Phantasy: idealisation, masculinity and the soldiers of empire', *Soundings*, 3 (1996), 145–60.

Day, G. (ed.), *Varieties of Victorianism: The Uses of the Past* (Basingstoke: Macmillan, 1998).

SELECT BIBLIOGRAPHY

De Groot, G., *Blighty: British Society in the Era of the Great War* (London: Longman, 1996).

Digby A. and P. Searby, *Children, School and Society in Nineteenth-Century England* (London: Macmillian, 1981).

Dunkel, H., *Herbart and Herbartianism: An Educational Ghost Story* (Chicago: Chicago University Press, 1970).

Dyhouse, C., 'Social Darwinistic Ideas and the Development of Women's Education, 1880–1920', *History of Education*, 5:1 (1976), 41–58.

Dyhouse, C., *Girls Growing up in Late Victorian and Edwardian England* (London: Routledge and Kegan Paul, 1981).

Elliot, B.J., 'The League of Nations Union and History Teaching in England: A Study in Benevolent Bias?', *History of Education*, 6 (1977), 137–46.

Elliot, B.J., 'An Early Failure of Curricular Reform: History Teaching in England, 1918–1940', *Journal of Educational Administration and History*, 12:2 (1980), 39–46.

Elliot, B.J., 'History Examinations at 16 and 18 Years in England and Wales between 1918 and 1939', *History of Education*, 20:2 (1991), 119–29.

Elliot, B.J., 'The Impact of the Second World War upon History Teaching in Britain', *Journal of Educational Administration and History* 26:2 (1994), 153–63.

Ellis, A., *History of Children's Reading and Literature* (London: Pergamon Press, 1968).

Ellis, A., *Educating Our Masters: Influences on the Growth of Literacy in Victorian Working Class Children* (Aldershot: Gower, 1985).

English, J., 'Empire Day in Britain, 1904–58', *The Historical Journal*, 49:1 (2006), 247–76.

Evans, E. and Penny Summerfield (eds), *Technical Education and the State Since 1850: Historical and Contemporary Perspectives* (Manchester: Manchester University Press, 1990).

Fulton, R., 'The Sudan Sensation', *Victorian Periodicals Review*, 42:1 (2009), 37–63.

Furedi, F., *Mythical Past, Elusive Future: History and Society in an Anxious Age* (London: Pluto Press, 1992).

Galbraith, G., *Reading Lives: Reconstructing Childhood, Books and School in Britain, 1870–1920* (Basingstoke: Macmillan, 1997).

Gard, A. and P.J. Lee, '"Educational Objectives for the Study of History" Reconsidered', in A. Dickinson and P.J. Lee (eds), *Historical Teaching and Historical Understanding* (London: Heinemann, 1978).

Gardner, P., 'Classroom Teachers and Educational Change 1876–1996', *Journal of Education for Teaching*, 24:1 (1998), 33–49.

Gardner, P., 'Reconstructing the Classroom Teacher, 1903–1945', in Ian Grosvenor, Martin Lawn and Kate Rousmaniere (eds), *Silences and Images: The Social History of the Classroom* (New York: Peter Lang, 1999), 123–44.

Gardner, P., 'Oral History in Education: Teacher's Memory and Teachers' History', *History of Education*, 32:2 (2003), 175–88.

SELECT BIBLIOGRAPHY

Glendenning, F.J., 'School History Textbooks and Racial Attitudes, 1804–1911', *Journal of Educational Administration and History*, 5:2 (1973), 35–44.

Glendenning, F.J., 'Attitudes to Colonialism and Race in British and French History Schoolbooks', *History of Education*, 3:2 (1974), 57–72.

Goldstrom, J.M. (ed.), *Education – Elementary Education, 1780–1900* (Newton Abbott: David and Charles, 1972).

Goodlad, G., *British Foreign and Imperial Policy* (London: Routledge, 1999).

Gordon, F., 'The Handbook of Suggestions for Teachers: Its Origins and Evolution', *Journal of Educational Administration and History*, 17:1 (1985), 41–8.

Grainger, J.H., *Patriotisms: Britain 1900–1939* (London: Routledge and Kegan Paul, 1986).

Grant, A. and Keith Stringer (eds), *Uniting the Kingdom? The Making of British History* (London and New York: Routledge, 1995).

Green, M., *Dreams of Adventure, Deeds of Empire* (London: Routledge, 1980).

Greenlee, J., '"A Succession of Seeleys": The "Old School" Re-examined', *Journal of Imperial and Commonwealth History*, 4:3 (1976), 266–82.

Greenlee, J.G., *Education and Imperial Unity, 1901–1926* (New York and London: Garland, 1987).

Gregory, D., 'British "War Enthusiasm" in 1914: A Reassessment', in Gail Braybon (ed.), *Evidence, History and the Great War* (Oxford: Berghahn, 2003), 67–85.

Grosvenor, I., M. Lawn and K. Rousmaniere (eds), *Silences and Images: The Social History of the Classroom* (New York: Peter Lang, 1999).

Gunning, D., *The Teaching of History* (London: Croom Helm, 1978).

Hallam, R., 'Piaget and Thinking in History', R. Hallam (ed.), *New Movements in the Study and Teaching of History* (London: Temple Smith, 1970), 162–78.

Hamilton, D., 'The Pedagogic Paradox (Or, Why No Didactics in England)?' *Pedagogy, Culture and Society*, 7:1 (1999), 135–52.

Harper, M., '"Personal Contact Is Worth a Ton of Textbooks": Educational Tours of the Empire', *Journal of Imperial and Commonwealth History*, 32:3 (2004), 48–76.

Harrington, R., '"The Mighty Hood": Navy, Empire, War at Sea and the British National Imagination, 1920–60', *Journal of Contemporary History*, 38:2 (2003), 171–85.

Heathorn, S.J., '"Let Us Remember that We, Too, Are English": Constructions of Citizenship and National Identity in English Elementary School Reading Books, 1880–1914', *Victorian Studies* 38:4 (1995), 395–427.

Heathorn, S.J., *For Home, Country and Race: Constructing Gender, Class and Englishness in the Elementary School, 1880–1914* (Toronto: Toronto University Press, 2000).

Hechter, M., *Internal Colonialism: The Celtic Fringe in British National Development* (Berkeley: University of California Press, 1975).

Hendley, M., *Organised Patriotism and the Crucible of War: Popular Imperialism in Britain, 1914–32* (Montreal: McGill Queens University Press).

SELECT BIBLIOGRAPHY

Hennock, E.P., *British Social Reform and German Precedents, 1880–1914* (Oxford: Clarendon, 1987).

Hobsbawm, E. and T. Ranger (eds), *The Invention of Tradition* (Cambridge: Cambridge University Press, 1992).

Hole, N., 'Nineteenth-century Method Manuals with Special Reference to English Literature', *Paradigm*, 7:2 (2003). Available at: http://w4.ed.uiuc.edu/faculty/westbury/Paradigm/ (accessed 13 May 2010).

Horn, P., 'English Elementary Education and the Growth of the Imperial Ideal', in J.A. Mangan (ed.), *Benefits Bestowed: Education and British Imperialism* (Manchester: Manchester University Press, 1988), 39–55.

Horsman, R., 'Origins of Racial Anglo-Saxonism in Great Britain Before 1850', *Journal of the History of Ideas*, 37:3 (1976), 387–410.

Howat, G.D., 'The Nineteenth-Century History Textbook', *British Journal of Educational Studies*, 13:2 (1965), 147–58.

Hudson, B., 'The New Geography and the New Imperialism: 1870–1918', *Antipode*, 2 (1972), 140–53.

Humphries, S., *Hooligans or Rebels? An Oral History of Working-class Childhood and Youth, 1889–1939* (Oxford: Blackwell, 1981).

Hunt, F., *Gender and Policy in English Education, 1902–44* (Hemel Hempstead: Harvester Wheatsheaf, 1991).

Hurt, J.S., 'Drill, Discipline and the Elementary School Ethos', in P. McCann (ed.), *Popular Education and Socialisation in the Nineteenth Century* (London: Methuen, 1977), 167–91.

Jackson, A. and D. Tomkins, *Illustrating Empire: A Visual History of British Imperialism* (Oxford: Bodleian Library, 2011).

Johnson, D., 'The Death of Gordon: A Victorian Myth', *Journal of Imperial and Commonwealth History*, 10 (1982), 185–310.

Jones, D. and T. Watkins (eds), *A Necessary Fantasy? The Heroic Figure in Children's Popular Culture* (New York: Garland, 2000).

Kearney, H., *The British Isles: A History of Four Nations* (Cambridge: Cambridge University Press, 1989).

Kennedy, P., *The Rise of the Anglo-German Antagonism, 1860–1914* (London: G. Allen and Unwin, 1980).

Kidd, C., 'Race, Empire and the Limits of Nineteenth-Century Scottish Nationhood', *Historical Journal*, 46:4 (2003), 873–92.

Kiernan, V., 'The British Isles: Celt and Saxon', in Mikulas Teich and Roy Porter (eds), *The National Question in Europe in Historical Context* (Cambridge: Cambridge University Press, 1993), 1–34.

Kumar, K., *The Making of English National Identity* (Cambridge: Cambridge University Press, 2003).

Kushner, T., 'Scientific Racism: History, Heritage, Gender and the (Re) Production of Prejudice', *Patterns of Prejudice*, 33:4 (1999), 67–86.

Kushner, T., 'New Narratives, Old Exclusions? British Historiography and Minority Studies', *Immigrants and Minorities*, 24:2 (2006), 47–51.

Kutzer, M., *Empire's Children: Empire and Imperialism in Classic British Children's Books* (London: Garland, 2000).

SELECT BIBLIOGRAPHY

Lammers, B.J., ' "The Citizens of the Future": Educating Children of the Jewish East End', *Twentieth Century British History*, 19:4 (2008), 393–418.

Langford, P., *Englishness Identified: Manners and Character, 1650–1850* (Oxford: Oxford University Press, 2000).

Larkin, P., *Island Story: Georgian and Victorian Britain* (Amersham: Hulton Educational, 1985).

Lawson, J. and H. Silver, *A Social History of Education in England* (London: Methuen, 1973).

Lawton, D. and P. Gordon, *HMI* (London: Routledge, 1987).

Lee, M., 'The Story of Greater Britain: What Lessons does it Teach?', *National Identities*, 6:2 (2004), 123–42.

Lewis, J., 'The Working Class Wife and Mother', in Lewis (ed.), *Labour of Love: Women's Experience of Home and Family, 1850–1940* (Oxford: Blackwell, 1986), 99–120.

Lieven, M., 'Bias in School History Textbooks', *Paradigm*, 2 (2000), 11–23.

Loeb, L.A., *Consuming Angels: Advertising and Victorian Women* (Oxford: Oxford University Press, 1994).

Lorimer, D., 'Nature, Racism and Late Victorian Science', *Canadian Journal of History*, 25:3 (1990), 369–86

Lorimer, D.A., 'Science and the Secularisation of Victorian Images of Race', in B. Lightman (ed.), *Victorian Science in Context* (Chicago: Chicago University Press, 1997), 212–31.

Low, E., 'The Concept of Citizenship in Twentieth-century Britain', in P. Catterall, W. Kaiser and U. Walton-Jordan (eds), *Reforming the Constitution: Debates in Twentieth-century Britain* (London: Cass, 2000).

Lowe, R., 'Personalities and Policy: Sadler, Morant and the Structure of Education in England', in Richard Aldrich (ed.), *In History and Education* (London: Woburn Press, 1996), 98–115.

Lunn, K., 'Reconsidering "Britishness": The Construction and Significance of National Identity in Twentieth Century Britain', in B. Jenkins and S. Sofos (eds), *Nation and Identity in Contemporary Europe* (London: Routledge, 1996), 83–100.

Lunn, K. and A. Day, 'Britain as Island: National Identity and the Sea', in R. Phillips and H. Brocklehurst (eds), *History, Identity and the Question of Britain* (Basingstoke: Palgrave, 2004), 124–36.

MacDonald, R.H., *Sons of Empire: The Frontier Movement and the Boy Scout Movement, 1890–1918* (London: University of Toronto Press, 1993).

MacDonald, R.H., *The Language of Empire: Myth and Metaphors of Popular Imperialism* (Manchester: Manchester University Press, 1994).

MacKenzie, J.M., *Propaganda and Empire: The Manipulation of British Public Opinion* (Manchester: Manchester University Press, 1984).

MacKenzie, J.M. (ed.), *Imperialism and Popular Culture* (Manchester: Manchester University Press, 1986).

MacKenzie, J.M., 'Heroic Myths of Empire', in J. MacKenzie (ed.), *Popular Imperialism and the Military* (Manchester: Manchester University Press, 1992), 109–38.

SELECT BIBLIOGRAPHY

MacKenzie, J.M., 'Empire and National Identities: The Case of Scotland', *Transactions of the Royal Historical Society*, 6th series, 8 (1998), 215–32.

MacKenzie, J.M., 'The Iconography of the Exemplary Life: the Case of David Livingstone', in G. Cubitt and A. Warren (eds), *Heroic Reputations and Exemplary Lives* (Manchester: Manchester University Press, 2000), 84–104.

MacKenzie, J.M., 'Irish, Scottish, Welsh and English Worlds? The Historiography of a Four-nations Approach to the History of the British Empire', in Catherine Hall and Keith McClelland (eds), *Race, Nation and Empire: Making Histories, 1750 to the Present* (Manchester: Manchester University Press, 2010), 133–53.

Madden, A.F.M., '1066, 1776 and All That: The Relevance of the English Medieval Experience of "Empire" to Later Imperial Constitutional Issues', in John Flint and Glyndwr Williams (eds), *Perspectives of Empire: Essays Presented to Gerald S. Graham* (London: Longman, 1973).

Maddrell, A., 'Empire, Emigration and School Geography: Changing Discourses of Imperial Citizenship, 1880–1925', *Journal of Historical Geography*, 22:4 (1996), 373–87.

Mandler, P., ' "In the Olden Time": Romantic History and English National Identity, 1820–50', in L. Brockliss and D. Eastwood (eds), *A Union of Multiple Identities: The British Isles, c. 1750–1850* (Manchester: Manchester University Press, 1997), 78–92.

Mandler, P., *History and National Life* (London: Profile, 2002).

Mandler, P., *The English National Character: The History of an Idea from Edmund Burke to Tony Blair* (New Haven: Yale University Press, 2006).

Mandler, P., 'What Is "National Identity"? Definitions and Applications in Modern British Historiography', *Modern Intellectual History*, 3:2 (2006), 271–97.

Mangan, J.A., ' "The Grit of Our Forefathers": Invented Traditions, Propaganda and Imperialism', in J.M. Mackenzie (ed.), *Imperialism and Popular Culture* (Manchester: Manchester University Press, 1986).

Mangan, J.A. (ed.), *Benefits Bestowed? Education and British Imperialism* (Manchester: Manchester University Press, 1988).

Mangan, J.A. (ed.), *The Imperial Curriculum: Racial Images and Education in the British Colonial Experience* (London and New York: Routledge, 1993).

Mannsaker, F.M., 'The Dog that Didn't Bark: The Subject Races in Imperial Fiction at the Turn of the Century', in David Dabydeen (ed.), *The Black Presence in English Literature* (Manchester: Manchester University Press, 1985), 112–34.

Marsden, W.E., ' "All in a Good Cause": Geography, History and the Politicisation of the Curriculum in Nineteenth and Twentieth Century England', *Journal of Curriculum Studies* 21:6 (1989), 509–26.

Marsden, W.E., 'Rooting Racism into the Educational Experience of Childhood and Youth in the Nineteenth and Twentieth Centuries', *History of Education*, 19:4 (1990), 333–53.

SELECT BIBLIOGRAPHY

Marsden, W.E., '"Poisoned History": A Comparative Study of Nationalism, Propaganda and the Treatment of War and Peace in the Late Nineteenth and Early Twentieth-Century School Curriculum', *History of Education*, 29:1 (2000), 29–47.

Marsden, W.E., *The School Textbook: Geography, History and Social Studies* (London: Woburn Press, 2001).

Martin, J., 'Making History: Grammar for Metaphor', in James Martin and Ruth Wodak (eds), *Re/reading the Past: Critical Functional Perspectives on Time and Value* (Amsterdam: John Benjamins, 2003), 19–57.

Mathison, Y., 'Maps, Pirates and Treasure: The Commodification of Imperialism in Nineteenth-century Boy's Adventure Fiction', in Dennis Denisoff (ed.), *The Nineteenth-Century Child and Consumer Culture* (Aldershot: Ashgate, 2008), 173–85.

May, T., *Great Exhibitions* (Oxford: Shire, 2010).

Mayer, A.K., 'Moralizing Science: The Uses of Science's Past in National Education in the 1920s', *The British Journal for the History of Science*, 30:1 (1997), 51–70.

McCarthy, H., 'The League of Nations, Public Ritual and National Identity in Britain, c. 1919–56', *History Workshop Journal*, 70 (2010), 109–33.

McClintock, A., *Imperial Leather: Race, Gender and Sexuality in the Colonial Contest* (London: Routledge, 1995).

McIntosh, P., *Physical Education in England since 1800* (London: G. Bell and Sons, 1952), 109–21.

McLeod, H., 'Protestantism and British National Identity, 1815–1945', in Peter van der Veer and Hartmut Lehmann (eds), *Nation and Religion: Perspectives on Europe and Asia* (Princeton, PA: Princeton University Press, 1999), 44–70.

Melman, B., 'Claiming the Nation's Past: The Invention of an Anglo-Saxon Tradition', *Journal of Contemporary History*, 26 (1991), 575–95.

Miller, B., 'Our Abdiel: The British Press and the Lionisation of "Chinese" Gordon', *Nineteenth Century Prose*, 32:2 (2005), 127–53.

Mombauer, A., *The Origins of the First World War: Controversy and Consensus* (London: Longman, 2002).

Morgan, K., 'The Boer War and the Media', *Twentieth Century British History*, 13:1 (2002), 1–16.

Nairn, T., *The Break-Up of Britain: Crisis and Neo-Nationalism*, second edition (London: New Left Books, 1977).

Nairn, T., *Faces of Nationalism: Janus Revisited* (London: Verso, 1997).

Nash, G., C. Crabtree and R.E. Dunn, *History on Trial: Culture Wars and the Teaching of the Past* (New York: Alfred A. Knopf, 1997).

Newsome, D., *The Victorian World Picture* (London: Fontana, 1998).

Newth, J.D., *Adam and Charles Black, 1807–1957: Some Chapters in the History of a Publishing House* (London: A. & C. Black, 1957).

Otley, C.B., 'Militarism and Militarisation in the Public Schools, 1900–72', *British Journal of Sociology*, 29:3 (1978), 321–39.

Paris, M., *Warrior Nation: Images of War in British Popular Culture, 1850–2000* (London: Reaktion Books, 2000).

SELECT BIBLIOGRAPHY

Parker, D., '"Something a Little Sterner and Stronger": World War One and the Enhancement of Bias in English Elementary Education', *Journal of Vocational Education and Training*, 52:3 (2000), 435–61.

Parker, J., *England's Darling: The Victorian Cult of Alfred the Great* (Manchester: Manchester University Press, 2007).

Peel, E.A., 'Some Problems in the Psychology of History Teaching', in W.H. Burston and D. Thompson (eds), *Studies in the Nature and Teaching of History* (London: Routledge and Kegan Paul, 1967), 173–90.

Pettman, J.J., 'Boundary Politics: Women, Nationalism and Danger', in Mary Maynard and June Purvis (eds), *New Frontiers in Women's Studies: Knowledge, Identity and Nationalism* (London: Taylor and Francis, 1996).

Phillips, D., 'Michael Sadler and Comparative Education', *Oxford Review of Education*, 32:1 (2006), 39–54.

Ploszajska, T., *Geographical Education, Empire and Citizenship* (Historical Geography Research Series, 35, 1999).

Pocock, J.G.A., 'British History: A Plea for a New Subject', *Journal of Modern History* 47:1 (1975), 601–21.

Porter, A., 'Religion and Empire: British Expansion in the Long Nineteenth Century', *Journal of Imperial and Commonwealth History*, 20:3 (1992), 370–90.

Porter, B., *The Absent-Minded Imperialists: What the British Really Thought about Empire* (Oxford: Oxford University Press, 2004).

Potter, S., *News and the British World: The Emergence of an Imperial Press System, 1876–1922* (Oxford: Oxford University Press, 2003).

Proctor, T., *Scouting for Girls: A Century of Girl Guides and Girl Scouts* (Santa Barbara, CA: Praeger, 2009).

Pryke, S., 'The Popularity of Nationalism in the Early British Boy Scout Movement', *Social History*, 23 (1998), 309–24.

Pugh, M., *The March of the Women: A Revisionist Analysis of the Campaign for Women's Suffrage, 1866–1914* (Oxford: Oxford University Press, 2000).

Quayle, E., *The Collector's Book of Boys Stories* (London: Studio Vista, 1973).

Reader, W.J., *'At Duty's Call': A Study in Obsolete Patriotism* (Manchester: Manchester University Press, 1988).

Readman, P., 'The Place of the Past in English Culture, c. 1890–1914', *Past and Present*, 186:1 (2005), 147–99.

Rich, P., *Race and Empire in British Politics*, second edition (Cambridge: Cambridge University Press, 1990)

Richards, J. (ed.), *Imperialism and Juvenile Literature* (Manchester: Manchester University Press, 1989).

Richards, T., *The Commodity Culture of Victorian England: Advertising and Spectacle* (London: Verso, 1991).

Riedi, E., 'Women, Gender and the Promotion of Empire: The Victoria League, 1901–14', *The Historical Journal*, 45:3 (2002), 569–99.

Roach, J., *Public Exams in England, 1850–1900* (Cambridge: Cambridge University Press, 1971).

Roach, J., 'History Teaching and Examining in the Secondary Schools, 1850–1900', *History of Education*, 5:2 (1976), 127–40.

SELECT BIBLIOGRAPHY

Robbins, K., 'History, the Historical Association and the National Past', *History*, 66 (1981), 412–25.

Robbins, K., *Nineteenth-Century Britain: Integration and Diversity* (Oxford: Clarendon, 1988).

Roberts, N., 'Character in the Mind: Citizenship, Education and Psychology in Britain, 1880–1914', *History of Education* 33:2 (2004), 177–97.

Robertson, A., '"Between the Devil and the Deep Blue Sea": Ambiguities in the Development of Professorships of Education, 1899–1932', *British Journal of Educational Studies*, 38:2 (1990), 144–59.

Robertson, A., 'Schools and Universities in the Training of Teachers: The Demonstration School Experiment, 1890 to 1926', *British Journal of Educational Studies*, 40:4 (1992), 361–78.

Robinson, W., 'The "Problem" of the Female Pupil Teacher: Constructions, Conflict and Control, 1860–1910', *Cambridge Journal of Education*, 27:3 (1997), 365–78.

Robinson, W., 'Historiographical Reflections on the 1902 Education Act', *Oxford Review of Education*, 28:2–3 (2002), 159–72.

Rose, L., *The Erosion of Childhood: Child Oppression in Britain, 1860–1918* (London: Routledge, 1991).

Rose, J., 'Willingly to School: The Working-Class Response to Elementary Education in Britain, 1875–1918', *Journal of British Studies*, 32 (1993), 114–38.

Rose, J., *The Intellectual Life of the British Working Classes* (New Haven and London: Yale University Press, 2001).

Rubinstein, D., 'The Socialisation of the London School Board, 1870–1904', in P. McCann (ed.), *Popular Education and Socialization in the Nineteenth Century* (London: Methuen, 1977), 231–64.

Rüger, J., 'Nation, Empire and Navy: Identity Politics in the United Kingdom 1887–1914', *Past and Present*, 185:1 (2004), 159–87.

Samuel, R. (ed.), *Patriotism: The Making and Unmaking of British National Identity*, 3 volumes (London: Routledge, 1989).

Samuel, R., *Island Stories: Unravelling Britain*, II, *Theatres of Memory* (London: Verso, 1998).

Sayer, D., 'British Reaction to the Amritsar Massacre, 1919–1920', *Past and Present*, 131 (1991), 130–64.

Schools Council, *Young School Leavers* (London: HMSO, 1968).

Schools Council 13–16 Project, *A New Look at History* (Edinburgh: Holmes MacDougal, 1976).

Searle, G.R., *The Quest for National Efficiency: A Study in British Politics and Political Thought, 1899–1914* (Oxford: Blackwell, 1971).

Selleck, R.J.W., *The New Education: The English Background, 1870–1914* (London: Isaac Pitman, 1968).

Shemilt, D., 'Beauty and the Philosopher: Empathy and History in the Classroom', in A. Dickinson, P. Lee and P. Rogers (eds), *Learning History* (London: Heinemann, 1984), 39–83.

Sherwood, M., 'Educating Racism', *Race and Class*, 42:3 (2001), 1–28.

SELECT BIBLIOGRAPHY

Silbey, D., *The British Working Classes and Enthusiasm for War, 1914–16* (London: Frank Cass, 2005).

Simpson, L., 'Imperialism, National Efficiency and Education, 1900–1905', *Journal of Educational Administration and History*, 16:1 (1984), 28–36.

Smith, A.D., *Myths and Memories of the Nation* (Oxford: Oxford University Press, 1999).

Smith, A.D., '"Set in the Silver Sea": English National Identity and European Integration', *Nations and Nationalism*, 12:3 (2006), 433–52.

Smith, J., '"No Subject ... More Neglected": Victorian Elementary School History, 1862–1900', *Journal of Educational Administration and History*, 41:2 (2009), 131–49.

Smith, M., *Empire in British Girls' Literature and Culture: Imperial Girls, 1880–1915* (New York: Palgrave, 2011).

Springhall, J., 'Lord Meath, Youth and Empire', *Journal of Contemporary History*, 5:4 (1970), 97–111.

Springhall, J., *Youth, Empire and Society: British Youth Movements, 1883–1940* (London: Croom Helm, 1977).

Springhall, J., 'Building Character in the British Boy: The Attempt to Extend Christian Manliness to Working-class Adolescents, 1880 to 1914', in J.A. Mangan and J. Walvin (eds), *Manliness and Morality: Middle-Class Masculinity in Britain and America 1800–1940* (Manchester: Manchester University Press, 1987), 52–74.

Stapleton, J., 'Citizenship versus Patriotism in Twentieth Century England', *The Historical Journal*, 48 (2005), 151–78.

Steele, I., *Developments in History Teaching* (London: Open Books, 1976).

Stevenson, J., *British Society, 1914–45* (London: Allen Lane, 1984).

Surridge, K.T., 'More Than a Great Poster: Lord Kitchener and the Image of the Military Hero', *Historical Research*, 74:185 (2001), 298–313.

Taylor-Milne, A., 'History at the Universities: Then and Now', *History*, 59:195 (1974), 33–46.

Thompson, A., *Imperial Britain: The Empire in British Politics, 1880–1932* (Harlow: Longman, 2000).

Thompson, A., *The Empire Strikes Back: The Impact of Imperialism on Britain from the Mid-Nineteenth Century* (Harlow: Longman, 2005).

Thompson, F.M.L., *The Rise of Respectable Society* (London: Fontana, 1988).

Tinkler, P., *Constructing Girlhood: Popular Magazines for Girls Growing Up in England, 1920–50* (London: Taylor and Francis, 1995).

Turnball, A., 'Learning Her Womanly Work: The Elementary School Curriculum, 1870–1914', in Felicity Hunt (ed.), *Lessons for Life: The Schooling of Girls and Women, 1850–1959* (Oxford: Blackwell, 1987), 83–100.

Vance, N., 'The Ideal of Manliness', in Brian Simon and Ian Bradley (eds), *The Victorian Public School* (London: Gill and Macmillan, 1975), 115–28.

Ward, P., *Red Flag and Union Jack: Englishness, Patriotism and the British Left, 1881–1924* (Woodbridge: Boydell, 1998).

Ward, P., *Britishness since 1870* (London: Routledge, 2004).

Ward, S., 'Echoes of Empire', *History Workshop Journal*, 62:1 (2006), 264–78.

SELECT BIBLIOGRAPHY

Watts, R., 'Education, Empire and Social Change in Nineteenth Century England', *Paedagogica Historica*, 45:6 (2009), 773–86.

Weedon, A., *Victorian Publishing: The Economics of Book Production for a Mass Market, 1836–1916* (Aldershot: Ashgate, 2003).

Winfield, S., 'Travelling the Empire: The "School Empire Tours" and Their Significance for Conceptual Understandings, 1927–39', *History of Education Review*, 40:1 (2011), 81–95.

Wodak, R., R. de Cillia, M. Reisigl and K. Liebhardt, 'The Discursive Construction of National Identities', *Discourse and Society*, 10:2 (1999), 164–5.

Wolffe, J., *God and Greater Britain: Religion and National Life in Britain and Ireland, 1843–1945* (London: Routledge, 1994).

Wolffe, J., *Great Deaths: Grieving, Religion, and Nationhood in Victorian and Edwardian Britain* (Oxford: Oxford University Press, 2000).

Wormall, D., *Sir John Robert Seeley and the Uses of History* (Cambridge: Cambridge University Press, 1980).

Yeandle, P.D., 'Lessons in Empire and Englishness: Further Thoughts on the English/British Conundrum', in Helen Brocklehurst and Robert Phillips (eds), *History, Nationhood and the Question of Britain* (Basingstoke: Palgrave, 2004), 274–86.

Yeandle, P.D., 'Englishness in Retrospect: Rewriting the National Past for Children of the English Working Classes, c.1880–1920', *Studies in Ethnicity and Nationalism*, 6:2 (2006), 9–26.

Research dissertations and theses

Brindle, P., 'Past Histories: History and the Elementary School Classroom in Early 20th-Century England' (unpublished PhD thesis, University of Cambridge, 1999).

Cook, T.D., 'Changing Attitudes to the Teaching of History in Schools, c. 1900–1970' (unpublished MPhil thesis, University of Lancaster, 1970).

Glendenning, F.J., 'The Evolution of History Teaching in British and French Schools in the Nineteenth and Twentieth Centuries, with Special Reference to Attitudes to Race and Colonial History in History Schoolbooks' (unpublished PhD thesis, University of Keele, 1975).

Manton, K., 'Socialism and Education, 1883–1902' (unpublished PhD, University of London, 1998).

Mizobe, A., 'Nationalism and School Textbooks: A Comparative Study of Britain and Japan, 1919–1955' (unpublished PhD Dissertation, University of Lancaster, 1997).

Ploszajska, T., 'Geographical Education, Empire and Citizenship, 1870–1944' (unpublished PhD thesis, Royal Holloway University of London, 1996).

Robinson, W., 'The Pupil-Teacher Centre in England and Wales in the Late Nineteenth and Early Twentieth Centuries' (unpublished PhD thesis, University of Cambridge, 1997).

Steele, I., 'A Study of the Formative Years of the Development of the History Curriculum in English Schools, 1833–1901' (unpublished PhD, University of Sheffield, 1974).

SELECT BIBLIOGRAPHY

Sutton, F., 'An Investigation into the Impact of Imperialism on the Teaching of History in the Elementary Day Schools of England and Wales' (unpublished MA Dissertation, University of Lancaster, 1995).

Syriatou, A., 'Educational Policy and Educational Content: The Teaching of European History in Secondary Schools in England and Wales, 1945–1975' (unpublished PhD thesis, University of London, 1996).

Wong, J., 'Continuity and Change in Citizenship Education in Twentieth Century England' (unpublished PhD thesis, University of Liverpool, 1991).

Yeandle, P.D., 'Lessons in History: Citizenship and National Identity in the Teaching of History in England, c. 1880–1914' (unpublished PhD thesis, University of Lancaster, 2007).

INDEX

Adams, John 27, 52–3
Adamson, John 34, 37, 53–4, 61–2, 64
Africa / Africans 32, 98, 108–12, 130, 163
Alfred, King of England 60, 90–1, 103, 121–2, 137, 141, 151, 163
Anglo-Saxon 5, 75, 77, 78–83, 89–90, 92, 97, 99, 106, 132, 138, 152, 160
  heritage 79–83, 89–90, 92, 106, 138, 160
  race 75, 77, 79, 97, 99, 152
  seafaring 5, 78, 89–92, 132, 152
Armada 80, 88–9, 122, 129
apperception 57, 70n.44

Baden Powell, Robert 60, 125
Barker, Ernest 10
Battle of Hastings 104, 122
Blondel 123–5, 141
Board of Education 2–3, 6, 22, 25–6, 28, 35, 108, 131, 150, 157, 161, 163
  Handbook of Suggestions, The 2, 107, 150, 151, 155
Boer War (South African War, 1899–1902) 33, 35, 86, 109, 127
Bray, Reginald 3–6
British 1–2, 4, 7, 9–12, 20, 32, 34, 36–8, 74–5, 77, 79–80, 82–3, 85–92, 97–102, 105–6, 108–12, 118, 131, 133
  Empire *see* imperialism
  English *see* English, the
  Irish 9, 11, 37, 75, 98–103, 105
  Isles 9, 36, 82–3, 138, 161

  nations 4, 9, 10, 92, 97, 162
  Scottish 9, 11, 37, 74–5, 98, 100–3, 105
  Welsh 9, 11, 15, 74–5, 98, 100, 103
Browning, Oscar 27–9, 37–8, 64, 100, 137
Buckley, Arabella 105, 110

Canada 79, 130, 133
Canute, King of England 60, 63, 141
China / Chinese 98, 108–9, 110
Christianity 41, 60–1, 64, 77–8, 83–7, 103, 119, 174
Clive, Robert (Clive of India) 87, 121, 130–2, 137, 163
concentric system *see* educational psychology
Cowham, Joseph 34, 37, 40, 58, 107
Cox, Thomas 34, 54–6, 63–4,
Cox, G.W. 83, 111
Crecy, Battle of 128–9

Danby, T.W. 26
Darling, Grace 25, 86, 135–7
Dodd, Catherine 27, 52–5, 57, 62, 65, 153
Drake, Sir Francis 88, 121–2, 163
Dunstan, Bishop 103

Education Acts 6, 21, 27, 87, 150
educational psychology 1, 2–6, 8, 11, 19–20, 24, 27–30, 40–2, 51–5, 57, 60, 62, 64, 66–8, 74–5, 78, 87, 89, 97, 99, 107, 109, 113–14, 123, 127, 129, 131–4, 138–40, 142, 150, 153–5, 164–5, 172–4, 179–81

[207]

INDEX

concentric system 54, 59, 61–2, 87, 130
  definition of 59–60
Herbartianism 2, 29–30, 41–2, 51–5, 60, 62, 64, 66, 68, 75, 78, 87, 97, 99, 114, 123, 127, 129, 131–4, 138–40, 153–5
  heroism and patriotic values 5, 19, 24, 27, 42, 52, 53, 67–8, 75, 78, 87, 109, 114, 120–3, 125, 127, 129, 131, 134, 140, 154–5, 172, 174
  moral and religious 4, 55, 57, 114, 150, 154, 164, 172–4
  pedagogy 11, 24, 42, 52–4, 68, 74–5, 109, 114, 134, 142, 165
  recapitulation 60, 62–3, 67–8, 74–5, 83, 97, 99, 109, 114, 121, 138–9, 153, 155
  definition of 60
  sympathetic interest 60, 62, 64, 66, 87, 89, 114, 123, 127, 134, 138, 140, 154
teaching of history
  debates in 1, 6, 8, 41, 52, 67–8, 107, 154, 164–5, 172–3, 179–80
  past practice 2, 6–7, 74, 179
  texts and methods 19, 24, 26–9, 42, 52–3, 67–8, 109, 153–4
  value of history 5, 8, 30, 40, 113, 107, 164, 172–4, 179–81
educational publishing 24–8, 35, 44n.35, 87, 126, 152–3
Edward I, King 100, 122, 136
Edward III, King 122, 136
Egerton, Hugh 79–80, 93n.22
Eleanor of Castile 100, 121–3, 135–6
empire 1–2, 4–5, 8, 11, 19–20, 30–9, 41–2, 63–4, 66, 68, 75, 77–81, 83, 86–8, 90–2, 97–102, 105–8, 110–2, 118–19, 126, 128, 130–1, 139, 147–51, 156–64, 172–4, 179–81
Empire Leagues 32, 157, 162

Empire Day 32, 36, 148, 157
English, the
  character 10, 66, 74–5, 81, 83–4, 89, 104–5, 120–2, 127, 129–30, 134, 140, 173
  Englishness 10, 79, 81, 85, 98–9, 101, 102, 105–6, 129, 139, 173, 178–80
  homeland 32, 40, 81–2, 91, 104, 122
  identity 1, 6, 10, 12, 75, 88, 97, 106, 112, 113, 139, 176
  race see Anglo-Saxon
enlightened patriotism 2, 4–5, 12, 20, 22, 37–9, 41–2, 52, 55, 64–6, 68, 74, 109, 114, 120, 140, 149–50, 158, 164, 174
  collective identity 121, 148
  definitions of 2, 39
  and Hebartianism 2, 52, 55, 64, 66–8, 123
  and imperialism 2, 4–5, 12, 19, 33, 35, 37–9, 41–2, 65–6
  moral and religious education 55, 64, 68
  national and civic identity 22, 38, 39, 41, 66, 174
  racial outlook 74, 109, 114, 174

Findlay, J.J. 26–7, 29, 52–4, 57–8, 61–3, 154, 158–9, 164
Finnemore, John 27, 40, 81, 89–90, 100, 104–5, 125–7, 129–40, 153, 171
First World War 3, 11, 27, 34, 36–7, 87, 136, 142, 147–9, 151, 155, 158–9, 163–4
Fletcher, C.R.L. 25, 35, 36, 78, 83, 89, 102

Gardiner, S.R. 27
Gender, as analytical category 85, 119, 121–2, 85–9, 140
Germany 19–20, 29, 52, 155–6, 158, 160
Gordon, General Charles 60, 87, 89, 109, 122, 130, 133–4, 152

INDEX

Gove, Michael 5–9
Grenville, Sir Richard 89
Gunn, John 39, 54, 57, 59, 120, 154

Hadow Report (1926) 108, 131, 159
Haldane, Richard Burdon 19–20, 39
Hasluck, E.L. 158, 160
Hayward, Frank 42, 52–3, 56, 62
Hearnshaw, F.J.C. 27
Hensley Henson, Herbert 156
Henty, G.A. 27
Herbart, Johann Friedrich 29–30, 51, 53, 57, 62
Herbartians and Herbartianism 1–2, 29–30, 41–2, 51–6, 58–9, 60, 62, 64, 66–8, 75, 78, 87, 89, 97, 99, 114, 123, 127, 129, 131, 134, 138, 140, 150, 153–5, 171, 173
  and chronology 59, 60, 138
  definition of 2, 29
  education for moral citizenship 29, 41–2, 51–2, 54, 56, 64, 87, 114, 123, 127, 129, 131, 140, 154, 171, 173
  extent of influence 51–4, 67–8, 150, 153
  in history teaching 29, 30, 41, 51, 54
  and imperialism 30, 41, 46
  and pedagogy 29, 30, 51, 53, 150, 155
  and race 60, 62, 89, 91, 99, 155, 171
  six objectives 55, 66, 123
  storytelling and role models 56, 59, 62, 64, 66, 127, 129, 131, 171, 134, 153
  sympathetic interest 51, 55–6, 62, 67, 154
heroes and hero-worship *see* educational psychology
Historical Association 20–1, 26, 31, 40, 113, 153, 157, 159–60
Holmes, Edmond 29
Howard, M.A. 54–5, 58
Howart, G.D. 27
Hubert 123–5

imperialism 1–12, 20, 22, 30–41, 43, 53, 61, 64, 66, 68, 74–82, 84–90, 92, 97–9, 104–5, 108–10, 113, 118–19, 121, 125–6, 130–5, 139–40, 142, 147–50, 156–7, 160–5, 172–6, 179–81
  crude 2, 4, 34–5, 37, 40, 43, 111, 113, 125, 164
  imperial values 4–5, 22, 36–7, 53, 64, 73, 75, 77–8, 86, 121, 135, 142, 149–50, 162, 174
  imperialists 4, 31–2, 35, 126, 148–9, 156
India/Indians 33, 91, 98, 108–11, 130–1, 151, 163, 175

Jena, University of 53, 62
Joan of Arc 123, 135, 136, 141
juvenile literature 27, 112, 119, 142n.5

Kipling, Rudyard 25, 35, 36, 78, 83, 89, 102, 111, 126

Landon, Joseph 29, 40, 54, 59, 62, 120
League of Nations 159–60, 162
Lucas, Sir Charles 32–3, 157, 162

Macdonald, R.F. 34, 54–6, 63–4
MacKenzie, John 2, 86, 88, 119, 151
Mantoux, Paul 34
Marten, C.H.K. 21, 26, 34, 126, 150
Meath, Reginald Brabazon 12th Earl of 36, 38, 147, 157
Montfort, Simon de 63, 103

National Curriculum 3, 6, 8, 108, 179–80
navy 87, 88–92, 150–1
Nelson, Admiral Horatio 87, 89, 121–2, 132–3, 137, 152–3, 163
Nightingale, Florence 121, 136
Normans 98, 100, 103–5
Norwood Report (1943) 161

INDEX

Oman, Charles 25
Opium Wars 109
otherness, as analytical category 106, 113, 177

patriotism 2, 4–6, 12, 20, 22, 30, 32, 34–9, 41–2, 52, 55, 64, 66, 68, 74, 99, 106, 109, 113–14, 118, 120–1, 123–5, 140, 147–50, 154, 156–8, 161, 164, 174–5, 180–1
  and citizenship 34–7
pedagogy *see* educational psychology
Philippa, of Hainault 122, 126, 135–6,
Piaget, Jean 60, 67, 153
Plassey, Battle of 109

Raleigh, Sir Walter 78, 89, 163
Raymont, Terence 23, 30, 39, 50, 54, 58, 125, 154
recapitulation *see* educational psychology
Royal Colonial Institute 2, 161

Sadler, Michael 20, 52
Salmon, David 25, 37, 54, 57–8, 63
Scouts 32, 119, 125–6
Seeley, Sir John Robert 40n.48, 79–80
Shropshire, Olive 21, 108, 160
Sidney, Sir Philip 60, 85–6, 121

Slavery 85, 98, 110–12
Starr, Mark 158
Stobart, J.C. 161

teacher training 21–2, 23–4, 27–30, 33, 37, 39, 45n.58, 50, 52, 55, 148–9
Tout, T.F. 27, 160
Trafalgar, Battle of 88, 132
Turner, Josiah 104–5

Ûfer, Christian 62

Vikings 85, 90, 103–4, 151–2

Waldegrave, A.J. 38
Wallace, William 123
Warner, G.T. 2
Webb, W.H. 20
Wellington, Arthur Wellesley Duke of 87, 121, 130, 133–4, 163
Welton, James 23, 39, 58, 126, 154
Wembley, Empire Exhibition 151
West Indies 111
Withers, Harry 3, 26, 30, 32–3, 37
Wolfe, James 121, 130–1, 133, 152, 163

York-Powell, Frederick 27

Ziller, Tuiskon 53, 62

EU authorised representative for GPSR:
Easy Access System Europe, Mustamäe tee 50,
10621 Tallinn, Estonia
gpsr.requests@easproject.com

www.ingramcontent.com/pod-product-compliance
Ingram Content Group UK Ltd.
Pitfield, Milton Keynes, MK11 3LW, UK
UKHW041140160426
5217IPUK00045B/35